ON ADAM'S HOUSE IN PARADISE

THE MUSEUM OF MODERN ART PAPERS ON ARCHITECTURE

On Adam's House in Paradise

THE IDEA OF THE PRIMITIVE HUT

IN ARCHITECTURAL HISTORY

JOSEPH RYKWERT

Distributed by New York Graphic Society Ltd., Greenwich, Connecticut

THE MUSEUM OF MODERN ART, NEW YORK

IN ASSOCIATION WITH

THE GRAHAM FOUNDATION FOR ADVANCED STUDIES IN THE FINE ARTS, CHICAGO

Copyright © 1972 by The Museum of Modern Art

All rights reserved

Library of Congress Catalog Card Number: 73–129553

Cloth binding ISBN 0–87070–512–1

Paperbound ISBN 0–87070–513–X

The Museum of Modern Art

11 West 53 Street

New York, New York 10019

Designed by Carl Laanes

Type set by Ruttle, Shaw & Wetherill, Inc., Philadelphia, Pa.

Printed by Halliday Lithograph Corporation, Hanover, Mass.

CONTENTS

To Roberto and Fleur

FOREWORD

ON *ADAM'S HOUSE IN PARADISE* IS THE SECOND IN A SERIES OF OCCASIONAL papers concerned with the theoretical background of modern architecture. Published in collaboration with The Graham Foundation for Advanced Studies in the Fine Arts, the series is independent of the Museum's exhibition program. It will continue to explore ideas too complex for presentation in exhibition form, and its authors will represent no single professional group.

The first book in this series was Robert Venturi's *Complexity and Contradiction in Architecture* (1966). The present book is in no way related to it, and yet a comparison of the two studies suggests some parallel concerns. Mr. Venturi wants to rid modern architecture of what he considers its compulsive preoccupation with purity of form and rational consistency. His critique of modern architectural dogma has had what might be called a therapeutic effect, not necessarily because he offered a persuasive alternative but because he deprived some of the dogma of its magically inhibiting force.

Therapy, however, in architecture as in life, operates most effectively when it discloses to the patient the root of his troubles. The modern movement in architecture has been richer and more complex than its critics have perhaps been willing to allow, but its dominating compulsion to conceptual purity can never be understood if it is regarded merely as the product of some perverse but peculiarly durable fashion. On this theme Professor Rykwert's history of the idea of the first house is especially revealing. Architects contemplating his account of the search for original purity will observe that the paradise we hope to gain is modeled on the one we think we lost. Our desire to recover it grows out of anxieties inseparable from the human condition. How these anxieties have been acknowledged or suppressed, during the pursuit of the prototype, constitutes a subliminal history of architecture and of much else: philosophy, politics, religion, and science.

— Arthur Drexler, *Director,*
Department of Architecture and Design

ACKNOWLEDGMENTS

THIS ESSAY WAS CONCEIVED IN A CONVERSATION WITH ROBERTO CALASSO and owes him a great deal, both in matter and in manner.

Michael Ayrton and Frank E. Brown discussed the theme with me on several occasions; they have read the text and made suggestions. George Baird, Françoise Choay, Christopher Cornford, Eric John, Alasdair MacIntyre, and Dalibor Vezely have discussed the matter with me at various times. Several friends and colleagues have made specific suggestions which I have followed: Günther Nitschke, Michael Podro, Tony Vidler, and Dudley Young.

I must thank Richard Miranda, Günther Nitschke, and Ludwig Glaeser for help with the illustrations.

The staffs of several libraries have borne patiently with my enquiries, particularly those of the American Academy in Rome, the London Library, and the Marquand Library at Princeton University.

I owe a great debt of gratitude to my friends at The Museum of Modern Art for undertaking this publication and for their patience in guiding it through the press, and to The Graham Foundation for Advanced Studies in The Fine Arts for giving it its financial support.

Maureen Reid has been very long-suffering in preparing the manuscript.

—J. R.

Pour en revenir aux sources, on devait aller en sens inverse.
—René Daumal, *Le Mont analogue*

Chapter 1: THINKING AND DOING

THE LORD MADE ADAM ". . . IN THE IMAGE OF HIMSELF/CREATED HIM IN THE image of God . . ." on the sixth day of His "great work. . . . Male and female created He them," we are further told.[1] God made Adam and Eve such that they might keep each other company, that they might have intercourse with each other: but also with Him when He "walked in the garden in the cool of the day."

This garden the Creator had Himself planted with "every tree that is pleasant to the sight and good for food."[2] Eden was no forest growing wild. A garden which man was to tend, "to dress and keep," presupposes an ordered disposition of plants in beds and terraces. Among the rows of trees and beds of flowers there must have been places to walk, to sit and talk. Perhaps the fruit of the trees was varied enough to satisfy all the human, or at any rate Adamite, desire for variety; and perhaps fermentation was not among Adam's skills; if anything like wine was taken in the garden, however, this would suggest jars and cups, and these, in their turn, stores and sideboards, so on to rooms, larders, and all that: a house, in fact. A garden without a house is like a carriage without a horse. And yet Scripture, so specific about the onyx found near Paradise, says nothing about this implied house which I have read into the text.

Much has already been read into the Good Book, and into the beginning particularly, and I hope that my modest inference will prove unexceptionable. I make it in the conviction that the shadow or outline of this inferred house has dogged many builders and architects, much as the enigmatically described plan of the garden, with its four rivers, has inspired so many decorators, weavers, makers of carpets, as well as gardeners. All of these have spun their fantasies round the framework of the lost plan, since every paradise must, as Proust sharply observed, necessarily be a lost one. Which implies, in the first place, that I will not be able to propose a specification of this first house to my readers. Yet, since the vision seems to have haunted everyone involved in building (long before building was distinguished from architecture), I would like to trace the way in which some recollection of the type has occurred in different contexts; and, from the haunting persistence of the vision, draw some conclusions about the nature of the first house.

I therefore propose first to investigate the arguments of some architects who are our near contemporaries, yet sufficiently removed in time to appear as historical figures, in order to show how the notion of a first house (*right* because it was *first*) was invoked by them as a justification: the first principle of their radical reforms. I shall then attempt to show how this notion, which may not have exhausted itself entirely yet — it will come up in some odd contexts — had an extended history and is certainly as old as architectural theory. Architectural theory may be said to have begun with Vitruvius, if only because no earlier

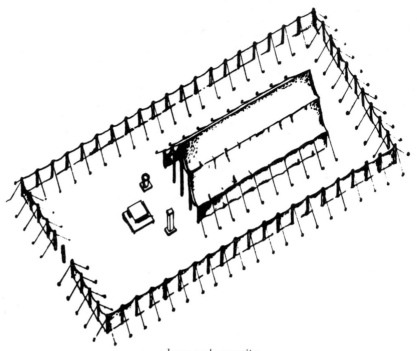

above and opposite:
Primitive temple—The Jewish Tabernacle in the Desert,
from Le Corbusier

literary evidence has survived. And since it is a notion which I wish to stalk, and not a thing, there would be no point in appealing to archeological evidence for its prehistory and origins. There cannot have existed a first house whose authenticity archeologists could certify. They could not even indicate where its site might have been located. To do this, as I have already suggested, they would have to find the Garden of Eden. There is another source available to me, however, beyond the theory; before the notion of a "first" house was a piece of conceptual apparatus, attempts were made to recall its form and its nature through ceremonies and rituals by people some still call primitive. The nature of my subject, therefore, forces me into paradox, since the first object of my search must be a memory of something which cannot but be lost.

An object which has always been lost cannot — in any ordinary sense of the word — be remembered. The memory of which we speak, however, is not quite of an object but rather of a state — of something that was; and of something that was done, was made: an action. It is a collective memory kept alive within groups by legends and rituals. But it seems also to have appeared in circumstances where normal historical transmission cannot be invoked to explain its communication and survival. It would almost seem to have some inherent connection with man's view of his works, and his shelter in particular. But before I attempt any general explanation I must illustrate my theme.

"Primitive man," so Le Corbusier introduces his ideal savage, "has halted his chariot: he has decided that here shall be his home ground. He chooses a clearing and cuts down the trees that crowd it in; he levels the ground about it; he makes a path to the stream or to the settlement of his fellow tribesmen which he has just left. . . . This path

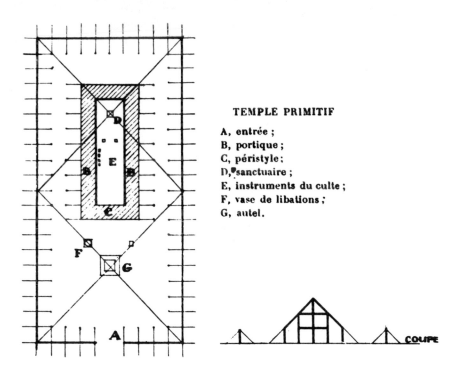

TEMPLE PRIMITIF

A, entrée ;
B, portique ;
C, péristyle;
D, sanctuaire ;
E, instruments du culte ;
F, vase de libations ;
G, autel.

COUPE

is as straight as his tools, his hands and his time will let him make it. The pegs of his tent describe a square, hexagon or octagon: the palisade [of the settlement] forms a rectangle whose four angles are equal. . . . The door of the hut opens on the axis of the enclosure, and the gate of the enclosure faces the doorway of the hut." Appealing to analogy, Corbusier describes the construction of the temple. And he concludes: "Look at a drawing of such a hut in a book on archeology: here is the plan of a house, the plan of a temple. It is exactly the same attitude as you find in a Pompeian house or in a temple at Luxor. . . . There is no such thing as a primitive man; there are only primitive means. The idea is constant, potent from the very outset."[3]

These chariot-riding and ax-wielding primitives are not as primitive as all that: they are barbarians rather than savages, according to the pedantic discrimination of modern archeological jargon, and belong to a Late Bronze or Early Iron Age society, if they are to be identified by their equipment and their ways as Corbusier describes them. But their exact situation in prehistory is not important. They are "first" men in this context, since they operate by the light of uncorrupted reason and instinct and so are able to employ a device apparently of the greatest elaboration: the tracés régulateurs, or geometrical guidelines, which enable the designer to operate a kind of geometrical rhyme using similar rectangles, and which Corbusier suggests all architects must use as "a protection against the arbitrary."

Because he operated by the light of instinct aided by reason alone, Corbusier's primitive builder could appeal directly to these very sophisticated means denied to the twentieth-century architect, whose thinking is shackled by artifice and distorted by prejudice. The tracés *régulateurs* are therefore justified: they are directly based on first principles, a product of unadulterated reason.

Corbusier's way of arguing here is not altogether new. His primitive man is one of a series of heroic archetypal figures whose ultimate prototypes people all myths. "In the beginning" these figures gave immediate expression to their inner nature, which, uncontaminated, was in unison with the fundamental laws of all creation. They were therefore able to devise the essential skills, and the constant imitation of these first actions led to all the basic human accomplishments. So Prometheus invented fire-making; Daedalus the saw—and sculpture; Palamedes the alphabet and gaming dice; Jubal the making of music; and Tubal-Cain all kinds of metal work.

In myth the hero-inventors are not rough, clumsy beginners, but famous and brilliant workmen. Although Daedalus was the first to cast bronze, he also managed to produce that famous honeycomb with bees on it, which was reckoned one of the great technical achievements of the ancient world. Like Corbusier's primitive builder, Daedalus had already mastered his method to perfection; later technical improvements merely elaborated on the essential skill. Corbusier's primitive also had this total mastery of method which twentieth-century architects have willfully neglected or wholly misunderstood. "They had forgotten," says Corbusier in the same place, "that great architecture is at the very origins of humanity and that it is the immediate product of human instinct."[4] This "immediate product of human instinct" is invoked by Corbusier at the beginning of his most famous book, *Vers une architecture*. Primitive builders had been able to fulfill the two essential conditions of great architecture: the first, that having measured by units man had derived from his own body (the inch, the foot, and so on), his buildings were made "in man's measure, to human scale, in harmony with man"; and the second, that "having been guided by instinct to the use of right angles, to axes, to the square and circle . . . [primitive man] could not create otherwise than by demonstrating to himself that he had created. For axes, circles, right angles are truths of geometry, they are the truths our eyes measure. . . . Geometry is the language of the mind."[5]

Primitive builders were not the only archaic exemplars in the 1920s and 1930s. Two or three film stars made careers by incarnating the noble savage: Tarzan was only the best known of such parts. The ancestor of Corbusier's "primitive builder," as of Tarzan or even Kipling's Mowgli, is the noble savage of the eighteenth-century *philosophes*. But the picture is more complex than such a simple genealogy might lead my reader to suppose.

Not even in modern architectural literature was Corbusier's appeal to the primitive isolated. In his short polemical book *Architecture*, published a few years after *Vers une architecture*, André Lurçat invokes the pile dwellings of the Late Stone Age in justification of the *pilotis* so favored by architects in the thirties to liberate the congested city terrain. Again, when he discusses mass production, Lurçat refers to the Greek temples as well as to the dwellings of the "Troglodytes." In general, "primitives" of this kind were invoked rather perfunctorily at a time when, as Lurçat himself put it, "everything [must be] rejected a priori, and then rehashed and created anew."[6]

In the United States the issue was even more immediate. "Primitive" man, there, was neither fossil nor the distant savage. The plains Indians had been confined to reservations only as a result of nearly a century of fierce campaigning. When Frank Lloyd Wright arrived in Chicago the Indian wars were a generation or two away. But he had brought with him ideas of a different kind about primitive living from the eastern seaboard: his parents had come from that transcendentalist background where city culture was despised and the virtues of life in a little hut in the woods extolled. Whatever urban transports may have inspired Whitman, to the high-minded New Englander the hermitage at Walden was a goal of pilgrimage.

To Thoreau, to Emerson, and to Hawthorne the little hut in the woods, and the advocacy of subsistence farming, was a reduction, to its essence, of the great Utopian tradition. And whatever Wright may have absorbed from and through his Chicagoan master, Louis Sullivan, it was to this patrician tradition that he owed his first and greatest allegiance.

Inevitably, the two "worlds" of ideas, and Wright's own position as a "gentleman-artist-architect" living among the commercial barons of Oak Park, produced a conflict, which Wright projected into a fabulized prehistory: "Go back far enough in time," he says in *The Living City*, a text first published in 1945, "mankind was divided into cave-dwelling agrarians and wandering tribes of hunter-warriors; and we might find the wanderer swinging from branch to branch in the leafy bower of the tree, insured by the curl at the end of his tail, while the more stolid lover of the wall lurked, for safety, hidden in some hole in the ground or in a cave: the ape? . . . The cave dweller became the cliff dweller. He began to build cities. . . . His God was a malicious murderer. . . . He erected his God into a mysterious covenant. When he could, he made his God of gold. He still does.

"But his swifter, more mobile brother devised a more adaptable and elusive dwelling place—the folding tent. . . . He was the Adventurer. His God a spirit: devastating or beneficent as he was himself."[7]

There is much more in this vein. The goodies and the baddies were not kept apart: "Conflicting human natures have conquered or been vanquished, married, intermarried, brought forth other natures; a fusion in some, still a straining confusion in others." The nomad—the reader will have recognized him by now—Wright offers as the proto-

type of the democrat, while the caveman/agriculturist is the embodi-
ment of the unfocused anti-democrat. Wright thought that "in the
affair of culture, shadow-on-the-wall has so far seemed predominant,"
because of the clumsy technologies and the ever-present violence of
older societies. But the recent developments both social and technical
have created new conditions: "So a human type is emerging capable
of rapidly changing environment to fit desires, one amply able to off-
set the big city of today: remnant of the great, ancient 'Wall.' In the
capability to change we have the new type of citizen. We call him
democratic."[8] And the new environment is foreshadowed in Wright's
Broadacre City, with which I cannot here concern myself. But I wonder how much this division of humanity into the earthy bad and the
spiritual tent-building good — itself a variation on the scriptural account of Cain and Abel — is reflected in the constant and sharp distinction which Wright's building always displays, between the
"liberated" and apparently unsupported planes of the roof, and the
deliberately heavy walls, walls formally identified with the earth
from which they so often seem to grow.[9]

Wright, who in his vision of the past separated all men into good
and bad, attempted in a sense to reintegrate these opposites in the
figure of those houses he so often built for people who must have
seemed to him to contain a strong dose of the shadow-on-the-wall
nature. He was perhaps alone among architectural theorists in believ-
ing that human nature is the conflation of two opposed tendencies
among our remotest ancestors.

Naturally, the appeal of the "primitive" differed from milieu to
milieu. It was fascinating if threatening in the United States; in Germany it had much less evident "notional" attraction. Little reference
to that sort of thing will be found in *Frühlicht*, the expressionist magazine run by the brothers Taut in the twenties; nor in *G*, that most sober
of all the *Sachlich* publications. Ludwig Mies van der Rohe, perhaps
the most distinguished of the latter's contributors, echoes such an idea
rather faintly in a late, American "utterance": Let us guide students over the road of discipline from materials, through function, to
creative work. Let us lead them into the healthy world of primitive
building methods, where there was meaning in every stroke of an axe,
expression in every bite of the chisel. . . ." It is of course the common-
sense view which one of the pioneers of *Sachlichkeit*, who had fought
in his earlier writings for what might be called the laicization of architecture, for the idea that all great architecture is the automatic product
of the program taking flesh in terms of building construction: "Create
from out of the nature of our task with the methods of our time; this is
our task," for "Architecture is the will of an epoch translated into
space; living, changing, new."[10]

Mies van der Rohe's oracular pronouncements are few and terse;

they rarely descend below the level of pious generality. An almost exact contemporary, Erich Mendelsohn, was more lavish with his words, and more explicit about ideas. Although he was very partial to the historical parallel, the "ultimate," the "natural" image for him was not the first home of primitive man. On the contrary almost, the models to which he appealed were from the animal kingdom; the city, he maintained, had to observe the same laws as the beehive and the anthill. Mendelsohn's early projects for planless, fantastic buildings drawn with an expressionist bravura have often been compared to the Futurist fantasies of Antonio Sant'Elia. But nature entered the Futurist manifestos differently: to provide images of the great vitality of the new features of the mechanized city. "Elevators should not hide away squashed like tapeworms in the stairwell; the stairs, which are now useless, should be abolished and the elevators climb up the face of the building like snakes of steel and glass . . ." says Sant'Elia.[11] In the Futurists' attempt to jettison their positivist heritage they replaced the natural model of the house with the "dynamic" machine; and yet the vision of evolution this invokes, and which conditions the new style, is itself based on a positivist interpretation of society and of nature. Mendelsohn leans much more directly on the positivist heritage. Although, of course, as he was working in Weimar Germany, the unaided reason of primitive man could not serve as a reliable archetype; the models to which he looked are described in the more elementary activities of animals — social animals in particular. Books on the architecture of animals (and, by a curious metonymy, of plants as well) had a great vogue in the second half of the nineteenth century. The Reverend J. G. Wood, the naturalist and popularizer, devoted a splendid, richly illustrated book to just such an idea in 1875. The title itself is interesting: *Homes without Hands, Being a Description of the Habitations of Animals, Classed According to Their Principles of Construction:* not, you may note, according to their inhabitants' way of life, or even their genetic alliances, so that nests of fish find themselves jostling birds' nests constructed in a similar fashion. The underlying idea inherent in this approach is spelled out explicitly in another popular manual, this time on architecture, *Les Merveilles de l'architecture,* published in 1880 as a volume in the *Bibliothèque des Merveilles* by André Lefèvre, a poet and writer on mythology and philosophy (and a translator of Lucretius, incidentally). He begins: "Architecture is not unknown to animals: the worm's hole, the ant's gallery, the bee's hive . . . the gorilla's hut, the house, the castle keep, the temple, and palace all satisfy the same need, infinitely diversified. A common law may be induced from them, and that is the law of adaptation. Utility is the ground of any architectural aesthetic. . . . The individual dwells as he is clothed . . . to defend himself from the inclemency and hostility which surround him . . ."[12] and so on.

Nests of the African Weaver, after J. G. Wood

Within this general current of nineteenth-century thinking the reader may find a direct contradiction of such speculations. "There could be no such thing as an animal architecture," says one positivist historian, who wishes to identify the concept of architecture with the notion of permanent duration, with monumentality. Although this is really fussing about nomenclature, yet the division between an architecture which may be classified according to materials or the methods of construction, like the nests of swallows and sticklebacks, must—even in positivist theory—be clearly distinguished from an architecture which is building with monumental intention, building for permanence. This distinction suggests another polarity. And in spite of the apparent superficiality of the point at issue, this is much more interesting.

~ The first habitations of man, it is generally held, were makeshift props against some rock face, which the first men devised to protect themselves against the weather and their various enemies. "Architecture . . . must have had a simple origin in the primitive effort of mankind to provide protection against inclement weather, wild beasts and human enemies. . . ."[13] So begins Banister Fletcher's A History of Architecture, from which generations of English-speaking architects conned their lessons in architectural history. And this would be the view still expressed by the generality; "It is singular," remarks the great French prehistorian André Leroi-Gourhan, considering this very point, "that the earliest surviving buildings are contemporary with the appearance of the first rhythmic marks . . . [although] the foundation of moral and physical comfort in man is the altogether animal perception of the perimeter of security, the enclosed refuge, or of the socializing rhythms: [so] that there is no point in seeking for a scission between animal and human to explain our feelings for the attachment to social rhythms and inhabited space . . . [yet] the little that is known [of pre-Homo sapiens habitations] is enough to show that a profound change occurred about the time which corresponds to the development of the control sections of the brain in strains relating to Homo sapiens. . . . Such archeological evidence [as there is] would seem to justify the assumption, that from the higher paleolithic period onwards there was an attempt to control the whole spatio-temporal phenomenon by symbolic means, of which language was the chief. They imply a real 'taking charge' of space and time through the mediation of symbols: a domestication of them in a strict sense, since it involves, within the house and about the house, a controllable space and time."[14]

The reader will have noticed the contradiction. On the one hand, the commonly accepted view, expressed by Mies, Mendelsohn, Choisy, and so on, of man slowly adapting the various makeshift arrangements which the inclemency of the weather imposed upon him (indeed, the

Gropius: Blockhaus Sommerfeld, Berlin, 1921

great positivist architectural historian Auguste Choisy thinks that
it was the onset of the Ice Age which forced men into shelters and
caves)[15]; and on the other hand, the paleontologist's insistence on the
conceptual, rather than the physical, difference between human and
animal habitations. It is the difference of conception, the attachment of
meaning to his task, that distinguishes man's first attempts in that
direction from those of the instinctually driven beasts. And this second view seems surprisingly like that which Le Corbusier expressed
in *Vers une architecture*. There is another reconstitution of the primitive house in a more immediately architectural context. The word
"primitive" appears in a number of contexts nowadays. The phylogenetic argument, to take one instance, suggests that the junior school-
child is passing through a development parallel to that of the paleolithic phase of prehistory, much as the fetus condenses the whole of
tertiary and quaternary evolution into a nine months' gestation. Anal-
ogously, the technological achievement of some exotic societies allows
incautious anthropologists to call "paleolithic" certain tribes in the
Australian bush or in New Guinea. In the same way, as late as the end
of the nineteenth century the agricultural laborer was seen as a kind
of "primitive," and moreover a "primitive" whose humble ways,
whose daily contact with the soil, with animals, guaranteed him a
more instinctive, a "truer" view of things. This view dominates the
writings of such nationalist heroes as Wyspiański, and the musical
researches of Bartók and Kodály, or the earlier paintings of a cosmo-
politan artist like Kandinsky. I draw attention to this climate of
opinion in order to "situate" more convincingly the curious house
which Walter Gropius and Adolf Mayer designed for a prosperous
timber merchant called Sommerfeld, in Dahlem, a Berlin suburb. It

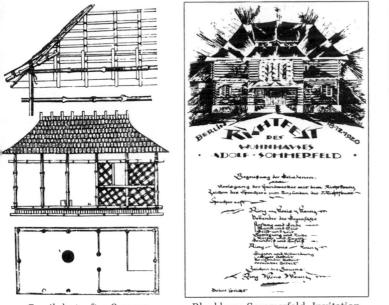

Log construction
in Byelorussia,
after Strzygowski

Caraib hut, after Semper

Blockhaus Sommerfeld. Invitation
to house-warming party.
Lithograph. Bauhaus Archive

has always been referred to as the *Blockhaus* Sommerfeld (using the German term), which has led people to forget that "*Blockhaus*" means log house, or even log cabin. In a way the choice of material was dictated by the client's profession, but in spite of this the house has always inspired special pleading. The "peasanty" detailing – the carved beam ends, for instance – as well as the use of a clumsy constructional method quite unlike anything else in Gropius's work, invites further examination.

There is something about the house which does recall certain earlier American work, particularly Sullivan's or Elmslie's. But Walter Gropius was very familiar with quite other aspects of the Chicago school, and at the time the Sommerfeld house was being finished, Gropius and Mayer were already working on the competition scheme for the Chicago Tribune Tower, which of all the projects submitted was the most sophisticatedly faithful to the earlier work of the Chicago school. This deliberate piece of extravagantly coarse, almost peasant building brings to mind a footnote of Semper's: "Even today Europe's over-civilized sons, when they wander in the primeval forests of America, build themselves log cabins."[16] The pioneering spirit of that remark fits well with the general atmosphere of pioneering renewal of the early days of German social democracy. Perhaps, too, the self-reliant businessman client scented some echo of the great American cabin-to-White House myth, social achievement in spite of the humblest origins: it was already popular before the 1914–18 war.

With all that, the house occupies a curious place in Gropius's oeuvre. Although it is illustrated in the Bauhaus commemorative book, there is no mention at all of it in Siegfried Giedion's "official" monograph on Gropius. And yet, my considerations apart, the house

23

was most important as being the first collective effort of the Bauhaus, the first building to exemplify the rousing slogan in the closing sentence of the Bauhaus manifesto: "Together let us conceive and create the new building which will embrace architecture *and* sculpture *and* painting in one unity and which will rise one day toward heaven from the hands of a million workers like the crystal standard of a new faith."[17] These words are, in the manifesto, illustrated by a wood engraving of a churchy, three-towered edifice, from the tops of whose towers shining stars illumine the dark. But in reality the teaching of the manifesto is demonstrated by the Sommerfeld log house, on which the architects collaborated with Josef Albers for the stained glass, Joost Schmidt for the wood carving, Hans Jucher for the metal reliefs and Marcel Breuer (still a student) for the furniture. And in a real way, this furniture, though made of bulky wooden members, contained the promise of Breuer's later development. The house itself is only indirectly related to later Bauhaus productions. The year after it was done, the Bauhaus produced another "total" effort, the *Haus am Horn*, which was built for the exhibition of 1923 and which departed radically both from current building practice and its Dahlem predecessor.

Nevertheless, the Sommerfeld log house requires interpretation. The Bauhaus authorities are no help in this matter. Gropius himself took great care to dissociate himself from the taint of primitivism. In a circular letter to his colleagues, he restates the essential aim of the Bauhaus as its *Urheber* (prime mover). It is a call to the realities of a creative contact with industry, and a condemnation of "some *Bauhäusler*, who cultivate a misunderstood Rousseauish return to nature. Someone who denies the world as it is should retire to a desert island. . . ." And later in the same essay the true Rousseauism is summed up in a sentence: "The architect has over-valued his usefulness . . . the engineer, on the contrary, untrammelled by aesthetic and historical prejudice, has arrived at clear, organic forms. . . ."[18]

But the Sommerfeld house belongs to the earlier, unregenerate Bauhaus of craftsmanship, of the handmade jobs. And the meaning of this strange exercise is not vouchsafed by its designers. I should like, therefore, to interpolate a passage by a later collaborator of Gropius's, Konrad Wachsmann, who published a book on timber architecture in 1930, still a long time before he was to collaborate with Gropius. Wachsmann devotes a chapter to the log house as a form of timber building. "It is," he says, "the most ancient way of building timber houses. Examples are known from prehistory . . . the log house represents the inner conception of the timber house, since the intrinsic value of the structural form apart, it shows the material qualities of timber in their purest form. In spite of all possible structural refinements, the principle of construction remains unaltered from the primitive log house of the ancients. . . ." And later, in the same chapter: "In

Lenin Mausoleum, second wooden stage

Lenin Mausoleum, stone building

spite of all technical aids, the construction of a log house will always be a craft procedure, which can only be carried out by experienced carpenters."[19]

Such ideas derive ultimately from the positivist historicizing of Semper, mediated particularly by Josef Strzygowski against the other historians of the Vienna school. Timber building, Strzygowski maintained, was the original building technique of his Indo-Germanic ancestors. Since wood is perishable, the whole world of primitive "northern" architecture was lost to the historian of art; and early in the century he set up a research institute in Vienna to study and record the remains of this archaic form of construction, which he saw as the original method of building throughout northern Europe and Asia: separated from the eastern Mediterranean and China by a belt of brick and of tent builders respectively. At times he would go even further: "Anybody who makes a comparative study of art on a geographical basis is practically driven to the conclusion that in the vast majority of countries wood was the original building material. . . ."[20]

Moreover, as against the frame and "stave" techniques, Strzygowski set out as a champion of the priority of log construction in the north. Now although Strzygowski's ideas on the matter were given definite form in lectures which he delivered in 1922–24, and published three years later, his research institute had been going for many years, and he had talked and written in this way for some time.[21] Gropius must have been aware of these ideas, as he had been to Vienna in the war years: they were certainly discussed in his circle. Strzygowski was sufficiently familiar with and sympathetic to the ideas which animated the Bauhaus, moreover, to be a member of the committee, formed in 1923, of the Association of the Friends of the Bauhaus.

Unexpectedly, this form of building is echoed in a near-contemporary construction which has never been adequately described or examined: the Lenin mausoleum. After the dismantling of a provisional monument, it was built in 1924 both to enshrine the embalmed body of Lenin and to act as a tribune for the great men of the Soviet hierarchy during parades in Red Square. Although its later stone form reproduced fairly closely the timber building which it replaced in 1930, yet it appears to be a modest construction. Anastas Schusov, who designed both forms, is on record as having conceived it as the tomb of some great primitive chieftain on the Mongolian steppes. A brief examination of the same architect's building for the Kazan station will show quite how nationalist and how consciously "primitive" Schusov's style could be. The Lenin tomb was in fact the first *permanent* ceremonial building of Soviet Russia, and it was from this origin, and not the brilliant concrete, steel and glass projects of Tatlin and Lissitzky, that subsequent Soviet architects took their cue.[22]

The return to an archaic form of construction, a form which remained unaltered in spite of all the possible refinements it suffered, seems to have been a conscious attempt to fuse the elements of style into a new unity by returning to a way of building which inevitably carried with it the seeds of a telluric, immemorial wisdom and rightness. In various forms this belief had quite surprising currency. In an essay which he published in his periodical *Der Andere* in 1909, and simply called "Architecture," Adolf Loos describes a visit to a charming lakeside mountain village, where "everything breathes beauty and peace. What's this, then? A false note disturbs this peace. Like an unnecessary screech: among the peasants' houses, which were not made by them but by god [his lower case], there is a villa. The work of a good architect, or a bad one? I don't know. I know only that peace, rest and beauty have fled.

"Before God there are neither good nor bad architects. . . . In towns, in the realms of Beelzebub, there may be fine distinctions, as there are even in kinds of crime. And I therefore ask: why is it that every architect, whether he is good or bad, harms the lakeside?

"The peasant does not. Nor does the engineer, who builds a railway to the lake, or plows deep furrows in its bright surface. They create in another way. The peasant has pegged out a patch of green meadow on which the new house is to stand, and dug a trough for the foundations. If there is clay in the neighborhood, then there will be a brick kiln to supply bricks; if there isn't, the stone round the edge of the lake will do equally well. And while the mason lays brick on brick, stone on stone, the carpenter has set up his rig. He is making the roof. What sort of roof? Will it be a beautiful roof or an ugly roof? He doesn't know. A roof.

"The peasant wanted to build a house for himself, his kin and his cattle, and he has succeeded. As his neighbor and his ancestor succeeded. As the animal succeeds, guided by its instincts. Is the house beautiful? Yes, just as beautiful as the rose and the thistle, the horse and the cow. I therefore ask again: why does the architect, be he a good one or a bad one, harm the lakeside? Because the architect, like practically every townsman, has no culture. He lacks the security of the peasant, who does have a culture. . . . I call culture that harmony [*Ausgeglichenheit*] between the inner and the outer man which alone guarantees sensible thinking and acting. . . ."[23]

But Loos does not take this part of his argument further. For him, in any case, the *art* in architecture is preponderant only in the tomb and the monument. Loos wants to show further that the artist is concerned with future generations, but craftsmen, such as the architect, with the present. The architect, he continues, must aim at creating a particular feeling in his spectator about the building he is designing. And he concludes, "When walking through a wood, you find a rise in the ground, six foot long and three foot wide, heaped up in a rough pyramid shape, then you turn serious, and something inside you says: someone lies buried here. *That is architecture.*"[24]

Loos does not say why it is that peasants and engineers are the ones who touch this elemental wisdom whatever they do. To him it seems self-evident that both categories of workers, by their particular circumstances, touch the telluric wisdom still available to those whose social situation does not condemn them to a rootless city life, as well as having access to the corresponding wisdom which continuity and its concomitant security confers on those who may otherwise be underprivileged.

Loos bore out his teaching in much of his building. His vision of architectural development led him to work one way in town, another in the country, and he certainly aimed at the simplicity, the *reduction* to elementals which the peasant enjoyed.

It would be easy to dismiss Loos, the *Blockhaus* Sommerfeld, Corbusier's ideas which I quoted earlier, and the other things as odd exceptions. But I would submit that these are examples of the thought and practice of most eminent and influential architects and historians: and that all the examples are crucial to the men who produced them.

Indeed, even a cursory reader might have noticed a curious feature in two of my quotations; that Le Corbusier in 1922 and Leroi-Gourhan forty years later (and starting from quite different premises) were really saying something rather similar. Their theme was the unity of mankind; and arising from it, their belief in the primacy of reason, which could in some sense be established at its purest at the very source: *en arche*. On the other hand, Loos and the *Bauhäusler* were talking about something quite different: about the hidden, secular, telluric wisdom that is concealed from the "civilized," the "privileged," and accessible only to the "primitive."

Yet both were in agreement on one thing. If architecture was to be renewed, if its true function was again to be understood after years of neglect, a return to the "preconscious" state of building, or alternatively to the dawn of consciousness, would reveal those primary ideas from which a true understanding of architectural forms would spring, or else an understanding of those elementary forms that architects must inevitably play as counters in a game, however simple or elaborate, in order to create the simplest as the most elaborate statements.

Chapter 2: NECESSITY AND CONVENTION

LOOS NEVER ATTEMPTED TO SET OUT A COMPLETE "BODY" OF ARCHITECTURE: he was not really a systematic thinker. Underlying his various essays there is, however, a fairly coherent, if changing and developing, set of beliefs about his art. As may be expected of a Viennese intellectual of his generation, what conditioned his thinking was a positivist ground against which he was always playing linguistic countertunes. Hence his coupling of the engineers' "instinctive" if irrational rightness (in response directly to need and condition) with telluric harmony: the assurance of the peasant dwelling, as of an animal construction. By having roots which grew deep into earthy necessity, this assurance guaranteed that form, visible form, was never perverted or twisted — as it was by the rootless urban dweller ever searching for a style. Following Gottfried Semper in this as in many other things, Loos equates style with ornament; even more, with a self-conscious desire for novelty, the indulgence of individual caprice. The peasant, it is worth noting, is allowed his ornament — forbidden to the civilized — by Loos: his work is governed by the immediate dictates of instinct reinforced by precedent, a stock of which the peasant acquires genetically. So the peasant need never articulate ideas about form and style. Form and style develop, when they develop rightly — unconsciously, spontaneously — through man's encounter with climate through craft: shades of Semper again.

When Loos published "Architecture," Alois Riegl's *Stilfragen*, with its attack on Semper's materialist position, was already fifteen years old. And it may be worth remembering that it was in that year, 1909, that Freud, who was paying his first visit to America, found his cabin steward reading *The Psychopathology of Everyday Life*, "which made him suspect that he [Freud] was famous."[1] *The Psychopathology of Everyday Life* had appeared in 1904; even if Loos himself had not read it by 1909, the ideas it contained would certainly have percolated to him by that time. In any case, he might already have come across the ideas about a "structured" — not quite in Freud's sense, of course — unconscious which Theodor Lipps had advocated so explicitly some twenty years earlier, though some notion of unconscious thinking had been bandied about much earlier, since Leibniz at least among German philosophers. But I return to Riegl, and his difference from Semper.

The difference arose on the matter of origins. Semper had set out, in systematic form, his ideas about the nature and meaning of ornament (and of art in general) at the beginning of his work *Der Stil*, which was perhaps the most influential single book published on the subject in the nineteenth century, and which still provides a source for the ideas of both historians and architects on the matter. Semper had maintained that the origin of all form in artifacts must be studied under two aspects:

"Firstly," he says, "as the result of the material service or use for which it is intended: whether this use is immediate, or only notional, to be taken in a higher, symbolic sense; secondly, as a product of the material used in its making as well as of the tools and processes which went into the making."[2] Even if this is not strictly speaking a materialist formulation, yet it certainly shows a positivist way of attacking the problem; indeed, when Semper comes to classify artifacts, he classifies them by their feel and durability. First comes that which is "elastic, tough, resistant to tearing, of the greatest stability"; secondly, that which is "soft, pliant [plastisch], capable of hardening, lending itself to a variety of shapes; and once hardened, retaining the shape it has been given"; thirdly, "rod-shaped, elastic, of remarkable strength relatively, that is, with respect to forces acting at right angles to its axis"; and fourthly, "strong, of a dense aggregate consistency, resistant to compression and fragmentation and therefore of high reactive capacity, so constituted that it may be given the desired shape by subtraction of parts from the main bulk or built up into a strong system out of regular fragments of the same substance. . . ."[3]

It is obvious that the categories of abstractly described substances in fact correspond to four groups of trades: weaving, ceramics, "tectonics" (i.e., carpentry), and "stereotomy" or masonry. The bulk of Semper's book is then aligned on this division. And, having axiomatically given logical priority to weaving, Semper deduces from his postulate that the first artifact (I interpret) is a knot or a daisy chain.[4] Naturally, when he comes to the origins of architecture, Semper must also see them in these terms: and so the obvious extension of the hypothesis is that the *logically* primary form of the house is the tent. "If climatic influences and other circumstances suffice to explain this phenomenon of cultural history, and even if we cannot deduce from it that we are dealing with a universally valid rule about the development of civilization, it nevertheless remains true that the beginnings of building coincide with those of weaving. . . . As the first partition wall made with hands, the first vertical division of space invented by man, we would like to recognize the screen, the fence made of plaited and tied sticks and branches, whose making requires a technique which nature hands to man, as it were. The passage from the plaiting of branches to the plaiting of hemp for similar domestic purposes is easy and natural."[5]

Notice the terminology: the easy gradual passage from the "natural" contrivance to the artifice. Semper goes on to examine the origins of architecture in terms of stick-and-cloth combination, in China and India, the Fertile Crescent and classical antiquity. The details of this examination do not interest me here, but the procedure of making each further development of the building that much more formal, that much more durable, has a curious lack of evident motivation about it. The three principles, which Semper proposes at the beginning of the book as providing the critical criteria for ordering variety into unity are: symmetry, as demonstrated by snowflakes; eurythmy, demonstrated by plants; and direction (by implication, purpose, physical function), exemplified by the animal kingdom and especially by man. These three criteria are the basis of all formal creation and formal perception: it is content, as far as art is concerned, which gives them unity.[6]

This rather dry summary does an injustice to Semper's great subtlety and insight. On this ultimate unity which "content" might provide, he has something to say at the very opening of the book. Man, he says, is not simply the naked ape in face of the elements: "surrounded by a world full of wonder and power, whose law man may divine, which he wants to understand but can never decipher or solve, which only reaches him in few fragmentary harmonies and which sets his sentiment in a constantly unresolved tension so that he conjures up the missing totality in play, he makes himself a tiny world in which the cosmic law acts in a tiny system, but an independent one — and within the system as a totality: in such play man satisfies his cosmogonic instinct. Hence music and architecture must not be thought of — although they originate in rhythmical regularity of time and space sequence: the daisy chain, the pearl necklace, the shell, the circular dance, and so on — as imitative: they are never imitative of the appearance of nature, but the highest, purely cosmic arts. And no other craft or art can be exempt from their legislative power."[7]

Arguing against Semper, Riegl accused the old man's "innumerable disciples" of traducing his doctrine by overemphasis on its materialist ingredient: and yet he sees Semper as a quasi-naturalist. "The naturalist-historical school, which seeks out the causal interrelations of every phenomenon, could not fail to be satisfied by a hypothesis which found — for a branch of human activity as eminently spiritual as artistic creation — a dominating motive, and an origin as fascinating for its naturalness as it was astonishing in its simplicity. . . . The materialist-naturalist conception of the world has had weighty consequences in the field of the study of art. It was thought that art could not have existed, from the beginning, as the highest expression of a spiritual development, but that there first had to be a technique directed to the achievement of merely practical ends. . . ." Riegl considers how the appearance of objects decorated with elementary geometrical figures, and the establishment of weaving as the first art, suggested that geometric styles of art were spontaneously generated from a technique.

"With an assurance," Riegl goes on, "which suggests that they were actually present and with their own eyes saw primitive men inventing the first forms of art while they were at work with their materials and tools, archeologists were able to explain the individual geometric patterns of the most ancient vases as originating in textile, metallic, stereometric techniques"—and so on. Having attacked the followers, Riegl returns to pay homage to the founder of the theory, and accepts Semper's essential position, but comments on the passage about the fence as the origin of architecture which I quoted earlier in this chapter. Indeed, Semper had made something of a concession there: the development from plaited sticks to the woven hem, he maintains, is natural, and then goes on: "That is also the origin of weaving, first using blades of grass, or natural vegetable fiber, later spun vegetable or animal threads. The natural differences in the colors of the fibers prompted the users to alternate colors: that produced pattern. Soon these aids given by nature were surpassed through the artificial preparation of materials, etc. . . ."[8]

Riegl takes this to be the crucial statement, for Semper implies that the discovery of a possible pattern in the "natural" weave prompted a higher stage of development but fails to show how this crucial insight is gained or operates. Man therefore did not come upon pattern by pure accident, as we might take Semper's text to suggest, but by a deliberate creative impulse. This is the contradiction which Riegl wishes to point out in Semper's theory. And of course he had one advantage over the earlier scholar, since Semper could only have learned of the discovery of paleolithic art when his great work was published: the paintings of Altamira were discovered in the year of his death. It is this discovery, and the continuing finds of mobiliary art in the caves, which suggests an alternative theory to Semper's, and which Riegl sums up by saying that "the beginning of all artistic creativity is the direct reproduction of natural objects aiming at the closest imitation of their appearance, a concrete manifestation of a psychological process." But he rejects both interpretations as avoiding the essential truth that "there is something in man which leads him to find pleasure in formal beauty, which neither we nor the followers of the school explaining the origin of the arts in technique and material are able to define, and that this something has stimulated—freely and independently—the geometric combination of lines, without the need of a material intermediary; whose introduction does nothing to make things clearer, but at the most will grant a miserable formal victory to the materialist conception of the world."[9]

The "indefinable something" which Riegl posits as the mysterious wellspring of art is the nearest he gets to situating the concept of *Kunstwollen* (which I translate as "artistic intention," despairingly), a concept which had a long career in spite of its rather nebulous origins. While it has its uses in teaching historians that artists of other ages were not necessarily links in a chain whose last and perfect link they were, it did little to relate this *Kunstwollen* to a coherent view of human nature: to give the psychology of art a context in a view of the whole physiology of human personality and of its historical transformations. It would perhaps have been impossible to do this at the end of the nineteenth century, when Freud was beginning to treat works of art as pathological specimens, and while Morelli was authenticating masterpieces by a method that depended on the recognition of conventionalized "deformations" of anatomical detail as the only true, because unconscious, artist's signature.

To focus the historian's and the aesthetician's view on the abnormal in the work of art was inevitable at the time. (And the theory of "pure visibility" as the ultimate value in approaching works of art was contrived between Munich and Vienna as well — though Croce actually gave it its name — to provide the idealist polar opposite of what Riegl called the technical-materialist view of the origin of art.) All this made the consideration of architecture very awkward: the awkwardness survives until our day. Even a work like Susanne Langer's *Feeling and Form*, dependent as it was on the German idealist tradition, displays this very awkwardness, particularly when extending the notion that art is the reproduction of natural models (but that these models show feeling, not structure) to architecture and to music.

Semper had set these arts apart from the rest. Pleasure in all art was a subcategory of the same feeling as the pleasure in the beauty and wonder of nature. The consciousness of rhythm, and therefore of a structuring of the universe, Semper finds in the most primitive of races: whether evidenced by the wreath or necklace in space, handclapping or oar strokes in time.[10]

Semper's book first appeared in 1860. In a primitive form, he had already arrived at his classification earlier when he formulated the plan for an ideal museum in London in 1852. His three or four years in London probably contributed to his thinking in other ways. It may well be that the initial impulse to his anti-idealist thinking had come from the "philological" historians, such as von Rumohr, whose first *Italienische Forschungen* had appeared in 1827. He would also have been familiar with French academic theory, particularly with Quatremère de Quincy's writings, which were causing much stir in the twenties and early thirties of the century. And he must have seen that strange paper on "The Poetry of Architecture," signed "Kata Phusin," and subtitled "The Architecture of the Nations of Europe Considered in Its Association with Natural Scenery and National Character," which John Ruskin had published in *Loudon's Architectural Magazine*, and in which he uses the English cottage and the Swiss châlet, the country house in Britain and in Italy, as instancing national character, as expressing a faith.[11]

The conception of the "national" character which architecture might have, as against the "international" style of the academies, was very much of the day. The year the first instalment of Ruskin's paper was published, the Houses of Parliament in London burned down in

Cottage near Altdorf, after Ruskin

a famous fire. The competition for the new buildings definitely specified that they should be in a "national style"; and the project chosen,
in which the neo-classical architect Charles Barry collaborated with
Augustus Welby Pugin, provided a perfect amalgam: a neo-classical
framework surfaced with fifteenth-century English ornament. Pugin
belonged to that second stage of the Gothic revival in which the barbarian aspect of Gothic had become consumed. For him it represented
another form of appeal altogether. It was indeed an appeal to the past.
But to an ideal civilized past, which had not descended to the false
values of the contemporary barbarian. The style of the fifteenth cen-

tury in England represented the perfect social-aesthetic condition to Pugin: when society cast no one out and the artist could keep his deserved place in it. The very architectural features of the buildings witnessed to this condition. It was the time when architecture got nearest to obeying the two essential conditions of true architecture: "1st that there should be no features about a building which are not necessary for convenience, construction or propriety; 2nd that all ornament should consist of enrichment of the essential construction of the building." And he saw these two conditions fulfilled, "strange as it may seem, in pointed architecture alone. . . . Moreover," he adds, "the architects of the middle ages were the first who turned the properties of materials to their full account, and made their mechanism a feature of their art." He turns to Greek architecture for a confirmation of his argument. "Grecian architecture," he argues, following the ancient authorities, "is essentially wooden in its construction . . . never did its professors possess either sufficient imagination or skill to conceive any departure from the original type . . . [it] is at once the most ancient and barbarous mode of building that can be imagined; it is heavy . . . and essentially wooden; but it is extraordinary that when the Greeks commenced building in stone the properties of this material did not suggest to them some different and improved mode of construction. Such, however, was not the case; they laid stone lintels, as they had laid wooden ones, flat across. . . . The finest temple of the Greeks is constructed on the same principle as a large wooden cabin. . . . The Greeks erected their columns like the uprights of Stonehenge. . . . The Christian architects, on the contrary, with stones scarcely larger than ordinary bricks, threw their lofty vaults from slender pillars across a vast intermediate space . . ."[12] and more in this vein.

The reason for which Pugin situated the ideal paradise, if not indeed Paradise itself (for was not the Reformation a second fall from grace?), in fifteenth-century England is a by-product of the new historicism. It is part of that historicization of myth which had begun a century earlier. The medieval past, the last medieval past, the time of the fully matured Gothic—which some of Pugin's successors would consider decadent—provides the combination of virtues to which architects must return to refresh themselves. Starting again from this ideal point, a new style, suitable to the present time, might develop. The return must be made: but Pugin, who was fully aware of the horrors of life in the new industrial towns (Contrasts came out in 1836, after a succession of cholera epidemics), fought for the return in formal terms alone. There is Ruskin's distinction. He too saw an ideal, a paradisal state somewhere in the Middle Ages: but he saw it not in terms of the forms it produced, and which could be reproduced in whatever way was easiest. What attracted Ruskin to the medieval situation was the relationship between the worked surface and the way it was worked, between the craftsman and his product. His hate was reserved not for the results of industrialization, but for the mechanization of the working processes as evidenced by mechanical surface. It was the worker's relationship to his product as well as to the social fabric which fascinated Ruskin in his later days. But already in that first essay I mentioned, "Kata Phusin" (according to nature) is making that sort of point. Houses erected in the country, the only ones in which the author is interested, must follow the customary ways of the countryman's building. They must "fit in" to the landscape, they must become part of it: that is the peasant's way, "since [the cottage] is ordinarily raised by the peasant where he likes, and how he likes; and therefore, as we have seen, frequently in good taste."[13] The whole argument sounds a little like a modified version of Loos's. The peasant cottage was given such exalted status by Ruskin because it was in a sense a part of nature, because the peasant could immediately mirror his national character in forms he derived from nature: that nature which Ruskin continuously scrutinized for the way in which surface revealed structure, and the structure the process of making. Clearly Pugin's formalism would seem contemptible to him, as did Pugin's vehement religious opinions. Ruskin was a naturalist: he was of Darwin's generation and intellectual climate, as Pugin was of Chateaubriand's and Overbeck's. If there was a man who provided a view of architecture which, however different, he felt had something to offer, that man was Viollet-le-Duc.

It can hardly be accidental that both men were fascinated by geology, that both were anti-clericals, that both had a strong attachment to social forms in spite of their radicalism, and that both found the appeal of Gothic through their concern for a national, even racial, character. This concern Ruskin owed to the idealist tradition to which he was heir, to Friedrich Schlegel in particular, as mediated by Coleridge and De Quincey. There is a sense in which the huts discussed by Ruskin in The Poetry of Architecture are as much exemplars of quasi-natural rightness, born of the mediation between nature and national character, as the Ancient Ballads had been to Wordsworth and Coleridge. Bishop Percy, dedicating his great collection of such ballads to the Countess of Northumberland in 1765, had indeed explicitly stated that he was offering the distinguished lady "rude products of our ancestors, products of nature and not of art."[14] Although in Bishop Percy's case this is no more than an allusion, the doctrine of the close correlation of art with climate, race and moral condition is established firmly by the theoreticians of romanticism, by Madame de Staël and by Chateaubriand particularly, and in a minor way by Hazlitt and De Quincey in England. The idea is developed by implication, though on a grander scale, by Carlyle, and of course is expressed by Ruskin in The Poetry of Architecture in a minor key. Even the most entrenched of academic theorists could not escape the idea. Quatremère de Quincy, whose first writings belong to an earlier age, had a second period of output and influence in the 1820s and 1830s. In the polemics his classical faith was diluted. He maintained, of course, that there was such a thing as absolute beauty, and he went on to argue that this beauty was attained by chosen races (that is, beautiful races), those which are acknowledged to be so by the general consensus of all generations. In particular, of course, to him this must mean the Greeks.

On this showing there is no progress possible in the arts: they advance by accumulation and not by development, and in such a view the primitive hut can only be thought of as a most miserable predecessor for the grand inventions of civilized people. In his two-volume *Dictionary of Architecture* Quatremère makes this point of view plain. He excludes from the appellation architecture any building that has purely material function; for no architecture is possible before the attainment of a certain material and moral standard. According to climate and custom, man adopted certain styles of buildings beyond the shelters nature made available to him, such as caves and trees; and wood must have seemed naturally and generally the building material for all primitive societies, as — Quatremère adds — has been proved by travelers who have come back from savage parts of the world. The hut was first built of branches, then of tree trunks, and this form of construction, as he points out, is still used in many European cities. But the use of timber or even of worked wood showed adherence to primitive forms of carpentry, "and that *symbolic hut* which was to become the type of architecture in Greece expresses nothing more than the first essays of the carpenter's art, that is, of a mechanical skill."[15] Although Quatremère believes this hut to have existed really, it was merely a product of natural circumstances: and the imitation of this "natural" model does not raise building to the status of architecture.

It was by emulating nature through taking up the proportions of the human body that the primitive Greek builders raised their craft to the status of great art. Quatremère finds it necessary to return to the argument in his dictionary, in the article *"Cabane."* He dismisses contemporary huts and cottages as either primitive and botched examples or vulgar reductions of more complex and important buildings, but he inserts the article only for its theoretical implications. In itself the hut is not the necessary germ of architecture; it may often prove sterile. It *did* prove conspicuously fertile in Greece, where the model hut had become a theoretical system "undoubtedly founded on primitive fact, but which had become a kind of canon both invented and real, to which the modifications, whether more or less necessary or probable, of already existing forms might be referred for justifying their validity [*vérifier la raison*] or to confirm a new usage." It is, in Quatremère's own phrase, "the rule for correcting abuse."

Quatremère's view was not universally accepted. His static and un-historical view of the past allowed for no progress and certainly not for the revolutionary genius, that popular figure in the first half of the nineteenth century. Quatremère's ideas were among the many things that Victor Hugo swept away. By the time Quatremère had reached authority, the young found him insufferable. He was shouted down in a famous riot at the Ecole des Beaux-Arts in 1826, and in 1829 his criticism of Labrouste led to the formation of an opposition party which, after the great changes of the following year, led to his increasing isolation.

Viollet-le-Duc in his turn, though he was teaching a doctrine substantially so different from Quatremère's, was to be shouted down in the Ecole des Beaux-Arts thirty years later, when he began that series of conferences in which his teaching was to be summed up. Viollet-le-Duc's unpopularity was also due to his devotion to the past, particularly to his vision of medieval architecture, and he was up against a new classical opposition. Like Quatremère, he produced a great dictionary, and though it was much longer, it was limited to French architecture in the Middle Ages. Viollet-le-Duc, like Quatremère, used the article on architecture to announce his basic tenets. Architecture, he says, may be divided into two parts: theory, which deals with all that is permanently valid, both the rules of art and the laws of statics, and practice, which consists of adapting these eternal laws to the changing conditions of time and space. It was the perfect incorporation of the eternal rational laws, both of art and of building science, in medieval architecture that so excited Viollet-le-Duc's admiration for medieval architecture.

Such a clear "structuring" of his material, such unshakable faith in the power of reason, gave Viollet-le-Duc enormous assurance as a historian. And he seems doubly assured when he is writing popularly, for a teen-age reader, as if he had actually seen the events with his own eyes, or rather with the eyes of two supernatural beings, Doxi, the dreamer and thinker (consequently the conservative), and Epergos, the doer and improver, who shows the men he and Doxi meet throughout their travels in space and time how to improve the habitations they have themselves devised by slow experiment—though at the beginning, "habitation" was hardly the word. Doxi and Epergos come upon "a dozen heavy-limbed beings, their skin a livid yellow, their skulls covered by sparse black hair which falls over their eyes, their nails hooked, huddled under a thickly growing tree, whose lower branches have been bent down towards the ground and kept in place with lumps of mud. The wind blows sharply and drives the rain right through this shelter. Some rush mats, some animal skins barely protect the members of these beings, who—by using their long nails—tear apart the fragments of animal flesh, which they instantly devour."[16] A little

"The First Building," after Viollet-le-Duc

later Viollet-le-Duc actually compares this very primitive shelter to a snake's nest, and what is more, he describes these beings as eaters of reptiles. Epergos is touched by their misery. Next morning he chooses two saplings within a few paces of each other. "Hauling himself up to one of them, he bends it down by the weight of his body, and pulling the top of the other one down with the aid of a crooked stick, and joining their branches together, he ties them with some rushes. The beings, which have now crowded round him, are amazed. But Epergos does not expect them to remain idle. He makes them understand that they must look for other saplings round about. Using sticks and their hands, they uproot them and bring them to Epergos. . . ."[17]

He shows them how to plait and tie the saplings into circular huts, caked with mud and floored with beaten earth. By the end of the day each family of this tribe (the Nairriti, Viollet-le-Duc calls them) wants a hut of the kind that Epergos has built.

Doxi does not think it right to interfere. " 'Why go against that which is done? Will you now teach the birds to build their nests, the beavers their huts in some other way than the one they already know? . . .' 'Who knows!' Epergos answers. 'Let us come back a hundred thousand days from now and see if these beings have forgotten my instructions to live as they did yesterday. If they have, I am wrong to interfere . . . but if they have benefitted from my advice, if the huts we find are better built than these, then I am right, for these beings are not animals.' "[18]

The reptilian action, the reptilian food of these Nairriti, is evidently chosen by Viollet-le-Duc to suggest a humble station on the evolutionary ladder. It is the crypto-providentially produced example of the two tied saplings which gives the first men that essential impulse from which all building starts: their first construction, the mud-weighted branches of the tree under which they shelter from the storm, is a construction plainly inferior to most animal dwellings of the kind the Rev. Mr. Wood has described in his book.

Histoire de l'habitation humaine was of course a late piece of popularization. And Viollet-le-Duc had, in a rather more serious tone of voice, gone into these matters in some detail when he composed, some twenty years earlier, his Lectures as professor at the Ecole des Beaux-Arts. He set out in these to "inquire into the reasons of every form — for every architectural art has its reasons; to point out the origin of the various principles which underlie them . . . to recall attention to the application which can be made of the principles of ancient art to the requirements of the present day: for the arts never die; their principles remain true for all time; humanity is always the same . . . its intellectual constitution is unchanged . . . while the various languages it employs do but enable it to express in every age the same ideas and to call for the satisfaction of the same wants."[19] Ruskin was all the talented amateur; his desultory, if extensive, education, his extended travels, his bouts of nervous illness, his personal fortune provided quite a different background to Viollet-le-Duc's thorough professional training at the hands of A. F. R. Leclère, his modest circumstances and fanatical dedication to his profession. Leclère himself had been a pupil of Percier, but had started his career in the atelier of Durand.

And while he almost immediately abandoned his first teacher's *atelier*, Durand's teaching influenced him as much as it did most architects of his generation.

Viollet-le-Duc was five when Durand's most popular and influential book, the account of his lectures at the Ecole Polytechnique, first appeared in 1819. The school had been founded twenty years earlier and it had aimed to form a new generation of architects, who would reject all that mythical baggage which the classical tradition, in spite of so many professions of reason, still imposed on the practicing architect. It was to produce designers guided in the first place by logic and conscious of the new techniques; competent and rational. "The architect's ability," Durand sums up his teaching succinctly, "lies in his ability to resolve two problems: 1, given a sum, to produce the most decent building possible, as in private building. 2, given the decencies required of a building, to produce the building for the smallest expense possible, as in public building."[20]

In spite of this bald assertion of Durand's, excision of the old values is not complete; tradition as well as reason teaches him the essential lesson: "Whether you enquire the reason or examine the monuments, it will be clear that pleasure could never have been the aim of architecture, nor architectural decoration its object. Public and private utility, the happiness and the preservation of individuals and of society . . . such is the aim of architecture."[21] Architecture, since it has to satisfy mankind's most urgent needs, must, by satisfying them, please. Nor is it at all necessary to search after effect in architecture. "If you dispose a building in a way appropriate to its use . . . will it not differ noticeably from any other building intended for some other usage? . . . If the different parts of this building, intended for different uses, are disposed severally the way they ought to be, will they not differ from one another?"[22] and so on. The one thing which must at all costs be avoided is imitation, a doctrine echoed later by Ruskin: "All imitation has its origin in vanity, and vanity is the bane of architecture," he writes, and urges the use of "natural and national forms only."[23] But the forms proposed by Durand are not *national*; they are on the contrary *rational*. Although he never explicitly says what the term might mean, at the climax of his exposition of the process of design (at the beginning of the third section of his *Précis*), he extols the variety that may be obtained by playing at combinations on a repertory of closed forms.[24] And that is the point at which the insidious — and contradictory — nature of the teaching which Durand got from his master Boullée becomes apparent. While Durand never states a priori his predilection for the elementary geometrical bodies (an idea to which I will refer later), it is clear that if exclusive appeal is made to the "elementary" geometry as providing a "rational" basis for formal invention, there will be little room for any ornament whatsoever. And yet, with all the manuals of architecture up to his time, and many later ones, Durand gives exact instructions about the setting up of the orders. This, however, he feels he has to justify in retrospect. Having explained the details of different columns and their possible applications, with reference to the properties of materials and the weather, he concludes: "Such are the forms and the proportions which the very nature of things has recommended to us for the principal parts of the orders as well as the habits which we have formed in either seeing the ancient orders or their imitations, and the care we must take not to tire the eye with strange proportions." He goes on to say that his economic system of architecture rests on a more solid basis "than the imitation of the hut or of the human body. . . . Simple and natural, it is as easy to remember as it is to understand."[25]

At the very outset of his essay he pours scorn on those writers on architecture whose art is "not that of building useful buildings, but of decorating them." Therefore, he goes on to say, they play about with orders which the ancients bequeathed us and most of Europe adopted; and these they reckon to be derived either from the imitation of the human body or of the primitive hut, which the majority considers the essence of architecture. It is for this idea that he reserves his heaviest sarcasm.

Chapter 3: POSITIVE AND ARBITRARY

THE MOST PROMINENT BUTT OF DURAND'S ATTACK WAS THE ABBÉ LAUGIER. Marc-Antoine Laugier, an ex-Jesuit *homme de lettres*, had busied himself with architectural matters a generation or so earlier. In 1753 he had published his first *Essai sur l'architecture*, which was reissued, with plates, two years later (just as he was leaving the Society of Jesus). Some years later, in 1765, he published a further book on the argument, *Observations sur l'architecture*, in which he revised some of his earlier opinions.

But Durand saw a convenient target in the earlier, and very much more popular, book: and it is on the issue of imitation that he, expectedly, takes issue with Laugier. The arguments which Durand thought it necessary to dismiss before he could get out his own view of architecture touched on the larger matter of mimesis, the imitation of nature in art. He sums up the offending attitude like this: "If architecture is to please through imitation, it must imitate nature, as do the other arts. Let us therefore see if the first hut made by man was a natural object; whether the human body may serve as a model for the orders; and finally whether the orders are an imitation of the hut and of the human body."[1]

I have previously given an account of Durand's attempt to dispose of the body-column analogy. As for the orders imitating the primitive hut, Durand chooses to open the argument in Laugier's allegedly self-condemning words, near the beginning of the first *Essai*. Laugier invites the reader to consider ". . . man in his earliest origins, without any other help, without other guide than the natural instinct of his needs. He wants a place to settle. Beside a tranquil stream he sees a meadow; the fresh turf pleases his eye, the tender down invites him. He approaches; and reclining on the bright colors of this carpet he thinks only of enjoying the gifts of nature in peace; he lacks nothing, he desires nothing; but presently the sun's heat begins to scorch him, and he is forced to look for shelter. A neighboring wood offers the cool of its shadows, he runs to hide in its thicket; and he is content again. Meanwhile a thousand vapors which had risen in various places meet and join; thick clouds obscure the air, and fearful rains stream in torrents down on the delicious wood. The man, inadequately sheltered by leaves, does not know how to defend himself against the discomfort of a humidity which seems to attack him on all sides. A cave comes into view: he slips into it; finding himself sheltered from the rain he is delighted with his discovery. But new defects make this dwelling disagreeable as well: he lives in the dark; the air he has to breathe is unhealthy. He leaves the cave determined to compensate by his industry for the omissions and neglect of nature. Man wants a dwelling which will house, not bury him. Some branches broken off in the forest are material to his purpose. He chooses four of the strongest, and raises them perpendicularly to the ground, to form a square.

On these four he supports four others laid across them; above these he lays some which incline to both sides, and come to a point in the middle. This kind of roof is covered with leaves thick enough to keep out both sun and rain: and now man is lodged. True, the cold and the heat will make him feel their excesses in this house, which is open on all sides; but then he will fill the in-between spaces with columns and so find himself secure.

"The little hut which I have just described is the type on which all the magnificences of architecture are elaborated. It is by approximating to its simplicity of execution that fundamental defects are avoided and true perfection attained. The upright pieces of wood suggest the idea of columns, the horizontal pieces resting on them, entablatures. Finally, the inclined members which constitute the roof provide the idea of a pediment. Note then what all masters of the art have confessed." But Laugier makes much more of this doctrine than its previous confessors. He makes it the cardinal point of his teaching. The second edition of the *Essai* shows architecture represented as a female figure pointing to this very same primitive hut, whose description I have just quoted, as the true examplar for architects.

The same passage continues: "Never has there been a principle more fruitful in its consequences; with it as guide it is easy to distinguish those parts which are essential components of an order of architecture from those parts which are only introduced through necessity or added by caprice." There are no arches, arcades, pedestals, attics, doors or even windows in the elemental cabin. Only the column, the entablature and the pediment are essential to it, and consequently to all architecture. The dictates of necessity, walls, windows, doors, etc., Laugier was prepared to consider as architectural elements. They contributed nothing to the essential beauty of the building; they were *licences*, a term which in earlier theory of architecture had been applied to ornamental features which had no antique sanction. But these were precisely what Laugier condemned utterly as the additions due to caprice. Even the pilaster, for which there was ample precedent in Roman antiquity, was to be abolished. Laugier went further: according to him, walls and pilasters should be relieved of the task of carrying loads, which should be confided to the proper column alone: in all this, it is the primitive hut which prompts and guarantees. "Let us never," Laugier admonishes his reader, "lose sight of our little hut."[2]

The earlier theorists of architecture, as I intend to show, made rather cursory reference to the connection between the origins of architecture and its principles. For Laugier origins had unique authority. Allowing for the inevitable differences between the two men, and the differing scale of their enterprises, this view of the authority of the primitive hut is not unlike that which Rousseau attributed to the family as the archetype of social organization. Whatever the authority which had been

The personification of architecture
and the primitive hut, after Laugier

attributed to the hut in earlier times, Laugier's view of it was sanctioned by reason appealing to contemporary anthropology. At the risk of demonstrating the obvious, I would like to spell out the difference between his account of origins and that of Viollet-le-Duc. Viollet-le-Duc's first men were brutish, bestial creatures, barely recognizable as humans; creatures who defended themselves against the violence of hostile nature by ineffectual makeshifts. Laugier's primitive man is quite at his ease with nature. The stream by which he settles flows gently, the meadow is green and soft. The sun may be excessively hot at times, the rain uncomfortably wet, but these are not the essential conditions of man's first existence; they are its accidents. And they are remedied by the construction of the hut, for which the cave and the forest are notional models. Hence this hut is built of column-like tree trunks and has no use for any clay or wickerwork; hence — too — it may be regarded as the mediation of nature to art through instinct and reason acting in unison. In all this Laugier's affiliations are evident. By the time of the *Essai* he was already moving at the edges of the Encyclopedist circle. Typically, he describes himself as *philosophe*, and it is *en philosophe* that he defends his right, against the overpragmatic practitioners, to state the rules and aims of an art like architecture.

I have already referred to a certain analogy between Laugier's method of arguing and Rousseau's. However, beyond the analogies, there are certain differences between the two writers on this very point which are worth noting. "I see," says Rousseau of his first men, "such as he might have been when he came from Nature's hand. . . . I see him replete under an oak, refreshed at the nearest brook, finding his bed at the foot of the very tree which had furnished him with his meal: and so his needs are quite satisfied."[3] Like so many descriptions of man's first state, this has a respectable classical ancestry: its immediate source seems to have been the discourse on the *Origins of Inequality*, which Rousseau wrote for the Academy of Dijon. Some years earlier, speaking to the same Academy on *The Contribution of Art and Science to the Refinement of Manners*, he had been more explicit: "It is not possible to reflect on manners and not wish to recall the simplicity of earliest times. Here is a calm riverbank, dressed by the hand of unaided nature, towards which the eye turns constantly, and which you leave with regret; here at a time when innocent and virtuous men wanted the gods to witness their actions, they lived together with them in the same huts. But soon men turned wicked, tired of the embarrassing onlookers, and relegated them to magnificent temples. Finally men chased the gods out altogether, so as to inhabit those temples themselves: or at any rate, the temples of the gods came to look very much like the citizens' houses. Then came the height of degradation, and vice was never carried so far as when it was seen, to speak figuratively, supported by marble columns and engraved on Corinthian capitals."[4]

You will note the calm riverbank, recalling the site of Laugier's first hut. Rousseau's hut stands, however, not for an architectural principle, but for a moral one. This was clear to everyone: as witness Kant's reference to these ideas in the *Critique of Judgment*, in a passage where he distinguishes between moral and utilitarian criteria of judgment on the one hand, and those of taste on the other.[5] Rousseau needs the metaphor to establish a different distinction: between savage and natural man, the origin and status of human industry, the nature of human property and the contingent problems of social organization and human aggression. In another essay, *On the Origin of Language*, Rousseau returns to the matter of primitive man's dwelling: "Their hut contained only their like: the stranger, the beast, the monster were all the same thing for him. . . . These barbarian times were the golden age not because men were united, but because they were separated. Everyone, it is said, thought himself the master of everything because no man knew or desired but what was to hand. . . . Men attacked each other at meeting, but they hardly ever met. The state of war was universal, but the whole earth was at peace." And he goes further: "Before land was divided among its owners, no one considered tilling it. . . . The first cake that was ever eaten was the communion of humanity. When men began to settle, they cleared a little ground round their hut: it was a garden rather than a field . . ."[6] and so on. But always it is from the family housed in its primitive hut that Rousseau conceives human society developing.

Three or four generations earlier, addressing a discourse on universal history to Louis XIV Dauphin — whose tutor and guardian he was — Bishop Bénigne Bossuet had assumed that building, like agriculture, husbandry and dress, had been taught to the earliest humanity by its Creator. For Bossuet, and for many later historians of human origins, man had never existed in a pure state of nature. When "natural man" became an essential item of philosophical equipment, an outwardly "*croyant*" thinker like Condillac was forced to postulate a second, postdiluvian fall, when the memory of the original didactic (and therefore de-naturing) revelation had been forgotten by certain families separated from the main body of humanity, in order that their "natural" behavior in the free world might be considered. Even Diderot had recourse to various subterfuges to distinguish the "man of creation" from the natural, innocent man.

The reason for which a return to origins became, in the eighteenth century, the precondition of all systematic thinking has been frequently ventilated. Here I might perhaps point out that the origins to which Rousseau returned to find the types on which constitutional thought was based assumed a "natural" condition before history, which was "primitive" and "original" in the notional rather than in the paleontological sense. The method which Rousseau employed and recommended to others in reconstructing the primal state of affairs was not archeological, but a priori speculation; even what we would now call anthropological fieldwork in search of the noble savage was only incidentally interesting to him.

However, Laugier's primitive man was not quite Rousseau's, although Laugier's primitive was also attained by speculation and not by data finding. But while Rousseau is not interested in the minutiae of building construction, Laugier has no concern for the social context of the first builder, whom he shows, Lockeian fashion, as being quite devoid of any innate ideas. In such a state of affairs, instinct and reflection respond directly to the pressures of hostile elements in nature by reproducing "constructions" which nature offers as models. The primitive hut, therefore, as Laugier conceives it, is a pure distillation of nature through unadulterated reason, prompted only by necessity. Here then was a guarantee against outworn, capricious custom as well as the vagaries of individual taste. More, it was the framework for a theory of architecture firmly based on nature, and entirely satisfactory to reason, a guide to all future architects, therefore, as well as to theorists and *philosophes*. It was a theory of architecture out of Newton (and Locke) by Condillac.

But the view of nature and of reason it took for granted was not altogether universal; even within the circle of the *philosophes* there was no uniform view of man's origin and of his destiny. Rousseau's moral view of origins looked back to man, whose manners were virtuous because he was born free and because he was content with those essentials which nature offered him; and to those conditions it might be possible to return by emulating the apparent outward circumstances of his existence, or, at any rate, by approximating to them as the millenianist visionaries had thought, centuries earlier. This is not quite Laugier's view. He does not exhort his contemporaries to dwell in the sort of hut he describes; nor does he even see any particular moral virtue in returning to a "natural" condition. I suspect that any such radicalism would have been quite alien to him. The primitive hut is *notionally* primitive. It is a demonstration of a priori reasoning, put forward as a criticism and a precept; it never spills over into an advocacy of "primitive life." Laugier's view might perhaps be closest to a "sensationalist" view, such as Condillac's — who no more than Laugier wanted a return to the life of first sensations — or even de la Mettrie's primitive materialism.

I do not wish to attribute too sophisticated or defined a philosophical view to Laugier. His view of the origins and nature of building could be located almost anywhere in the Encyclopedic spectrum. If Durand finds it absurd, it is not so much because Laugier's reasoning is faulty, but rather because his postulates are incomprehensible seventy years later. In the intervening period, however, Laugier's teaching gave the generation of architects who read him a sense of their part in the intellectual ferment of their time, and a sense of their social mission. It affected such staid professionals as Jacques-Ange Gabriel as well as the visionaries and utopians, and affected them in a way in which the polite rectitudes of Jacques-François Blondel could never have done: Laugier's little hut had been built on Rousseau's riverbank.

Yet in the middle decades of the eighteenth century Laugier's was the prevalent view in France. Elsewhere, and in France a generation earlier, a somewhat different view of human society and of man's destiny prevailed. Its most brilliant representative was Leibniz; in idiosyncratic form, it was asserted by Vico; and it is tentatively explored by Montesquieu, while somewhere behind hovers Bossuet's majestic construction of human history. It is a view which takes man to be an active partner in a process involving the individual and society — a continuous society from Adam onwards — collaborating with providence towards the working out of some high, and as yet unknowable, eternal purpose.

Most familiarly, this view is represented, in caricature, by Voltaire's Dr. Pangloss. This figure of fun had a near contemporary who attempted to formulate an architectural theory: a Venetian Carmelite, Carlo Lodoli, whose name is often coupled with Laugier as that of two representatives of protofunctionalism. But their views are very different. Laugier and Lodoli were both polymaths; but while Laugier busily published tracts, sermons, history, Lodoli came to be known as the modern Socrates because he never published anything at all. He corresponded with Vico, whose famous autobiography he commissioned, and with Montesquieu. But his own writings, including — so it is said — his treatise on architecture, were confiscated on his death by the Inquisitors of the Republic, since he was suspected of entertaining seditious ideas. They were placed under a leaking roof in the Piombe, and rotted into illegibility.[7] His thought is therefore known only through the writings of his disciples, Andrea Memmo and Francesco Algarotti.

While Algarotti gave a rather sophisticated account of his mentor's teaching, Memmo claimed to be a fundamentalist. His chatty, button-holing book gives the reader the whole Lodoli doctrine about *how to build with scientific solidity and an elegance which is not capricious,* in the words of the title. The book first appeared in Zara in 1786 and had an immediate Roman reprint. But Lodoli had died, an old man, in 1761. Algarotti's essay, adulterated though it was, had been composed before Lodoli's death.

Laugier and Lodoli's attitude, in common with some of the most remarkable thinkers of the eighteenth century, ignored or condemned current practice as corrupt and set out remedies by reference to first principles. This noted, they diverged immediately. Memmo registers this when he discusses the question of the origin of the orders. Having quoted the Vitruvian passage about the subject extensively, he cuts the canonic author down to measure: "Father Lodoli held that if Vitruvius should have had a more lively and wide-ranging intelligence, he would have recognized that to compose his architectural history it would be essential that he leave his retreat and visit . . . ancient Etruria, the realms of Naples and Sicily, no less than Egypt and Greece . . . so that he might have offered other insights, so that some wise man guided along by new ways may have realized that where people started to build in stone and brick, they would never set out to imitate huts. And because of that it could not be said with all certainty and for all cases (considering the *true* history of architecture) that it was an imitative art; even less that what it had to imitate was that first wooden construction. While if the first architectural invention was to have been imitated, then, as [the first invention] dictated by human intelligence and not by nature (since in Oriental countries stone was first used in building), the hut should not be accepted as a model by anyone who thinks of it as the first artifact to replace nature: all the less since a first invention is not usually the best. . . ."[8] In that inbred way eighteenth-century *literati* enjoyed, Memmo records that he had read with great approval the letter which Antonio Paoli (who was to publish the first survey of the temples of Paestum) had sent to another antiquarian, Carlo Fea, now remembered chiefly as the Italian editor and translator of Winckelmann, and which appeared as an appendix to the third volume of Fea's edition. Memmo sums up: "He [Paoli] proves, with the support of the authority of the sacred texts as well as the most ancient profane authors, and from those monuments which are still standing, that among the Orientals the first architecture was of stone. The Egyptians were the first to build in stone, that the Egyptians passed it on to the Phoenicians and to the Tyrrhenians or Etruscans, so this art of construction addressed itself to its primary object, which is the solidity and endurance of buildings."[9] Paoli thought, and evidently Memmo found this in agreement with Lodoli's ideas, that the primitive Doric order originated in Egypt; that columns, in combination with arches, had been used in the palace of Ahasuerus (a very telling point against Laugier, this); that Etruscan architecture had originated before the orders had been thought of; and that the canon of the three orders had not been formulated properly until the time of Pericles. The Homeric poems indeed make no mention of stone buildings: they do not eulogize architects, but carpenters. And Paoli in his turn quotes another contemporary writer, David le Roy, who maintained that the mastery shown by Greek carpenters in the building of timber houses was quite outstanding. "But I cannot really under-

Design for the Venetian Embassy, Istanbul,
attributed to Andrea Memmo, Fondazione Cini, Venice

stand," Paoli goes on, "how he [le Roy] might say in praise of such a
nation that it provided us with an example by translating directly into
stone that which had hitherto been worked in wood; I cannot see how
proportions which are suitable to working in wood might possibly be
adapted to stone."[10]

Paoli was writing in the 1780s: Lodoli and Laugier were both dead,
but the issue about which they differed was very much alive. It was
given a new relevance by the incipient nationalism of the day. Against
the newly discovered Greek prototypes—which had hitherto meant
Roman architecture—certain Italians championed Etruscan originality and independence of the Greeks. This Etruscan originality could,
moreover, be given immemorial ancestry, back to the first stone architecture of the Egyptians—invented in 549, after the flood, according
to the popular chronology composed by George the Syncelles in the
eighth century—and hence could be seen to derive directly from the
same source as Greek architecture.[11] The Romans, as the direct heirs
of the Etruscans, therefore became the mediators of the mainstream of
architectural tradition, in which Greek architecture was a mere tribu-
tary. This was more than just a matter of national pride to Italian antiquarians committed to chronicling and amplifying the treasures of
their long-suffering and politically fragmented nation.

These speculations conflicted with many subscriptural chronologies, drawn up in the seventeenth century; even the great Newton himself published one, which he was at times even tempted to consider his greatest achievement. Most such writers seemed to follow the Spanish Jesuit Villalpanda, who maintained that there could be no true, or stone, architecture before the Temple in Jerusalem (for which, after all, the Lord Himself dictated the specification to King Solomon), yet Egyptian architecture and Egyptian things generally had always had an enormous fascination, and the claim of the Egyptians to be the first of all the civilized nations had support even from Scripture. Hieroglyphs, familiar in Europe since they covered the faces of those obelisks which punctuated the topography of Rome, had a particular fascination. There had been various attempts to decipher them, and to reconstruct their meaning. They were thought to carry an ancient secret wisdom to which the key had been lost, or at any rate mislaid. All hermetic writers referred to them. Various artists thought that they had found this key; Bramante, to take an early instance, composed a hieroglyphic inscription. The allusions to Egyptian architecture in ancient authorities, such as Pliny, Tacitus and the geographers, were eagerly examined to provide reconstructable descriptions.

The passion for things Egyptian was not limited in the eighteenth century to Italy. Rousseau himself echoes older ideas about the hieroglyphs in his essay *On the Origin of Language.* "Since we have learned to gesticulate we have forgotten the pantomimic arts, for the same reason that, for all our fine grammars, we no longer understand Egyptian symbols . . . that which the ancients said most vividly they did not express in words, they showed to the sight." And further on in the same essay: "It seems most probable that the first gestures were dictated by need, the first words forced out by passion . . . the genius of Oriental languages, the most ancient languages that we know, gives the lie to the notion of a didactic progression which has been read into their development. The language of earliest man is described as if it were a language of surveyors: but we see that it was a poet's language."[12]

Although Rousseau is here concerned with an issue which was fundamental to eighteenth-century philosophy and has again become actual, I wish to point out here only that his illustrations are drawn from a field which was particularly fascinating in the eighteenth century: the Isaiac speculations of the early Freemasons and Rosicrucians have their correlatives in such masterpieces as *The Magic Flute.* For historians of architecture, Egyptian architecture had a dual fascination: if the Egyptians had invented stone buildings, then this stone architecture incarnated their immemorial wisdom. The Etruscans, having learned stone building and the wisdom it enshrined from the Egyptians, had left on Italian soil more noble exemplars for the moderns to emulate than the newly discovered Greek buildings could provide, since they were derived from timber huts. Some, like the engraver-architect G. B. Piranesi, took this argument further. Piranesi was the most ardent of Romanizers, or rather, he and whoever it was that wrote the texts he dwarfed by the vast etchings which accompanied them: whether the Jesuit Contucci alone, or (as Focillon surmises) a committee of cantankerous Italian scholars defending the national patrimony,[13] or even Piranesi himself. Whoever it was, the architectural virtue which the etchings seemed to extol above others was that *magnificenza*, which of course the timber-copying Greeks could never attain. Piranesi managed to depict the remains of antiquity as so convincingly magnificent that travelers (for instance, Goethe and Flaxman) familiar with them from his etchings would complain at the smallness and even the squalor of the ruins themselves.

Piranesi reserved his particular fury (and he could be *very* crabby) for David le Roy, whom Memmo had lightly trounced. The doctrine according to which stone building descended from timber construction he rejected as absurd and misleading. The refutal recurs in the great work on the magnificence of Roman architecture; it informs the malicious notes on a letter of the French connoisseur and critic Mariette, published as an article in a Parisian literary periodical; and it is exposed to ridicule in the "Dialogue on Architecture," which opens with one of Piranesi's favorite targets, a remark of Montesquieu's that "a building charged with ornament is an enigma for the eyes, as a confusing poem is an enigma for the mind."

In Piranesi's view the architect was free to "invent" ornament: that is, adapt vases, cameos, candelabra, and so on to his purpose. Fantasy could have free range — over any fragments of antiquity — since variety was the end of ornament. And in ornament the eye had the separate pleasure which doubled that essential one that bare architecture gave. But Piranesi also had another end in view: to establish the superiority of Roman art as derived from the native Etruscans and, more remotely, from the Egyptians who had first devised a stone architecture, as against the Greeks who derived their temples — so Vitruvius had it — from primitive wooden huts. Piranesi therefore took great pains to refute the position he attributed to the "rigorist" architects, that they would have everyone "to live in wooden huts, in which some believed the Greeks found the norms for adorning their architecture."[14] Again le Roy does duty as chief target. But behind le Roy there now looms the ubiquitous Laugier.

There is no evidence that Piranesi had actually read Laugier's *Essai*, though he must have come across the little book and the ideas derived from it frequently enough among his acquaintances at the French Academy. The book was certainly familiar to Francesco Milizia, whose reasoning sometimes reads like that of Protopirio, the younger protagonist of Piranesi's dialogue called *Parere sul'architettura*. This

Piranesi: Plate XIV, from *Carceri*

dialogue is the centerpiece of the *Remarks on Mariette's Letter* (from which I have just quoted). Protopirio is a rather fumbling and inexperienced dialectician, easily routed by the other protagonist, the robust Piranesian master Didascalco. The latter whips himself into a fury, and having proved — in crypto-Laugierian fashion — that the new rules will not allow any of the usual features of any building, he asks, rhetorically, "Well, choose, Signor Protopirio, which will you knock down? The walls or the columns? You won't answer? I'll knock the lot down. Start with buildings without walls, then buildings without columns, or without pilasters, without friezes, without cornices, without vaults, without roofs: all flat, flat, a vacant lot."

The fluency, the malicious temper and the sharp turn of phrase sometimes recall the more flippant Memmo; moreover, the Piranesian concept of *magnificenza* probably owes something to Lodoli. But more interesting is the contrast between the prim frigidities of the Milizian Protopirio and the structurally magnificent architecture whose pleasures are echoed and varied by a free, fanciful ornament (an ornament which pollulates all over it), concealing the suspicion that this architecture shows Lodoli's doctrine stood on its head. I have no doubt that Piranesi had been familiar enough with Lodoli's ideas in his youth. His uncle and mentor, Matteo Lucchesi, was an associate, even a partner, of Temanza, the pedantic neo-Palladian, one of Lodoli's more acrimonious and persistent opponents.

It was Piranesi's primary contention that the Romans had learned architecture from the Etruscans, not the Greeks; Roman architecture was to him overpowering in its nudity as well as its grandeur. He described, of course, bridges, aqueducts and roadworks as well as temples and tombs; and admired particularly such vaulted constructions as the *Cloaca Maxima* and the "emissarium" of Lake Albano,

Piranesi: Egyptian chimney-piece, from *Cammini*

which, a century earlier, the Jesuit mythographer Athanasius Kircher
had attributed to the work of demons.[15] The superb, economic use of
stone, "according to its nature," seemed as admirable to him as the
huge size and bareness of the buildings. Lodoli might have put it this
way; indeed, the same point is translated into visual terms in Piranesi's
best-known suite of etchings, the *Carceri*, those vast structures whose
very scale, considered in terms of contemporary building funds, at
once removes them into the realm of theater decoration, and which
must be the nearest approach to a Lodolian style of architecture.

Piranesi planned a great work on the introduction and progress of
the fine arts in Europe, in which he intended to vindicate the Romans,
the Etruscans, as well as the Egyptians against the claims of the Greeks.
He never got beyond the introduction. But he returned to the matter
of Egyptian architecture in his introduction to a set of designs for
chimneypieces, most of which were huge and in the Egyptian style.
Although in the preface to these etchings he never firmly committed
himself to an opinion about what the Etruscans learned from the
Egyptians (perhaps because le Roy, his *bête noire*, had already said so
much about it), he nevertheless eulogized the mystery and majesty of
Egyptian monuments, and the impressively sacred character of their
hieroglyphs. The whole preface reads almost as if it were a commentary on Vico's aphorism: "The earliest men first felt without articulat-
ing, then articulated the wonder and emotions of their souls, and
finally reflected with a pure mind."[16] Though there is a more insidious
purpose in Piranesi's mind than there was in Vico's, for in a sense the
whole output of *Vedute*, *Magnificenze* and *Carceri* is a vast *memento
mori* for a greatness which once was and perhaps shall never be again,
cannot be again. He aimed not only to use the vastness and sublimity
in the Burkeian sense, he actually maintained (in the *Cammini*) that

the pain of terror was an essential element of enjoyment: "Out of fear springs pleasure," he says in justification of those vast ornamental machines covered with undecipherable hieroglyphs and flanked by inscrutable, quasi-human "supporters" which would have dwarfed the largest, most palatial hall.[17] Clearly this may be taken to echo Burkeian sentiments. The sublime, Burke thought, was "a sort of delight full of horror, a sort of tranquility tinged with terror."[18] Since art deals with the two ranges of passion: those concerned with social intercourse, in which beauty is an essential ingredient, and those aroused by ideas of self-preservation, in which terror and pain prevail, he found that an appreciation of the sublime is stimulated when the terror of threatened self-preservation is recalled in tranquility. While Burke argued the importance of the sublime on an a priori consideration of psychology, the part terror had played in the origins of the arts, and of speech in particular, had been "historicized" by the Neapolitan historian Giovanni Battista Vico, in a way which I shall describe later.

As for the Romans' debt to the Greeks, Piranesi did recognize that the Greeks had some influence on Roman architecture, but this, he thought, was not only a late influence, it was also decadent and damaging since it led to the chaotic ornamentation of later imperial building.

Lodoli would not have found this attitude alien. He himself (or rather Memmo, following Paoli, and claiming the old master as authority) maintained that the Etruscans got their skill in stone construction from the Egyptians as well as the Phoenicians. The Greeks, in this view, having remained attached to timber forms, produced an unreasonable and highly defective architecture. It was a favorite aphorism of Lodoli's that truth was more ancient than the ancients, more ancient than the Oriental peoples or the Greeks, or their porticoes and their huts. Therefore, he said, "not only the most impartial philosophers, but also antiquarians should love her. . . . Now since I doubt," he would go on, "if reasoning should not ever give preference to truth over antiquity, even if truth were not the most ancient of the two, I will continue to consider if those first ancients, whose example we wish to follow, had perfected all that there was to perfect: that is, if they had harmonized in stone all those proportions which together combine the greatest possible strength with the greatest possible beauty."[19]

The architect's skill, Lodoli thought, should concentrate on the mechanical working of the structure: "Architecture is an intellectual and practical science which aims to establish by reasoning the good custom and the proportions of artefacts, and to discover through experience the nature of the materials which compose it."[20] However, as reported by his admirers, Lodoli shows only the most perfunctory concern with the way the building is to be used. He did have made what he called an "organic" chair, in which the seat and the back were

Primitive huts. Fig. I, Colchian huts; fig. II, Phrygian huts.
Reconstructed after Vitruvius's description by Claude Perrault

hard and concave, to take the shape of the human body. Demonstrating
it to the possessor of one of the largest Venetian palaces, he pointed
out its advantages: "The Sanmichelis and the Palladios imitated the
ancients as did those workmen who made your huge armchairs, without ever enquiring what unadulterated common sense alone might
simply dictate and obliged everybody to be uncomfortable. Carve,
varnish and gild as much as you like to satisfy your necessary [sic]
luxury, but without forgetting comfort and toughness. And could
houses not be made as reasonable as these chairs? Sit down on this
chair, then sit down on the other, and you will at once prove to your-
self if it is more comfortable to follow the authority of the ancients, or
to abandon it for reason."[21]

And yet Lodoli was not a utilitarian. Necessity was not dictated by
utility; it was dictated by reason considering the laws of structure in
relation to material. Ornament was a matter of taste and usage (l'uso
fa legge, as Piranesi put it in his Dialogue). In this he went against the
precepts of a theorist to whom he owed so much, the abbé de Cordemoy. Cordemoy appeared to be permissive about ornament; and yet
for him good taste, which alone dictated ornamental forms, had to be
squarely based on the example of the ancients. Cordemoy's interpretation of the ancients went back to Claude Perrault's rule of the orders,
which he had set out in his treatise on the same subject as well as in
his edition of Vitruvius, which had set a standard of splendor and
scholarship for a century—the edition to which Lodoli inevitably also

referred, and which the Marchese Giovanni Poleni, in his first Vitruvian bibliography, praised above all others.[22] But it is worth remembering that Perrault's respect for the ancients was not single-minded; he reckoned to have translated Vitruvius freely and improved his prose. His attitude to Vitruvius was of a piece with all he stood for: his brother and close associate, Charles, had been the protagonist of the "moderns" in that "quarrel between the ancients and moderns" which was the *cause célèbre* of literary Paris in the later seventeenth century, and his chief opponent had been Boileau.

It must be said at once that even the "moderns" did not reject the imitation of ancient examples. This was in any case a commonplace of contemporary historiography. History was generally taught and learned as an exemplar; hence the fascination with Plutarch. The difference between the "moderns" and the "ancients" lay very much in the amount of liberty in the treatment of the past which the emulator was allowed. To the "moderns" reason was independent of history, transcended it, proceeding from a *"cogito."* For the "ancients," and I abbreviate to the point of caricature, reason was immanent in history, more particularly in ancient history, which ran on the rails of an almost atemporal mythical sequence.

Hence Claude Perrault as a "modern" allowed himself to "rationalize," to simplify the proportions of the orders into a single canon.[23] Only a few years earlier Roland Fréart, Sieur de Chambray (whose brother Paul, Sieur de Chantelou, wrote the famous account of Bernini's visit to Paris), found it necessary, in his handbook of the orders, to provide some fifteen to twenty examples for each order as they were found in ancient buildings and specified in contemporary handbooks.

Perrault had not so many scruples. The orders did not belong to the essence of architecture, after all: the essence was to produce those beauties which he thought "positive and convincing."[24] And these were opposed to "arbitrary" beauties; these last depend on an intention (*volonté*) to give a certain proportion, form and figuration to things which could have some other one without being deformed, and which are not rendered pleasant for a reason which might be evident to everyone, but only by custom, and by the connection which the intelligence makes between two things of a different nature, "which principle is the natural foundation of faith; this is only the effect of a prejudice, a good opinion we have of someone who, when he assures us of a truth which is unknown to us, disposes us not to doubt him. . . ."[25]

The "positive, convincing and rational" beauties are of a different nature, according to Perrault: "Richness of material, the greatness and magnificence of the building, the just and careful execution, and *symmétrie* which [in French] signifies the kind of proportion which produces evident and striking [*remarquable*] beauty: for there are two kinds of proportion, of which one is difficult to perceive, consisting of

Simplified canon of the orders, after Claude Perrault

a rational relationship of the proportioned parts, such as that of the sizes of the different parts to each other or with the whole. . . . It is the other kind of proportion which is called *symmétrie* and which consists of the relationship which the parts have together because the equality and parity of their number, of their size and of their situation, is an obvious matter, whose deficiency one can never fail to observe."[26]

Perrault makes it quite clear here that the "positive and convincing" beauties require only common sense for their accomplishment, while the other, arbitrary ones require the trained architect's skill. "Good taste is based on the knowledge of the first beauties as well as the second, but it is certain [*constant*] that familiarity with arbitrary beauty is more proper to the formation of what is known as taste, and that it alone distinguishes true architects from those who are not such."[27]

And yet the foundation of arbitrary beauty is evanescent: "Neither imitation of nature, nor reason, nor common sense are . . . the explanation [le fondement] of those beauties which are perceived in the proportions, disposition or the arrangements of the part of a column. And no other explanation may be found of the pleasure which is found in them than custom."[28] Since the orders are—in one sense—the by-product of changing fashions at various historical moments, Perrault saw no reason why there should be all the confusing varieties of ancient and modern systems: and he reduced the five orders to a single simplified rule.

Interestingly enough, Charles Perrault, Claude's brother, gives a graphic illustration of this same argument in his *Parallel of the Ancients and the Moderns* which appeared five years after the *Ordonnance*. The *Parallel* is in the form of a longish conversation between a *Président*, an *Abbé* and a *Chevalier*. They discuss the arts and sciences at length. When they come to architecture, the *Président* maintains that the famous buildings they have seen are only so because they are faithful copies of the antique, while the *Abbé* maintains that imitation had nothing to do with it, the modern buildings being much superior. The *Président* thinks this is to show ingratitude towards the inventors of architecture, since without all the accouterments of the orders they would not be so beautiful. And here the *Abbé* concurs, but, he says, "If in a speech there had been no metaphors, no apostrophes, no hyperbole, nor any other rhetorical figure, this speech could not be regarded as a work of Eloquence: [and yet it does not follow] that those who formulate the rules according to which these rhetorical figures work are to be preferred before the great orators who used them . . . the case of the five orders of architecture is the same . . . the praise of a good architect is not that he used columns, pilasters and cornices, but that he used them with judgment." The *Président* takes up the comparison between rhetoric and architecture. "It is natural," he says, "for man to make rhetorical figures; the Iroquois make them, and that more abundantly than the best European orators. But these same Iroquois do not employ columns . . . in their buildings."

The *Abbé* agrees that the Iroquois do not use the classical orders, "but they use tree trunks, which are the first columns that men used, and they make their roofs project beyond the wall, which forms a kind of cornice. . . ."[29] While the *Président* elaborates this argument, a disagreement occurs about the further analogy to the human body. The *Abbé* denies that any such analogy can be detected between the orders, whose origins are arbitrary and their continuation due to convention. The difference between them is simply due to the fact that when the ancients had rejected all those tree trunks which were too stumpy and low, and those which were too tall and weak, they were still left with a great variety of serviceable trees, and hence the variations in proportion between the orders. This leads him to a rehearsal of the argument between "positive" as against "arbitrary" beauties, in which Charles Perrault—speaking through the *Abbé*—closely follows his brother. He rejects the *Président*'s attempt to foist any complicated system of optics on the ancients. Nor does he admit the analogy between the classical orders, whose proportions may vary a great deal, and the modes of classical music, so precise in specifying intervals. Rather, he says, "the five orders of architecture, well measured and well drawn, were in everybody's hands, and it was easier to take them from the books in which they are engraved than it is to look up a word in the dictionary."[30]

The *Abbé* then proceeds to praise modern stone cutting, for which there was a passion in France (where treatises on descriptive geometry applied to stone cutting were published in quantity) as exemplified by Claude Perrault's façade of the Louvre. This, he maintains, compares very favorably with the brick and plaster vaults of the ancients. It is this sort of remark which was to provoke Piranesi's rage: even if in other respects, as in his treatment of the architect's responsibility for ornament and surface proportion, he very much follows in Perrault's footsteps.[31]

The reader will now have realized how pervasive the form of the Perraults' argument had become. Not only Piranesi, but Cordemoy, Lodoli, and many others had taken it up. Laugier had also used it — but he turned it on its authors.

I have already alluded to Vico's share in shaping such ideas. His writings were not widely known until the nineteenth century, but his beliefs about the origins of architecture have a certain interest here. He too believed that the ancients were not possessed of any specially revealed wisdom. The Greeks and Egyptians moreover were not, according to him, to be taken as "the" ancients. There were four great ancient "gentile" nations: the Egyptians, the Scythians, the Chaldeans and the Chinese, who were descended from Noah's sons; not by his legitimate progeny, who were the Hebrews, and who (because of their orderly life and clean habits) continued to grow in the stature of which God had created Adam and Noah after him, and which is ours. The bastard children of his sons were dropped by their dams and nourished by nitrate salts from their own feces, in which they rolled helplessly at first, and then, hardened by the life of the primeval forest, they turned into giants living according to nature—a curious pre-echo of Condillac's second fall. About their dwellings he has not much to say. Caves and huts he mentions, like the architectural theorists, and that they tended to be situated by perpetual springs. He does mention that the Etruscans were instructed by the Egyptians. But there is another idea which is peculiar to him.

The natural postdiluvian men believed themselves alone in the world. Sometime after the Flood, when the moisture had dispersed, dry exhalations or else a fiery substance went up into the air from the earth and produced thunder and lightning. This, Vico thinks, must have been catastrophic. The few giants, raising their eyes upwards, saw the sky, "and since human nature is so constructed that it attributes its nature to effects . . . and since their nature was as of men full of robust bodily forces, who expressed their violent passions by shouting and groaning [brontolando], they imagined that there was in the sky a great animate body. . . ."[32]

Fear is the origin of the consciousness of the other. Vico thought so: there have been many more recent historians of religion who have held this view, if in a more sophisticated form. But in the eighteenth century this particular emotion became involved with thoughts of pleasure, and of aesthetic pleasure in particular. This complex feeling certainly inspired Piranesi's vast autopsies of the detritus of Roman magnificence; his creation of complex and overwhelming spaces in which dwarfish figures were incarcerated, drained or perhaps even tortured; and those vast chimneypieces in the Egyptian style decorated with made-up hieroglyphic inscriptions (Champollion was to decipher the Rosetta Stone some thirty years later). The sense of mystery evoked by the indecipherable combinations of signs obviously intended to be read was in itself thought beautiful: the very strangeness, the grandeur of Egypt, suggests Piranesi's already quoted remark, "Out of fear pleasure springs," which Vico might have echoed.

Another of Vico's ideas (though it has remoter ancestors) is canvassed by Quatremère de Quincy (to whom I referred in the previous chapter) in his earliest serious book, a treatise on Egyptian architecture.[33] He held at that time that there can be no such thing as an absolute original architecture, an idea which — as I pointed out earlier — he was to modify. There were, on the contrary, three archetypes of building: the tent, the cave and the hut or carpenter's work.

The tent is adopted by the Chinese and the Scythians; the architecture it leads to, however, is too light and finicky to allow of imitation. The cave is the Egyptian archetype; it leads to an architecture which is too heavy and too undifferentiated for approval. The timber frame, which was adopted and perfected by the Greeks, is alone worthy of imitation. The idea is developed further by early nineteenth-century writers. Soane, in his lectures to the Royal Academy in 1809, followed the principal French academic theoretician, Jacques-François Blondel, fairly closely when it came to recounting the origin of the three kinds of architecture, but he related the kind of primary dwelling to the principal human pursuits: hunters in caves, shepherds in tents, farmers in proper huts.[34]

The reader may recall that here, in nuce, is the historical geography of architecture as it was to be developed by Semper and systematized by Strzygowski. To return to Quatremère, however; he saw that timber was the perfect material for an architecture which was both differentiated and solid. Before the hut could be imitated in stone it had to be reasoned and developed. So much ingenuity was stimulated and spent on this refining that "the school of carpentry in itself could make a reasoned art out of Architecture." And he goes on, "The transposition of wood into stone is therefore the principal reason for the pleasure which Greek architecture gives us, and this pleasure is the very same which we find so desirable in other arts of imitation."[35]

Naturally, Quatremère rejects Lodoli's arguments out of hand, and by name. It is Memmo's Lodoli he attacks. Lodoli's other disciple, Count Francesco Algarotti, he mentions with approval; and yet, although Quatremère agreed with Algarotti about the particular virtue of timber-frame construction, in the matter of imitation he differed. To Algarotti architecture seemed to be an entirely different case from painting, poetry or music. "These have, in a certain sense, merely to open their eyes, contemplate the objects around them, and base a system of imitation upon them. Architecture, on the other hand, must raise herself on high through the intellect, and derive her system of imitation from ideas about more universal things, things far removed from human sight. It might almost be said with good reason that she has the same place among the arts as metaphysics has among the sciences. But in spite of the differences between the arts, architecture's perfection is in the same point as the other arts, that is that her productions must have variety and unity."[36] A smug commonplace concludes the high-sounding preamble. And indeed the conclusion of the whole essay is equally smug: "Even if the architects lie, and the philosopher has preached [Lodoli is the philosopher meant here], this will also be a case of saying that the lie is more beautiful than the truth."[37]

Algarotti lumps together Egyptian, Chinese and Greek architecture. In Chinese architecture there are columns without capitals, as in the Greek there are columns without bases, both demonstrating the early state of carpentry building, as does the Egyptian custom (and oddly enough Algarotti quotes Scamozzi as his authority here) of having columns with neither base nor capital.

Altogether, Algarotti argues, timber construction is the only form of building which is *reasonable*. If the nature of stone was to have been followed, it would have been impossible to have decent-sized openings, since stone lintels must inevitably be short. Arches, of course, could have been built instead, but although nature provides a model for these in caves, they would have reduced building to a boring uniformity.

Algarotti made a brief reference to Laugier, and it is obvious that, in spite of his deference to "the philosopher," or simply "philosophy,"

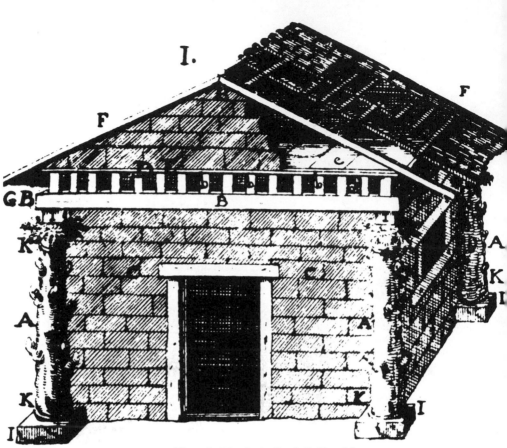

The primitive hut, after J.-F. Blondel

which introduces the opinions of Lodoli, he is much more influenced by Laugier. Curiously enough, in the matter of fluting he defers to Frézier, Laugier's opponent, and to another theorist, Jacques-François Blondel, for whom the whole matter of origins is reduceable to a brief reference at the beginning of his vast and vigorous treatise: "Men first doubtlessly made themselves shelters against the severities of the seasons and the attack of ferocious beasts. To this end they built themselves huts and cabins: reeds, cane, tree branches, their leaves, their bark and clay were almost the only materials which they employed to build their dwellings.

"As the families grew, their formless dwellings grew larger. Men had no sooner felt the needs to which society gives birth than they learned to provide themselves with more comfortable and more enduring dwellings. At this time also their dwellings, which had hitherto been spread out in vast deserts, changed into hamlets, these soon became burghs, and these last in turn towns. As soon as men were gathered in towns they had to defend themselves against the attacks of their neighbors. Strong earthworks were set up against them, walls were built, moats dug and towers raised. Not satisfied with the produce they found in their own climes, men wanted to enrich themselves with whatever nature made the furthest countries bring forth.

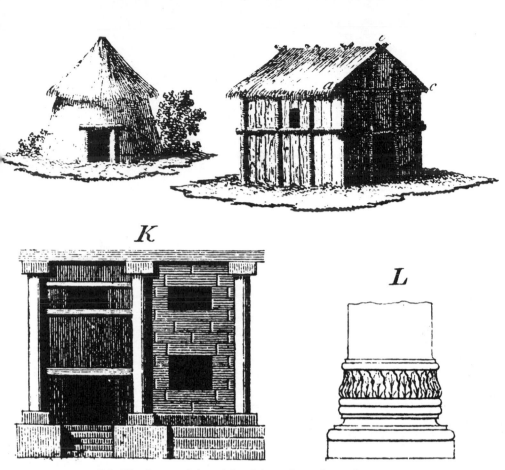

Primitive huts and the origin of the orders, after Milizia

. . . Such is the origin of the three kinds of architecture: civil, military and naval."[38]

This terse summary was in a sense the precursor of Durand's, since it grew out of a course of lectures; but where Durand found it necessary to spend pages on refuting the mimetic view of architecture and all the speculation that had been spun throughout the eighteenth century round the savage hut, Blondel could still be content with a laconic reference. He had very approximate ideas about the further progress of his art. The Egyptians, he thought, began building with woven reeds, the Greeks with sun-dried clay. While the Greeks progressed to wood, and created the true "antique" architecture, the Egyptians, for lack of wood in their country, "lapsed" into stone and marble, without passing through the essential carpentry stage. All this is unexceptionable. It may be worth noting, in the first paragraph, the Rousseauish reasoning, stripped of any moral overtones, and therefore almost inverted. But more curious is a footnote to this paragraph: "At the end of the fifteenth century, and at the outset of the sixteenth, the town of Moscow had not one house built of stone, only huts built of wood logs covered with moss. Houses in Perou are built in the same way today. Those of the Icelanders are built of small pieces of stone or rock bounded with moss and slurry. The Abyssinians build their huts only of daub composed of earth and straw. In the Monomotapa the dwellings are all of wood. Finally, there are people who, either because they do not have other materials available, or because they lack a certain kind of intelligence, build their huts out of the bones and skins of quadrupeds and marine monsters."[39]

In Blondel's book this kind of information remained an aside. The grand style had no need to take account of the irrelevant: the primitive and nonclassical past generally. Writing two generations later, Quatremère de Quincy, for all his devotion to the Greeks, found it necessary to systematize his material and integrate it into his main argument, in geographical terms, as I have already shown.

In the intervening generation this classification was going to be tied to the prevailing industry of a primitive society, but meanwhile an influential writer attempted a conciliation of the different attitudes. This was Francesco Milizia, the "Don Quixote of absolute beauty," disciple of Mengs and Winckelmann, and the enemy of all things baroque. In the preface to his *Lives of the Most Famous Architects* (which first appeared in Rome in 1768), he had already supposed that building was an inevitable product of the human instinct: "Man is impelled to build without much reflection, as he is impelled to drink, to preserve himself and to perpetuate himself, and as the beasts are impelled to song, to flight or to swimming. And what a distance there is between instinct and art, and between art and science!

"Many centuries were spent in huts, some conical, some cubical, in various modifications. This first way of building, which is not yet a real craft, and much less a science of building [that is, architecture], has renewed itself repeatedly, even in the most cultivated parts of Europe. . . . Building now in one way, now in another . . . seeing to commodity first, then to firmness, and finally to beauty . . . the art of building was finally developed. . . . The rudiments of this art were probably laid down in Asia and in Egypt . . . [in Greek monuments, however] there seems to appear something more than just art; there seems to be implied here a passage from art to science."[40]

Milizia defines art as "a system of knowledge reduced to positive and invariable rules, independent of capricious opinion," while science is "the knowledge of relationships which a certain number of facts may have to each other." Such facts are discovered by the senses alone, but Milizia proclaims that the primitive character of their first discovery should not lead us to despise our remote forefathers' efforts. "Although they were simple and coarse workmen, they must be looked upon as the greatest minds of their times. Had Palladio lived before the Flood, the whole effort of his genius might perhaps have been directed to putting together some miserable hut . . . as the great Newton, who discovered how to measure the whole universe, and calculate the infinite, might have exhausted all the resources of his understanding in counting up to ten. . . . Every art, and every science is born of necessity, and receives from the desire for improvement its slow and obscure growth. It is the business of philosophy to perfect them."[41]

All this serves as an introduction to the familiar hypothesis, briefly stated by Milizia, that if the Greeks were the first masters of the science and the art of building, they must have started with the hut in mind and before their eyes, and that, having improved it, they translated it into stone.

The orders, in Milizia's view as in Perrault's, were differentiated because of the range of tree sizes. He adds a personal note in suggesting that arches and vaults were derived from brackets, which may have been added to the tree trunks at an angle to carry more weight. He proceeds to derive every detail of stone construction, down to stairs and their balustrades, from the construction of a timber hut. In the matter of walls he is not quite as radical as Laugier. They were first made, he thought, either of boards, or of logs, or of unworked stone, which produced the various kinds of wall surface. And the conjunction of wall and column is the source of "bas-relief" architecture, in which the column is not standing proud of the wall but is more or less buried in it.

"Architecture, therefore," he continues, "is an art of imitation, as are all the other arts. The only distinction is that some of them have a natural model on which their system of imitation may be based. Such a model architecture lacks, but she has an alternative one offered to her by the natural industry of men when they built their first dwellings." The method will consist in "imitating for our use and delight a choice of natural perfect parts, which compose a perfect ensemble, such as may not be found in nature. Nature never forms a perfect ensemble, at least not to our way of thinking, but has strewn here and there perfect products which a man of taste and genius chooses and combines in the way most suitable to his subject, and forms it into a measured whole [*tutto compito*] which is that known as 'beautiful nature' [*Bella Natura*]."[42]

It is the remoteness and the difficulty of reconstructing the original quasi-natural model which leads to the frequent lapses of architecture into decadence. Milizia proposes nine principles which, he says, are "positive, constant and general, because they belong to the very nature of the thing and to good sense, and taken together they constitute the true essential beauty of architecture. But if they are lost sight of, then farewell Architecture. It is not science nor art, but turns into fashion, caprice and madness."[43]

The first principle is symmetry, more or less as Perrault defined it; then unity and variety, governed by the Vitruvian term "eurythmy." The third is the familiar principle of decorum. The fourth, stated almost in Lodoli's terms, is that, architecture being the daughter of necessity, everything in it must appear to be necessary and "every-thing which is done for ornament alone is vicious." In the fifth principle the orders are justified as not being ornament, but rather the skeleton of the fabric; they may therefore be defined (and here Milizia uses italics for emphasis) as "necessary ornaments produced by the very nature of building," to which all other ornament must be subject. Again, since ornament must result from necessity, nothing must be seen which has not its proper job in the building, and which is not integrated into the structure; "hence whatever is represented must also be functioning." Therefore, seventhly, "nothing must be done for which good reason may not be given." In the eighth principle, what is meant by reasons is spelled out: they must be derived from the origin and analysis of "the primitive natural architecture, the hut, which in turn gave rise to the fine art of imitation, that is to civil architecture. Everything," and this passage is italicized again, "must be founded on the true or on the plausible [verisimile]. That which cannot exist in truth and in reality may not be approved, even if it was made for the sake of appearance."[44] The last principle echoes Lodoli again; the authority of the past may never be used to block someone who is following reason alone.

The preamble to the *Lives of the Most Famous Architects* is expanded in the preface to the treatise on civil architecture. Again, it is dominated by the notion of ideal beauty, whose formulation Milizia derived from French authors; perhaps from the abbé Batteux's treatise, *Les Beaux-Arts réduits à un même principe*. This "Newtonian" strain attempts to incorporate ideas taken syncretically from Lodoli, Laugier, Blondel, and other salient theorists. Milizia's reading was wide, and he quotes copiously. But although he does not depart at all from the doctrine I have already transcribed, he does provide further definitions of the essential ideas. Having restated that the perfection of architecture, as of the other fine arts, is the imitation of *"Bella Natura,"* he goes on to say that imitation is "the artificial representation of an object; blind nature does not imitate, it is art which imitates. . . . Imitation may be rigorous or free. He who imitates nature, rigorously and faithfully, just as she is, is—as it were—no more than her historian, but he who composes her, exaggerates, alters and beautifies her, is her poet."[45]

Further on he amplifies this: to imitate "beautiful nature" is the same as imitating a choice of natural parts, each perfect in itself and composed into a perfect whole, such as may not be found in nature. The man of taste and genius, having observed nature well, will choose those parts which seem to him best, dispersed here and there among natural phenomena, and most suitable to his subject; these he will make into a well-knit whole. This well-knit whole is that which is called beautiful nature. The whole thing is imagined, but its ground is wholly natural. "All is nature," says Pope, "but nature reduced to perfection and to method. This is free imitation, or poetic imitation."

Art, says Milizia, takes those objects which, though they are more vivid in their natural state, evoke more pleasure when imitated, "because imitation puts the right distance between them and us, so that we experience the emotion without being disturbed by it. . . . Hence those arts which are called fine arts [belle arti] which have for their object beautiful nature [Bella Natura]. Now, the first savage artifact, the hut, is the exemplar of architecture, since it is from this rustic model that architecture must choose the most beautiful parts, imitate them well, ennoble them, dispose them in a natural fashion and one which is also consonant with the use of the building, so that from the variety of members, combined with proper regard to the aim, a delightful whole might result."[46]

Having rehearsed the familiar stuff about the principles which should govern architecture, Milizia ends with an invocation to architects not to forget the humble origin of their art, lest they become like the appalling nouveaux riches, who make themselves ridiculous by pretending to noble origins.

All my quotations have come from the first volume of Milizia's treatise, which is concerned with beauty in architecture. The second volume deals with commodity, the third with building construction. Milizia deliberately inverts the order of concepts in the Vitruvian tag: commodity, firmness and delight. The relegation of building construction to the last volume did not mean that the book lacked technical information; the little treatise was extremely popular and was used by many architects as much for the learning of the first as for the technical information contained in the last. But the reader who remembers Durand's strictures against the notion of architecture being an art of imitation may see in Milizia, whose treatise was republished for the fourth and last time long after Durand's lecture, a surviving witness to the vitality of this idea.

But Durand's master, the visionary and teacher Etienne-Louis Boullée, was already aware of other difficulties in such a view of architectural origins as was offered by Milizia. He directed his attack at a more prominent and formidable, if dead, opponent: Claude Perrault. Boullée reargued a famous academic disputation in which the elder Blondel, François (no relation to Jacques-François, the "younger" Blondel), had failed to present the argument for the natural origin of architectural beauty properly, and Perrault's argument had to be answered all over again.[47] Art mediated raw nature through taste, Boullée thought. "Taste is a fine, delicate discernment of objects which are connected with our pleasures. It is not enough to show us the objects of our pleasures; it is by choice that they are stimulated within us, and that it ravishes all our hearts."[48]

Taste is manifest through grace. The rich materials which were so dear to Perrault, Boullée excludes from among his criteria. Generally, as one might have expected from a positive worshiper of Newton ("Spirit sublime! Vast, profound Genius! Divine being, Newton!"),[49] problems of method cluster round the way in which perception led to the notion of regularity. Boullée testifies that himself, having studied irregular bodies, he recognized that "regularity alone could give men a clear idea of the forms of solids, and determine their domination, which . . . is the result not only of regularity and symmetry, but also of variety,"[50] thus providing the three essential ingredients of beauty, though beauty is recognized by a familiar criterion. "We qualify as *beautiful* those objects which have the most analogy with our organization, and we reject those which, lacking this analogy, do not agree with our way of existence."[51] A remark that Boullée supports with a comment presumably taken from Condillac, although its ultimate source, unknown to Boullée, was Locke.

It would be out of place here to see how the sphere turns out to be the perfect object within the specified criteria, and hence an obvious form for the Newton Cenotaph. More interesting is the idea that the notion of recurrence is more ancient than architecture itself. Boullée does not envisage men groping after the form of the first hut as a result of instinctive urges: "Conception is essential for execution. Our first fathers did not build their huts until they had conceived an image of them. It is this product of the mind, it is this creation which constitutes architecture."[52] In faintly echoing Alberti's division between conception and execution, Boullée was defending the art of architecture against those who saw it as coincident with building construction. The appeal to the conception of that first hut, not its ramshackle fabric, was the true model for the architect. The idea to which Boullée turned suggests that it is the essential form which nature yields to us through the perception of regularity which we must imitate in our buildings. And he returned to this primitive hut when the essence of architecture was to be conveyed. In a summary account of how architecture was to be taught, he suggested that "if one was to proceed with method . . . the simplest building, such as the rustic hut of which Vitruvius makes mention, should be offered to the eyes of beginners. The students are to draw this hut in different ways in order to familiarize themselves with the essential architectural concepts, and only then allow them to pass to more complex buildings."[53] What form was this rustic hut "according to Vitruvius" to take? I shall have more to say about the Vitruvian text, of course. But here I would like to refer to the way the primitive hut was described by Sir William Chambers, a near contemporary and possibly an acquaintance of Boullée's.

Chambers, writing in the 1750s, was considerably more conventional, at the outset at any rate, than Boullée. "At first," he says of the first men, "they most likely retired to caverns, formed by nature in rock, to hollow trunks of trees, or to holes dug by themselves in the earth. But soon, disgusted with the damp and darkness of these habitations [shades of Laugier!], they began to search after more wholesome and comfortable dwellings. Animal creation pointed out both materials and methods of construction; swallows, rooks, bees and storks were the first builders. Man observed their instinctive operations. He admired, he imitated, and, being endowed with reasoning faculties and a structure suited to mechanical purposes, he soon outdid his masters in the builder's art.

"Rude and unseemly, no doubt, were his first attempts; without experience or tools, the builder collected a few boughs of trees, spread them in conic shape, and covering them with rushes, or leaves and clay, formed his hut: sufficient to shelter its hardy inhabitant at night or in seasons of bad weather. But in the course of time, men naturally grew more expert; they invented tools to shorten and improve labour; they fell upon neater, more durable modes of construction, and forms better adapted than the cone to the purposes for which their huts were intended. . . . That the primitive hut was of a conic figure is a reasonable conjecture, from its being the simplest of solid forms and most easily constructed. Wherever wood was found, they probably built in the manner above described, but as soon as the inhabitants discovered the inconvenience of the inclining sides, and the want of upright space in the cone, they changed it for a cube, and as it is supposed, proceeded in the following manner."[54]

What now follows is the description, echoing Vitruvius, of the building of the primitive hut out of Laugier, more or less. That this form of construction was later to be imitated in stone and to become the source of Western architecture seemed to Chambers an obvious matter, to be mentioned only in passing. But the emphasis on the geometrical form of the hut is certainly remarkable. Chambers makes it extremely schematic. The passage is not from a conical, tentlike hut to a square one with a displuviate roof, but to a flat-topped cube; it was only later, as a third development, that "the form of the roof, too, was altered, for being, on account of its flatness, unfit to throw off the rains . . . it was raised in the middle . . . after the form of a gable roof."[55]

Chambers is so concerned with ornament — and with the orders in particular — that he has very little to say about proportions generally, so little that he does not take sides as between the "ancients" (with whom one would expect him to sympathize) and the "moderns," that he quotes Blondel and Perrault impartially as general authorities. It may well be that the idea of the conical and cubical hut is a gloss on Perrault's illustration of the Phrygian and Colchian in his great edition of Vitruvius.[56] It is worth noting that a contemporary of Chambers, Robert Morris, advocated an extremely rigid attitude to the geometrical

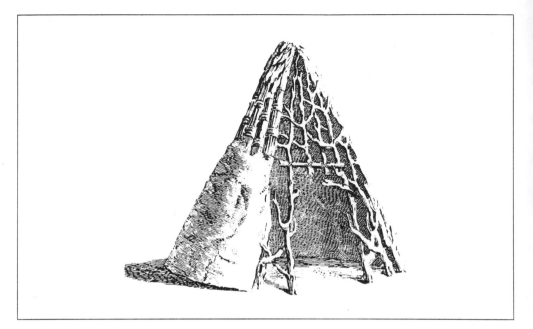

this page and opposite:
Primitive huts and the origin of architecture, after Chambers

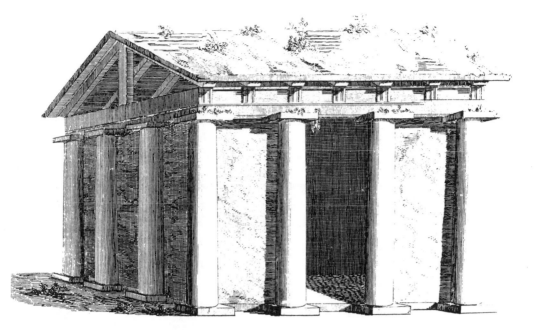

elements of composition. He suggested that the cube should become the element whose permutations in different sizes and numerical combinations should be the only essential compositional instrument.

In Boullée's mind, as in Chambers's, there is an ambiguity about the priority of the reality of the primitive hut over its idea — both the logical and the historical priority. If Boullée's idea of the priority of the concept over execution is taken historically, for instance, an impossible chicken and egg situation will result. And yet it was essential for these two writers to make a distinction which later, and even contemporary, theorists took in their stride. Such epistemological problems do not worry Milizia, Laugier, or Lodoli; even Algarotti, for all his Newtonism, does not prefer the geometrical concept of the hut in time to the hut itself. It is the extreme revolutionary, and the backward-looking academician, who see nature providing the conceptual model for the hut before the necessity of shelter forced men to build themselves huts.

J. M. Gandy: *Architecture: Its Natural Model.*
Watercolor. Sir John Soane's Museum, London.
This was to be the first illustration for a history of architecture;
the others were never done, nor was the text written.

Chapter 4: NATURE AND REASON

SPECULATIONS ABOUT MAN'S ORIGINS WERE NOT LIMITED TO THE SORT OF theoretical and philosophical writings I have discussed so far. The tone and manner adopted were sometimes very diverse. Two Scottish judges, whose lives span the eighteenth century, had very curious ideas upon the subject. Lord Kames, the more sober and the earlier of the two, believed that man was born with his accomplishments built in, as it were, and that he fell from civilization for a second time not after the Flood, but as a result of the confusion of tongues at the Tower of Babel.[1] After this fall, moral sense had to be recultivated, leading men up to the perfection reached in eighteenth-century Britain. Lord Monboddo had a rather more complex view of things. Primitive man, he thought, lived in perfect harmony of mind and body; social intercourse and progressive civilization (for man is the only creature capable of progress) had debilitated the body and sharpened the mind, and would lead in the last days, which were not distant, to a final degeneration of the body and triumph of the mind, which would in turn be followed by a modified apocalypse.

On the nature of the first men, Monboddo had very definite views. The orang-outang was, according to him, a surviving example of what our ancestors were: "I will add further upon the subject of the Oran Outan that if an animal, who walks upright, is of human form, both inside and outside, uses a weapon for defence and attack, associates with its kind, makes huts to defend himself from the weather, better, I believe, than those of the New Hollanders, is tame and gentle . . . has what I think is essential to the human kind, a sense of humour, who, when he is brought into the company of civilized men, behaves with dignity and composure, altogether unlike a monkey . . . and lastly, if joined to all these qualities, he has the organs of pronunciation and consequently the capacity for speech, though not the actual use of it, if, I say, such an Animal is not a Man I should desire to know in what the essence of a man consists, and what it is that distinguishes a Natural Man from the Man of Art?"[2]

To Monboddo, as to Francesco Milizia, the capacity to build is part of man's natural equipment, more essential than speech. But he does not enlarge upon it; indeed, in spite of this charming hypothesis, he is not committed to a definite view of the primitive hut. He did inevitably come in for much ribbing. Thomas Love Peacock's Sir Oran Haut-ton, for instance, the nonspeaking parliamentary candidate of highest principle in *Melincourt*, is a parody of Monboddo's primitive man. Dr. Johnson was briefer and more direct, as was his way. "I attempted," says Boswell, "to argue for the superior happiness of the savage life. . . . J: Sir, there can be nothing more false. The savages have no bodily advantages beyond those of civilised men. . . . No Sir, you are not to talk such paradox: let me have no more on't. It can't be certain, far less can it instruct. Lord Monboddo, one of your Scotch judges, talked a great deal of such nonsense. I suffered *him*, but I will not suffer *you*. Boswell: But Sir, does not Rousseau talk such nonsense? J: True Sir, but Rousseau *knows* he is talking nonsense, and laughs at the world for staring at him. B: How so, Sir? J: Why Sir, a man who talks nonsense so well must know that he is talking nonsense . . ."[3] and so on. But then Dr. Johnson was convinced that "conjecture as to what it would be useless to know, such as whether men went upon all fours, is very idle."[4]

Some writers, however, took such speculation in a somewhat different and more empirical fashion. Daniel Defoe's Robinson Crusoe, for instance, was a civilized man reduced to a state of nature by the development of his circumstances. When he was first wrecked, he followed the eighteenth-century scheme for primitive men and climbed a tree for the night. "All the remedy that offered to my thoughts . . . was to get up into a thick bushy tree . . . which grew near me, and where I was resolved to sit all night . . . and getting up into [the tree] endeavoured to place myself so that if I should sleep, I might not fall; and having cut me a short stick for my defence, I took up my lodging."[5] When he comes to build a proper house, he again proceeds according to the books. He finds a suitable site first, then, fearing hostile nature, he employs his thoughts "wholly about securing myself either against savages . . . or wild beasts . . . and I had many thoughts about how to do this, and what kind of dwelling to make, whether I should make me a cave in the earth or a tent upon the earth: and in short I resolved upon both."[6]

Crusoe was not entirely reduced to a state of nature. He had screws, saws, gunpowder, tarpaulins and worked timber. He also had a fund of moral commonplaces and prejudice; but it was the sight of growing corn, the basic agricultural phenomenon, which first inspired him with religious sentiments beyond his morality, sentiments which were reinforced by the experience of an earthquake. Unfortunately, when he makes his "bower" in the countryside, Crusoe gives little information about its construction: he is much more explicit always about fences and palisades than about the physical aspect of the dwelling. It is obvious, however, that if a simple sailor such as Crusoe, when stranded on a desert island, will rehearse the theoretical development of primitive man, the dwelling in the tree, the cave/tent model of the house, religious terror at earthquakes and thunder, gratitude for grain, domestication of animals, and so on, it should also have been possible to reconstruct some of the procedures the philosophers had spoken of and see if they corresponded with experience. The philosophers encouraged this idea by their own experiments. Rousseau himself spent some time in an idyllic rural retreat on the island of St. Pierre, near Berne, and later at Ermenonville, though they both turned out to have rather "civilized" snags. At a more absurd level there is Lord Monboddo's "air-bath," which may be taken to be returning him to a primitive, Adam-like vigor (he would get up at four o'clock in the morning and walk about his room naked in front of an open window before returning to bed).[7] The fascination with Russian baths at the end of the eighteenth century belongs to this world of ideas,[8] as does the interest in water for therapy; so too do Basedow's and later Pestalozzi's ideas on education, from which so much of modern educational theory derives, as well as the ideological background of modern sport; all are directly associated with Encyclopedic Adamism.

As far as architecture was concerned, there was also an obvious subject for experiment in this direction. This was the business of "developing" the orders. In the fifteenth and sixteenth centuries, before the orders were ruthlessly "canonized" by Serlio, inventing a new order was no problem. But in the seventeenth century, a new order meant — almost — tampering with revelation; especially since at the outset of the century a Spanish Jesuit, Juan Bautista Villalpanda, published, in his vast commentary on Ezekiel, his reconstruction of the order which had been used in the Temple of Jerusalem, and which was allegedly based directly on divine precept. Although Fréart de Chambray thought that this particular order was only suitable to churches dedicated to virgin martyrs (since it united the maidenly grace of the Corinthian with the robust strength of the Doric), it was appealed to with great earnestness by many architects. Throughout the seventeenth and eighteenth centuries there were several attempts to re-create the order of the Temple (eleven barley-sugar columns, allegedly from the "Golden Gate" of the Temple, are still in St. Peter's; one of them, known as the *Colonna Santa* because Our Lord is said to have leaned on it, is in the Chapel of the Pietà), with all sorts of curious results. Later I shall have more to say about the influence of Villalpanda's ideas, and the many speculations on the Temple in Jerusalem.

But in the latter part of the sixteenth century, and in the seventeenth, the political climate was very favorable to various attempts at creating a new "national" order on the "antique" model. There were Spanish and French orders more particularly; in 1672 there was a competition declared for the French order, to be used in the attic story of the courtyard of the Louvre. The prize was 3,000 livres and was won by no less a person than Colbert himself. But national orders were attempted by many other designers. In the eighteenth century, inevitably, the whole ideology of order making was transferred to nonclassical architecture; Gothic and Chinese orders were produced by the score.

The purists had to turn back to nature, of course, not only notionally. "Blondel, Perrault, Girardon, Desgodetz, as well as other artists, worked at . . . producing an order both elegant and rich, which would characterize the Nation . . . but most limited their efforts to varying the

The order of the Temple in Jerusalem,
after Villalpanda's description, from Freart de Chambray

Of the Temple of Jerusalem

Colbert: The French Order,
winning design in a competition of 1672, after Wildenstein

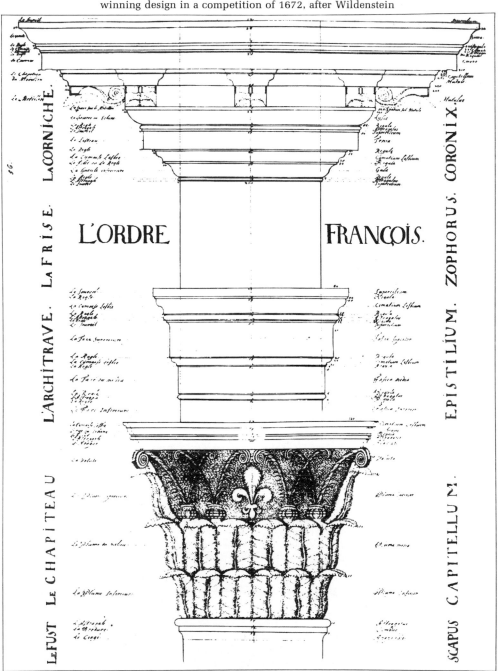

Corinthian capital . . . they forgot that, in order to compete with the Greeks, they should not imitate them closely, but go right back to the primitive theory, which is Nature herself" — this is how Ribart de Chamoust, a French gentleman, dedicates his work on *The French Order Found in Nature* to "the Nation." Some years earlier he had presented the manuscript of his book to Louis XVI, and made much of the accidental nature of his "discovery."

Now the order which Ribart proposed was "lighter, more slender, and more ornamented than the others." It was also, unlike the others, to be grouped in threes, arranged triangularly, for reasons as curious as the results of this device; but it is primarily the discovery which is of interest to me. Ribart is circumstantial, both in telling the story and in his reasoning. "I was taking a walk in a wood on my estates, in a valley which opens onto the Marne. Some young trees, growing in threes, although planted by chance . . . formed a sort of natural chamber, hexagonal and unusual. At this spectacle, my original idea about the change of volumes [*changement des masses*] was reawakened and fortified, all the more since I saw it 'squared' with all that I had already entertained of a French order. Perrault, I said to myself, coupled columns and pleased everyone . . . why, disposing them in threes as are these trees, should I awaken less interest, since, like him, I will only augment their beauty, which results from that severity and closeness so much sought after by the ancients, while on the other hand I will facilitate their separation for which the moderns have sacrificed all? I walked about the hall with a deal of pleasure and adopted it as archetype. Some time later, returning to the place, I almost imitated the ancient people of Achaia, in their composition of the Doric [order]. I had the trees of the chamber cut just above where they branched out . . . and all at the same height. I had the distance between them spanned by wall plates or lintels, then had beams placed above that, then a ceiling and a roof, and so I rediscovered the Greek type, but under a new species and with considerable differences. The next spring, the tender shoots which grow at the branching of lopped trees formed truer capitals than those of Callimachus. Some thick roots, naturally twisted . . . marked the bases; a lawn my miller had laid out by the side of his stream foreshadowed the stylobate. . . . The need for an agreeable location to hold the party [*fête*] which Friendship celebrates at my place [*chez moi*] every year suggested my choosing this hall in preference to any other. I had it decorated with garlands of flowers, and it naturally took on the shape of those country temples which used to be dedicated to love."[9] The landscape and the method of construction echo closely (allowing for the changed social circumstances, the carpenter, the miller and the gentleman-architect) the descriptions of primitive building quoted from Laugier and Rousseau, and I have no doubt Ribart sounded the echo only half-consciously.

The prototype and the full development of the French order,
after Ribart de Chamoust

TYPE DE L'ORDRE FRANÇOIS.

L'ORDRE FRANÇOIS DEVELOPPE.

Unfortunately, I cannot discuss here the elaborate imagery of the order; how the triple columns represented the three Graces, how the branching of the trees transformed into three *fleurs-de-lys*, the justification of the garlands being substituted for flutes, and so on; but I would like to emphasize the "sub-Newtonian" character of the "discovery," and the curious, almost scientific jargon Ribart chooses to employ. The order is *almost* not of his devising. He happened on this thing, which is implicit in nature, and *truer* (the word is his) than the late Corinthian invention of Callimachus.

It is also *national*. This last word is of course relatively new. Samuel Johnson — a tainted source in this context — lists two meanings for the word: public as against private, and "bigoted to one's own country."[10] But even the French Academy Dictionary does little better, though the word had already much more currency in French than in English. In the increasingly eclectic situation in the second half of the eighteenth century, the concept of "national" slowly came to mean "other than classical"; the French Revolution created a citizen army, a national army. The word was already used in that sense in French: the army recruited by a sovereign from among his subjects, as against foreign or mercenary troops. "National" architecture arrived at about the same time and made a similar distinction: the native-born, the spontaneous, the natural, as against the foreign, the imported, the strange. Hence justifications of national orders, such as Ribart's, had little future. But the historical method adopted by him was used in almost exactly the same way in Britain to justify and vitalize Gothic architecture by Sir James Hall, a Scottish geologist. He lived a generation or so later and I doubt very much if he had seen Ribart's book. He himself read his first paper on the origin of Gothic architecture before the Royal Society of Scotland (of which he was to be president for many years) in April, 1797, although the book from which the paper is an extract did not appear until 1813.

Hall believes, in his old-fashioned way, that the principle of imitation is essential to architecture. Stone, however, has no ornamental forms proper to its nature, nor has the act of building any immediate apparent forms to imitate. Hence the imitation of the wooden hut, which imposes a constraint within which the artist's licence may operate. On his return from his Grand Tour in 1785, Hall was struck by the beauty and stylistic coherence of many French Gothic buildings, and familiar as he was with the theory of the origin of the orders, he thought that "some rustic building, differing widely from the Grecian original, might have suggested the Gothic forms." He decided to investigate the matter, when he, too, came upon a happy accident. His journey through that part of France happened to be just after vintage time. The peasants were "collecting and carrying home the long rods or poles which they make use of to support their vines, or to split into

this page and overleaf:
The origins of Gothic architecture, according to Sir James Hall

hoops; and these were to be seen in every village, standing in bundles, or waving, partly loose, upon carts. It occurred to me that a rustic dwelling might be constructed from such rods . . . bearing a resemblance to works of Gothic architecture."[11]

The discovery involved Hall in an experiment, which, as he points out, is true *histoire raisonnée*, since he is verifying a hypothesis about the past by re-enacting it and hopes that his researches will lead to literary or archeological discoveries which may either confirm or

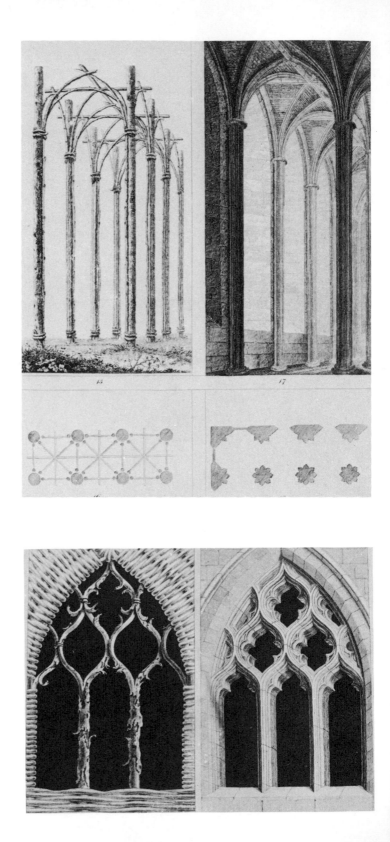

refute it. The system is simple. A row of equidistant poles of more or less the same height is fixed in the ground, as in various accounts of the origin of the orders. But to each of these "Gothic" poles, a surround of pliant willow rods is applied and fixed. When the opposite willow rods are brought together and tied, the resulting form is something like a groined vault, strong enough to carry a thatched roof, say. Small variations in the joining of the willow rods provide the models for varieties of arching and vaulting. Hall assumes the complexity to have been progressive: so the pointed arch, the clustered column, the branching roof, "the three leading characteristics of Gothic architecture," have been accounted for.[12]

The sides of the building are filled with upright rods on which in-and-out split willow rods are plaited horizontally, and probably caked with clay where that is available. Where windows are required, the matting is omitted, and this means that the windows are inevitably mullioned. Indeed, the upright rods, which are not rigid, may be tied together in various ways where they are free. And so another feature, tracery, is explained.

The experimental verification had to be made. "Finding that all the essential parts of Gothic architecture could thus be explained . . . I was desirous of submitting the theory to a kind of experimental test. . . . With the help of a very ingenious country workman [John White, cooper, in the village of Cockburnspath in Berwickshire], I began this in Spring 1792, and completed it in the course of the winter following." Hall is convinced that the method is so simple that it could be executed anywhere, with the help of almost any sharp instrument: "A set of posts of ash, about three inches in diameter, were placed in two rows, four feet asunder . . . then a number of slender and tapering willow rods, ten feet in length, were applied to the posts . . . and formed into a frame which, being covered with thatch, produced a very substantial roof, under which a person may walk with ease."

But this building was not, any more than Ribart's, a static, rigid construction. "In the course of spring and summer, 1793, a great number of the rods struck root and throve well. Those of the door, in particular, produced tufts of leaves along the bent part, exactly where they occur in stone-work. . . . I have likewise had the satisfaction in the course of last autumn [1796] of finding one entire cusp formed by the bark in a state of decay, in a place corresponding exactly to those we see in executed Gothic works."[13]

Although the foliation was not quite as abundant as Hall had hoped, he had justified, to his own and his friends' satisfaction, the timber origin of most Gothic forms. He had also actually copied, turning the method inside out, certain stone features (such as the porch of Beverley Minster, in Yorkshire), and felt fully justified in his procedure. Curiously enough, although Hall is explicit about the method of con-

The Gothic Hut, built by Sir James Hall

struction, the identity of each feature and the examination of existing monuments, he does not suggest where or how the change from timber to stone took place, or where the original huts had been devised, or by what sort of peoples, although it is quite clear from his description that it might have been in England, or anywhere else in the center or north of Europe.

Hall's motive in going through this elaborate exercise is his conviction that, before the rise of Gothic architecture proper, its principal features had appeared in "a more ancient style," and he hopes "to restore to Gothic architecture its due share of public esteem" by showing how it derives from a simple timber original, and is consequently systematic, "its authors having been guided by principle, and not, as many have alleged, by mere fancy and caprice."[14]

Essentially, the method for testing the hypothesis about the origins of Gothic architecture, to demonstrate that a "national" style is reasonable, systematic and natural, is almost identical with the attempt to enlarge the classical repertory, some twenty years earlier, by the "discovery" in a natural context of the truly "national" extrapolation from the ancient orders.

It is therefore hardly surprising that within a few years Hall's theory was contemptuously dismissed by Friedrich von Schlegel. It has been assumed, I think rightly, that this is the paper (the full book was not yet published) that Schlegel found on his return from his "Gothic" tour in 1805 to Paris, and to which he refers: "Among many learned novelties and scientific treatises [I found in the library] one on Gothic architecture, by an Englishman [sic]. How strangely must the brains of some individuals be organised! This writer imagines himself to have made an entirely novel discovery in tracing the foliated, tree-like form of Gothic architecture, the lofty, avenue-like aisles, the leafy vaulting and the universal similitude of every part, to the vegetable productions of nature. Yet, instead of recognising in this the love of natural beauties . . . he explains everything materially, from the imitation of I know not what existing objects, the rude efforts of savage industry, rustic cottages of interwoven osiers, basket-work of various kinds, and similar arbitrary suppositions."[15] Schlegel condemns the attempts to find the original forms of Greek architecture in such "rude contrivances, suggested by the necessities of savage life"; he finds the analogy between such a theory of Gothic origins and an equally unproven theory about Greek architecture gratuitous. Romanesque architecture, he further points out, shows no traces of its origins in wickerwork or suchlike. Gothic architecture develops from early Christian and Romanesque, by the operation of the Gothic spirit.

In his philosophical lectures — which owe so much to the two Schlegels — Coleridge condenses this argument and sums it up in his own way: "I cannot imagine a more expressive symbol and as it were analogy of this [commencement of modern times as opposed to the ancient] than by placing before my eyes the palace of the Imperial Goth, Theodoric, frowning opposite the Christian temple that alone overlooks it and the magnificence of Greek and Roman art. . . . I imagine that temple, too, removed with all its Greek and Roman associations, and nothing remaining but Christ and the Cross, and instead of it a cathedral like that of York, Milan or Strasbourg with all its many chapels, its pillared stems and leaf-work, as if some sacred grove of Hertha, the mysterious deity of their pagan ancestry, had been awed into stone at the approach of the true divinity and thus dignified by permanence into a symbol of the everlasting gospel. I hear the choral thanksgiving rolled in peals through the solemn aisles, or the chant of penitence and holy piety from veiled and consecrated virgins sobbing and dying away in its dark recesses among strange grotesques."[16]

Schlegel would have found this rhapsody sympathetic, I imagine; it represents an attitude much closer to his own thinking than Hall's pedestrian tinkering with rods and withies. Now Hall was aware that his idea might not be original, though he claimed that his verification was. At the time of his Grand Tour — when he first conceived his hypothesis — he had not, or so he says, yet read Francis Grose's *Antiquities of England and Wales* (1773–89), in which views similar to his were sketched, although Grose in fact had essentially different views of Gothic origins. Hall was, however, acquainted with the generally vegetable and forest view of Gothic origins which, he seems to think, "originated with Dr. Warburton."[17] The reference is to Warburton's commentary on Pope's Epistle to Lord Burlington (of which more later), which is closer to Coleridge than to Hall. But this association should not obscure the essential differences between them. There was a break between Coleridge and Warburton. The "positive" imitation of primitive working method and unenduring materials in nobler stuff did not appeal to the theorists of the nineteenth century. Ten years before Hall visited the French cathedrals, Goethe had gone to Strasbourg. He was a young man, and he describes himself as having his head full of the familiar book learning about architectural criticism and the canons of good taste. It was all blown away by his first sight of Strasbourg Cathedral. "With what unexpected sensations did the sight surprise me, when I came upon it! A total, huge impression filled my soul — for it was composed of a thousand harmonizing details which I could taste and enjoy, but neither recognize nor explain. The joy of heaven is like that — so they say."[18]

Goethe's essay appeared in 1772, and again in an anthology of Herder's in the next year. To an enthusiastic young man the conflict between judgment and impression was so violent that Goethe had to attack those who misled him, and he attacked them in the person of their mentor, none other than Laugier, whose book had appeared in

German some years previously. The primitive hut, says Goethe, is no model for the architect. In any case, "Dear Abbé," as he addresses Laugier, "the column is in no way an essential part of our dwelling. Our houses do not consist of four walls on four corners. They arise from four walls on four sides which are there instead of columns, and exclude all columns, and where these are stuck on, they are a burdensome superfluity." He apostrophizes architects in general: "Multiply, pierce the huge walls which you are to raise against the sky so that they shall ascend like sublime, overspreading trees of God, whose thousand branches, millions of twigs and leaves . . . announce the beauty of the Lord, their master. . . ."[19]

In *Dichtung und Wahrheit*, Goethe was to go back to the overpowering impression which the cathedral at Strasbourg, rising among the crowded low houses, had made on him. He had traveled from Leipzig, where he presumably came across Laugier's doctrine, and even his book, perhaps through the painter Adam Oeser, Winckelmann's friend. To dissociate himself from Laugier's view, Goethe invokes the analogy between the woods and forests of the north and the high Gothic vaults which Warburton had made popular in literary circles. In this anonymously published prose-poem, he was attacking not only Laugier but also the Zurich "physiological" art-historian Johann Georg Sulzer, who had attempted to formulate "objective" canons of taste. Neither is mentioned by name, though Goethe's critics knew well enough to whom he was pointing.[20] The issue comes up again in Goethe's correspondence with Schiller and Humboldt in 1795, when the matter of the criteria by which works of architecture are to be judged is debated between them.[21] Although Schiller's line is almost pre-Hegelian, Goethe takes a more complex view and attempts to formulate imminent architectural criteria to be sought in a building; and later still, when reworking his Italian notes, Goethe comes across the theory of the timber origin, in Rome, where he records it being advocated by Schinkel's correspondent, the archeologist Aloys Hirth.[22] He records it now conversationally, without the earlier animus. Hirth, he remembers, manipulated his examples well in support of the curious theory, though others maintained that this excessive devotion to rules was unnecessary, and that "in architecture, as in everything else, there was a place for the tasteful fiction with which the artist must never dispense."

It is tempting to recognize an echo of Algarotti's teaching here, though perhaps it is only an echo of the Horatian "*Sic veris falsa reminiscet.*" But Goethe is at his chattiest and gives no further details. When he had occasion to return to Hirth's ideas later (*Der Sammler und die Seinigen*), he wanted to dismiss Hirth's notion of "characteristic"-and-contingent as the essential ingredient of beauty.

And yet Hegel was to find Hirth, with his old-fashioned ideas about the imitation of the hut in stone, useful. To Hegel architecture was the original and in that sense the least "spiritual" art. It is hardly surprising that the only architect he actually mentions by name in the *Aesthetik* is Vitruvius (unless one excepts the Emperor Hadrian), and this in a work in which sculptors and painters, never mind musicians and poets, come in for a lot of individual attention.

Anyway, to him too the analogy of the vaulted Gothic church appeared striking and acceptable: "If you entered the interior of a medieval cathedral it did not represent to me the strength and mechanical efficiency of the carrying piers and of the vaulting resting upon them, but rather a forest vault, whose ranks of trees incline their branches towards each other and intertwine. A crossbeam requires a firm point of support and a level setting; in Gothic architecture, however, the walls rise up free and independent, as do the piers, which spread out in several directions as they rise, and meet, as if by accident. That is: although the vault does in fact rest on the piers, the purpose of carrying the vault is not expressly shown or asserted for its own sake [*für sich hingestellt*]. It is as if they [the piers] did not carry any weight: as in a tree the branches are not carried by the trunk, but appear to have the form, in their slight inclination, of continuing the trunk and of building a leafy roof out of their twigs. . . . And yet all this is not to say that Gothic architecture truly accepted trees and woods as its model." Naturally, Hegel considered this image incidental to the "aesthetic" effect which Gothic builders intended. The whole contrast between interior and exterior, the fragmented walls, the slender columns, and the vast areas of window supporting huge vaults, all this has a supernatural aim: "The columns grow slender, ever thinner, and rise so high that the eye cannot take in the form at one look, and is forced to wander about and fly upwards until, reaching the softly curving vault, it rests at the crossing of the arches. Just as the soul, at first unquiet, troubled, rises gradually from its ground of the finite to heaven and finds its rest in God alone."[23]

Even from this passage it is clear that for Hegel the "meaning" of a building was quite independent of the way it was made—I shall return to this point—and of the way it was used; even of the immediate associations it evoked. The meaning had to be found in the transcendent concept which the architecture "incarnated"; a concept whose value would be the overwhelming element in one's estimate and apprehension of the particular architectural forms.

This is perhaps not entirely fair to Hegel, who is at his least happy and familiar with this matter in the *Aesthetik* when dealing with architecture. Oddly so, since in his view—as I said earlier—architecture is the "original" art, on the temporal scale at least: "The first aim, the prerequisite, of art is that a conception, a thought, should be produced by the mind and presented by man as an artifact [*ein Werk*]; as in speech concepts exist in their own right which man presents and makes understandable to others."[24] Later, he says, even more explicitly, of a public, "monumental" building, that it comes into being for no other purpose than to express the highest through itself; it is therefore an independent, self-justified symbol of an idea touching directly on essential nature, a universally valid thought, a manifestly clear if silent statement addressed to the spirit.

The notion that the primitive hut is essentially true to nature (or whatever the justification for its archetypal role may have been) cannot have any real importance to Hegel, who makes the point explicit. Aloys Hirth's argument about the timber origin of the hut, and the form-dictating nature of timber (to be worked into beams and columns), is reiterated at length when Hegel embarks on a discussion of classical architecture. Stone, he goes on, does not suggest its own use as timber does; if anything, stone in large quantities suggests the idea of hollowing out. Since, moreover, stone has no forms proper to it, it may be shaped into any. Hence stone is the right material for the earlier symbolic architecture as well as for the later romantic. Timber, "because of the directional nature of the tree trunk, seems more immediately suitable to be used for that strict adherence to purpose, and that regularity which is the principle of classical architecture . . . but . . . classical architecture does not limit itself to timber construction; on the contrary, when it has been perfected to the point of producing beauty, it constructs its buildings in stone."[25] The characteristics of the two materials modify each other, it is true, but in essence Hegel presents information collected from the commonplace eighteenth-century treatises, which he might have received from Hirth in a digested form.

However, Hegel takes me away from my theme. For him the primitive timber hut, imitated in stone, is no "Urbau," no paradisal, nor (in the sense I have so far used it) original construction. It hardly belongs to architecture proper as far as Hegel is concerned. Yet Hegel thought that architecture not only had traceable origins but was historically the first art. Although he senses the fascination of the idea of origins, he chastely refuses to commit himself on a subject where empirical information is deficient and conjecture inevitable. Moreover, "such simple beginning is, as far as its content goes, something of such little importance that it must appear as something completely accidental to philosophical discourse."[26] The idea of the hut or cavern as the original architecture belongs to the realm of popular speculation, which may have charm but does not absolve the philosopher from looking for explanations within the limits of history.

The first aim of art, then, as Hegel sees it, is "to formulate, to give form to (gestalten), the essentially objective, the natural world, the external environment of the spirit, so as to give meaning and form to that which has no soul (*dem Innerlichkeitslosen*), which, however, will remain exterior to it since this form and meaning are not immanent to the object."[27] Form and meaning are therefore transcendent; for the artist, as far as the object itself is concerned, it is a physically present work of art. Hence neither the use of a building nor its *facture*, nor even the metaphorical echoes the building may provoke (viz., the forest cathedral), are directly aspects of meaning and form, but belong to the generalized *Innerlichkeitslose* in which form and meaning are infused.

I cannot here sum up how this leads Hegel to the triple division of architectural history into a symbolic epoch in which architecture becomes independent; the classical, in which it leaves the fashioning of the individual image to sculpture and becomes independent, an inorganic setting; and finally, the romantic (Moorish, Gothic or German), in which the various civil or religious functions are only indirectly related to the mysterious life of the buildings themselves.[28] Hegel does indeed enumerate the first buildings known to the history of architecture; they are the stepped towers of Mesopotamia, the obelisks, pyramids and sphinxes of Egypt, and they are not to be regarded too highly. "The ideas which are accepted as content in them are — this is true of symbolism generally — as it were unformed conceptions, elementary . . . confused abstractions of the life of nature, mixed with notions about spiritual function, without ever being focused, in terms of idea, as the states of a single subject."[29] Clearly, then, for Hegel the house could never represent nature in the way in which it did for Laugier and for earlier theorists; moreover, that kind of representation of nature could only form a metaphoric element in the building. It was too closely incorporated with the procedure of construction to allow of the kind of symbolization Hegel required of architecture, and which he described in his account of a Gothic cathedral. Elsewhere he took up a more explicit attitude to the business of the basic, commonplace building and nature. In the introduction to the *Philosophy of History*, Hegel discusses one of the fundamental ideas which animates his assessment of the historical process. History is an account of that activity which may be understood as the "middle term of the syllogism, one of whose extremities is the universal essence, the *idea*, which reposes in the penetralia of the spirit; and the other the complex of external things — objective matter. That activity is the medium by which the universal latent principle is translated into the domain of objectivity.

"I will endeavor," says Hegel further, "to make what has been said more vivid by examples. The building of a house is, in the first instance, a subjective aim and design. On the other hand we have, as means, the several substances required for the work, iron, wood and stone. The elements are made use of in working up this material: fire to melt iron, wind to blow the fire, water to set wheels in motion in order to cut the wood, etc. The result is that the wind, which has helped to build the house, is shut out by the house; so also the violence of rains and floods, and the destructive powers of fire, so far as the house is made fireproof. The stones and beams obey the laws of gravity, press downwards, and so high walls are carried up. Thus the elements are made use of according to their nature, and yet to co-operate for a product by which their operation is limited. Thus the passions of men are gratified; they develop themselves and their aims in accordance with their natural tendencies, and build up the edifice of human society, so fortifying a position for right and order *against themselves*."[30]

I have taken this trivial example from a vast discourse on history, but I have quoted it to demonstrate a point about Hegel's schemata rather than to further the understanding of the essential Hegelian notions, for which the reader must turn to the text from which I extracted this passage. But I wish him to note this: until a few years before Hegel used this example, it would have been an unthinkable one: although the house was used to exclude the elements, as well as various enemies, it was never thought of as being *against* nature. For the elements, in their hostile manifestation, were only that aspect of nature against which men found in nature itself the remedies for human weakness. A radical shift has taken place. And it was curiously enough Durand's *Lectures* that give this shift emphatic expression in terms of architectural theory.

GOTHIC EXCURSUS

A NUMBER OF WRITERS WHO HAVE BEEN QUOTED—GOETHE, HEGEL, COLERIDGE —saw the Gothic cathedral as echoing not some primitive hut but a wood, or even a forest. Now innumerable references can be found in the literature of the time, and later, to vaults like forests glades, and vice versa. William Empson, writing more recently in his *Seven Types of Ambiguity*, comments on a line of Shakespeare's seventy-third sonnet:

Bare ruin'd quiers, where late the sweet birds sang,

that these words, and all "those boughs which shake against the could" of the preceding line, suggest an obvious parallel. "The comparison holds for many reasons: because ruined monastery choirs are places in which to sing, because they involve sitting in a row, because they used to be surrounded by a sheltering building crystallised out of the likeness of a forest, and coloured with stained glass and paintings like flowers and leaves. . . ."[1] Here, and in the rest of the paragraph, Empson lays out the whole apparatus of the metaphor, ap-

Drawing for ornament, from sketchbook of Villard d'Honnecourt

parently as true for Shakespeare as it was for him. And yet I doubt very much if the wood-choir metaphor would have seemed quite as *obvious* to Shakespeare as it was to Empson.

We know a deal about the symbolism of medieval churches from books like Durandus of Mende's treatise about the rules of the divine office and the various notes left by such patrons as Suger, or master-builders like Villard d'Honnecourt, which refer to much other symbolism (the church as the city of God, as earth and heaven, as a *"summa,"* as a human body, etc.), but a reference to the church as a forest is hard to find. Villard does indeed, in his notebook, show some very fancy vegetable ornament, particularly for carving, but when he does invoke an analogy to plant forms he associates it in the time-honored fashion with the human body.

I suspect that the men of the Middle Ages would have been puzzled by some of Hegel's descriptions of their thinking, as well as by the way in which Gothic architecture was classified and described by writers on art like Schlegel. To Schlegel there was a polarity in art between "sidereal" and "vegetal" styles, which did not coincide exactly but was parallel to "classical" and "romantic." On his showing, and in terms not altogether unlike Hegel's, he identified the product of the intensely "sidereal" thinking of medieval master-builders as "vegetal." Not that the analogy between vault and wood was original.

In the eighteenth century, the *locus classicus* of the metaphor was found in Bishop Warburton's commentary (in his monumental edition of Pope) on the Fourth Epistle in the *Moral Essays,* the one to Lord Burlington. At the seemingly irrelevant point when Pope apostrophizes the pedantic peer:

> Yet shall [My Lord] your just, your noble rules
> Fill half the land with Imitating fools,
> Who random drawings from your sheets shall make
> And of one beauty many blunders make;
> Load some vain church with old Theatric state,
> Turn Arcs of triumph to a Garden-gate . . .

Warburton chooses to interpose an argument about the church and triumphal arch: "for the one being for religious service, and the other for civil amusement, it is impossible that the profuse and lascivious ornaments of the latter should become the modesty and sanctity of the other." The objection to the different character is reinforced, in Warburton's mind, by the fact that the church ornament is essentially for the interior, whereas the pagan is for the outside. And he goes on: "Our Gothic ancestors had juster and manlier notions than [these] modern mimicks of Greek and Roman magnificence, which, because the thing does honour to their genius, I shall endeavour to explain. All our ancient churches are called, without distinction, Gothic, but erroneously. They are of two sorts; the one built in Saxon times, the other during our Norman race of kings. . . . When the Saxon kings became Christian, their piety . . . consisted of building churches at home and performing pilgrimages to the Holy Land. . . . Now the architecture of the Holy Land was Grecian, but greatly fallen from its ancient elegance. Our Saxon performance was indeed a bad copy of it. . . . But our Norman works had a very different original. When the Goths had conquered Spain, and the genial warmth of the climate and the religion of the old inhabitants had ripened their wits and inflamed their mistaken piety . . . they struck out a new species of architecture unknown to Greece and Rome; upon original principles and ideas much nobler than what had given birth even to classical magnificence. For this northern people, having been accustomed, during the gloom of paganism, to worship the Deity in GROVES . . . when their new religion required covered edifices, they ingeniously projected to make them resemble groves, as nearly as the distance of architecture would permit. . . . And with what skill and success they executed the project . . . appears from hence, that no attentive observer ever viewed a regular avenue of well-grown trees, intermixing their branches overhead, but it presently put him in mind of the long Visto through a Gothic cathedral. . . .

"Under this idea . . . all the regular transgressions against art, all the monstrous offences against nature, disappear; everything has its reason, everything is in order, and an harmonious Whole arises from

the studious application of means, proper and proportioned to the end. For could the Arches be otherwise than pointed when the Workman was to imitate the curve which the branches make by their intersection with one another? Or could columns be otherwise than split into distinct shafts, when they were to represent the stems of a clump of trees? On the same principle they formed the spreading ramifications of the stone work in the windows, and the stained glass in the interstices; the one being to represent branches, and the other the leaves, of an opening grove; and both concurred to preserve that gloomy light which inspires religious reverence and dread. Lastly, we see the reason of their studied aversion to apparent solidity in these stupendous masses, deemed too absurd by men accustomed to the apparent as well as real strength of Grecian architecture. . . . But when one considers, that this surprising lightness was necessary to complete the execution of the architect's idea of a Sylvan place of worship, one cannot sufficiently admire the ingenuity of the contrivance. . . . Such as is here described was GOTHICK ARCHITECTURE. And it would be no discredit to the warmest admirers of Jones and Palladio to acknowledge it has its merits. They must at least confess it had a nobler birth, though a humbler parentage, than the GREEK and ROMAN ARCHITECTURE."[2]

I must apologize for the inordinate length of this quotation. Even though some of Warburton's prolixities have been excised, it remains a verbose but important document. It is nice to think, at any rate, that Warburton — who in the year this was published changed a Gloucester prebend for one at Durham, and was ultimately to return to Gloucester as its bishop — had a real liking for Gothic architecture. The reader will no doubt have recognized several ideas that have already appeared in quotations from Hegel and Goethe. Both knew this text directly or indirectly, and it must certainly have been at the origin of Coleridge's rhapsody. The theory of the Moorish origin of Gothic architecture Warburton attributes to Wren's *Parentalia*, though it had appeared almost at the same time in Fénelon's *Dialogue on Eloquence*. It was popularized in Evelyn's preface to Fréart de Chambray's *Parallel Orders*, and it goes back no doubt to the generalized condemnation of all things Greek and Gothic in painting and architecture so fashionable in the fifteenth century.

I do not really wish to consider the way in which the notion of "Gothic" architecture developed, both as an idea about the past and as a way of working. Here I am concerned with the transformation of the model, the archetype, for architecture; and in this connection it seems worth mentioning the earliest surviving instance of the "wood" model for Gothic architecture.

It appears in a report about the state of Roman architecture, written to an unnamed Pope — perhaps by Raphael and/or Baldasar Castiglione to Leo X, perhaps (though I do not think so) by Peruzzi. At any rate,

above: Tree column and vault, Bechyne Castle, Bohemia,
after Börsch-Supan

left: The tree column, after P. de L'Orme

right: Bramante: Column of loggia, Basilica of S. Ambrogio, Milan

Tree arch, Ulm Cathedral

the author laments the way in which the barbarians, once they got to Rome, stripped ancient structures of marble and even brick for their own use. The barbarians, so this author points out, even succeeded in corrupting Greece, the source of "the inventors and perfect masters of all the arts," so that it became the home of an atrocious style. "Next, in almost every country, the German style of architecture appeared . . . [it] often used cramped and poorly constructed small figures for ornament, and — worse still — strange animals, figures and leaves out of all reason, as corbels to support a beam. Nevertheless, this architecture had a certain justification: it originated by the taking of branches of uncut trees, binding them together and bending them to construct pointed arches. Although such origins are not wholly contemptible, yet the construction is weak, because the huts made of tree trunks set up as columns and linked so that their tops and roofs (which Vitruvius describes in his account of the origin of the Doric order) can bear much more weight than pointed arches, which are two-centered. . . . Aside from the weakness of a pointed arch, it lacks the grace of our style, which is pleasing to the eye because of the perfection of a circle. It may be observed that nature herself strives for no other form. . . ."[3]

At the risk of restating the obvious, I must point out that Raphael, or whoever wrote the report, does not offer the reader a starry-eyed, overwhelming vision of Gothic architecture: there is no northern gloom here, no pagan sacred groves. Gothic architecture originates in a rustic form of roofing. Raphael appears to have more in common with Sir James Hall than with the romantic admirers of Gothic architecture. But there is also a puzzle here. The author of the report speaks of the origins of Gothic architecture as if he were alluding to a commonplace. There are of course a number of references to Celtic and German sacred woods and shrines, which were all conveniently collected by Philip of Cluver,[4] and these would no doubt have been familiar to seventeenth-century writers, certainly to Wren, Evelyn and Warburton. But of all the texts about such shrines, the only one on which pseudo-Raphael might have based his notion of the vault originating in branches that have been tied together is Lucan's description of a shrine in the woods near Marseilles, whose "interlacing branches enclosed cool central space" (*Lucus erat, longo numquam violatus ab aero / Obscurum cingens connexis aere ramis*).[5] As far as medieval texts are concerned, the symbolism of the forest simply does not occur in them. There are many references to symbolism connected with plants in patristic and scholastic literature, but none that would warrant the "forest" theory. Durandus of Mende's *Rationale*, for instance, the obvious source, has no interest in it, although he is full of argument about symbolism, and later writers borrowed much from him. If anything, the attempt to link so obvious a feature of the church building to the pagan shrines would have met with great disapproval. But from St. Bonaventure onwards, particularly in the mystical literature of the fourteenth century, much reference is made to symbolism connected with particular plant growth. There is, earlier, the odd plant form in a building, more ambitious than the foliage of a capital or of a roof boss. There is the rare literary reference to the church building as a paradise, but too rare and too obscure to make anything of. Of course, there are two obvious and ancient tree symbols: the Cross as the tree of life, and the "Tree of Jesse."

And then, towards the end of the fifteenth century, there was a vast increase in the use of plantlike ribs and columns. Whether an explicit theory arose in the fifteenth century to promote such a development is difficult to say. It may well have developed in emulation or as an echo of Vitruvius's account of the orders which, further south, had a more radical influence at that time. It is worth recording, however, that the text of Vitruvius was familiar in the Middle Ages (in spite of the legend of Poggio's discovery of the manuscript) and was particularly valued as a technical handbook, though it seems also to have been bound into one volume together with books on number symbolism, such as Cicero's short book on the *Dream of Scipio*, or Augustine's and Boethius's treatises on music.

In any case, pseudo-Raphael produces the "locked branches" theory not to invoke the sublimity of Gothic architecture, but as a possible extenuating circumstance for its shortcomings. Although Gothic architecture is technically poor, he seems to be saying, without rule or measure, crude rustic stuff, yet it has the redeeming feature of being derived from what seems to have been a *natural* operation. But since it is a human operation, the origins of Gothic architecture are again in human dealings with nature, not in "found" natural features, apprehended by the builders and translated at once into stone. Therefore, it is a way of understanding nature, of approaching it, of mediating it through a technique, even if it is of the simplest.

Now in Warburton, in Hegel, in Coleridge, what was being admired was the immediate dependence of Gothic architecture not on art but on nature proper; on a nature that was not mediated at all, either by the builder's working method or by the conceptualization. The Gothic cathedral is not a symbol, and I use this term in Charles Sanders Peirce's sense rather than Hegel's, but an image, a direct mirroring: or rather the solidification, the petrification of a wood. Hegel conceives the spectator as being submitted in the cathedral to a gamut of sensations which the forest *might* have induced in order to achieve the desired emotion.

I have already indicated that this seems to me to presuppose a radical change in the way architecture was being looked at. But here is a chance to view the change from another angle, for the generalized disapproval, though not always undifferentiated, of Gothic architecture underwent a radical change about the middle of the eighteenth century in another way. In Britain certainly, and elsewhere in northern Europe, even in France, there was an interest in an indigenous architecture, rooted in antiquarian lore and revaluing the surviving monuments of a glorious medieval past. What was a toy to Horace Walpole and a sensation-tickler to William Beckford was to become a passion and an industry. In the great age of sentiment this change could not be justified by any appeal to a recent, recorded, historical past. The appeal must of course be beyond history, to natural man, as was Sir James Hall's way, or preferably to nature untouched by human hand.

A curious sidelight on this situation is provided by Bishop Thomas Percy, who in 1765 published a book which was to become the source book of the early English ballad, and which had a traumatic impact on the English poetry of the time, *Reliques of Ancient English Poetry*. With mock modesty, and apparently half-sincere embarrassment, Percy dedicates the book to the Countess of Northumberland, "and hopes that the barbarous productions of unpolished ages can obtain the approbation or the notice of her who adorns courts by her presence, and diffuses elegance by her examples."

The excuse follows: "But the impropriety, it is presumed, will disappear when it is declared that these poems are presented to your LADYSHIP not as labours of art, but as effusions of nature, shewing the first efforts of ancient genius, and exhibiting the customs and opinions of remote ages."

"Not as labours of art, but as effusions of nature." That, in a sense, is what the romantic critics admired in Gothic cathedrals. And yet their picture of nature corresponded nowhere to that of the cathedral builders. And curiously enough, the change is reflected sharply by the shift in the attitude to ruins.

Ruins, until the middle of the seventeenth century, meant classical ruins, and the ruins of Rome in particular:

> Who lists to see what ever nature, arte,
> And heaven could doo, O Rome, thee let him see
> In case thy greatness he can gesse in harte,
> By that which but the picture is of thee.

So Joachim du Bellay invites the pilgrim (in Spenser's translation) to reconstruct the greatness gone from the crumbling, dusty remains. And this process is to teach him both admiration for Roman greatness and a salutary lesson about the vanity of human fortunes:

> For if that time make end of things so sure
> It als will end the pain which I endure.[6]

But the eighteenth-century writers on ruins rarely affected such profundities. After du Bellay's grandeur it is a terrible comedown to return to poor Lord Kames, who has already appeared in the preceding chapter; but he also thought much about ruins. Ruins, artificial ruins, came into vogue as melancholy reminders of sentiments such as Bellay's, but by the 1760s, when Kames and Percy wrote, they had become merely a form of superior garden ornament, for all their possible overtones. Kames exercised his mind on a question of taste which occupied some of his contemporaries: Gothic or Classical? On balance, Kames preferred Gothic since Gothic ruins demonstrated the triumph of time over strength.[7] The classical ruin, however, shows the triumph of barbarism over taste, and at once invokes a "historical" recollection, makes an appeal to prose reading, while the Gothic ruin is clearly connected with epic, with timeless myth, with Lord Kames's (and, by the same token, with Lady Northumberland's) mystical and heroic ancestors. It is hardly surprising that Spenser's *Faerie Queene* had such a revival about this time. King Arthur's Camelot was sometimes seen as the nearest thing Britain had to a lost paradise.

The invention of fire, after Cesariano

Chapter 5: REASON AND GRACE

AT THIS POINT I CANNOT AVOID A DISCUSSION OF THE TEXT TO WHICH ALL THE writers I have quoted are forced to allude, and which must be regarded as the source of all the later speculations about the primitive hut: that of Vitruvius on the origins of architecture. Writing probably about the time of Augustus, Vitruvius gives a circumstantial account of the origins of his art, and uses it as an apologia for the way his book is ordered.

"The men of ancient times," he says, "bred like wild beasts in woods and caves and groves, and eked out their lives with wild food. At a certain moment it so happened that thick, crowded trees buffeted by storm and wind, rubbed their branches together so that they caught fire: such men as witnessed this were terrified and fled. After the flames had calmed down, they came nearer, and having realized the comfort their bodies drew from the warmth of the fire, they added wood to it, and so keeping it alive they summoned others and pointed it out with signs showing how useful it might be. In this meeting of men sounds were uttered at different pitch, to which, through continued daily exercise, they gave customary value to the chance syllables. Then, by pointing to the things in most common use, they began to talk to each other because of this accident. Since the invention of fire brought about the congress of men, and their counsel together and cohabitation, and since many people now met in one place, and had moreover been given a gift by nature above that of other animals, that they did not walk with their heads down, but upright, and could see the splendor of the world and the stars; and since they could make whatever they wished with their hands and fingers easily, some of that company began to make roofs of leaves, others to dig hollows under the hills, yet others made places for shelter in imitation of the nests and buildings of swallows out of mud and wattle. Then, observing the construction of others, and by their own reasoning adding new things, as time went on they built better dwellings. Since men were of an imitative and docile nature, glorying in their daily inventions, they would show each other the results of their building; and so, employing their abilities in competition, they gradually improved their judgment. At first, setting up forked posts, and putting withies between them, they finished their walls with mud. Others built walls out of dried clods, framed with wood, and covered with reeds and leaves to keep out rain and heat. When, during the winter, the roofs could not resist the rains, they devised gables, and smearing the inclined roofs with clay, they made the rain water run off."[1]

Vitruvius then mentions barbarian and primitive nations whose habits confirm this description, and quotes in particular detail the way huts are built by the Colchians who lived in Pontus, that is, the Crimea, and the Phrygians of northwest Turkey; the first in tall huts of logs with pyramidal roofs, the second in burrowed hollows covered by

EX PRIMA MVNDI HOMINVM AETATE AEDIFICATIO · MVLTI ENIM AB
ANIMALIBVS EXEMPLA VITAE CONSERVAME OZ IMITATI SVNT & C͏ᴬ

The building of the primitive hut, after Cesariano

wood and reed roofs, which in turn are covered with earth. At Marseilles he seems to have seen roofs covered with earth and straw
kneaded together. He ends the section by invoking two monuments:
"In Athens there is, on the Areopagus, an example of ancient building
roofed with clay to this day. Also on the Capitol, the hut of Romulus
will remind you of the ancient ways and their meaning, as will, on the
citadel, the thatched roofs of the shrines. By these mementoes [signa]
we may have an idea of the ancient invention of building, reasoning
that they were similar. But when men had got their hands used to
building, and had attained to art by constant practice of their cunning
skills; when industry had so accrued in their minds that those who
were keener in it claimed the status of craftsmen . . . then also from the
construction of buildings by degrees they went forward to other arts
and disciplines, and passed from a savage life in the wilds to civil
humanity. But when improving their minds, they looked further;
when their ideas had become more generous because of the variety of
their crafts, instead of huts they began to build houses with brick walls
set on proper foundations, or of stone, with timber tiled roofs, then by
their careful observation they were led from their confused and wandering ideas to the certain reasoning of symmetry."[2]

By this passage, Vitruvius justifies his plan for what he claims was
to be the first complete treatise on architecture. Having in the first
book enumerated the essential — and many — accomplishments of the

The building of the primitive hut, after *Vitruvius Teutsch*

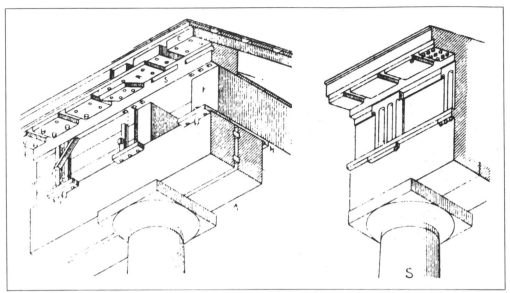

Stone and reconstructed timber origin of Doric order, after Choisy

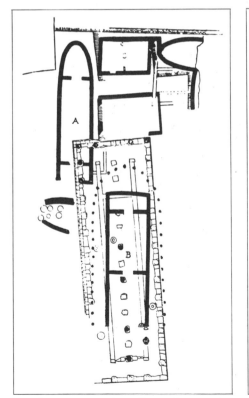

The sanctuary of Apollo at Thermum, after Kawerau. A, the Aegean megaron; B, the early Hellenic megaron with its peristyle of posts. The 7th-century temple which was built over it is drawn in outline.

Reconstructed origin of the Ionic order, and the caryatid porch, after Cesariano

architect; having discussed the primary notions concerned with sites, building rituals and all that, he uses the passage about the origins of architecture in the first hut to introduce the chapter dealing in detail with various building materials. But in the third book, on coming to the problem of ornament, he returns to the matter of how "the confused and wandering ideas" were turned into the "certain reasoning of symmetry."

Symmetry, he explains, is the establishing of a general proportional relationship in a building, a temple in particular, by using the module, that is, half the diameter of the column selected as the mathematical unit throughout the building. The model for this method is the idealized human body, *hominis bene figurata ratio*.[3] Vitruvius follows this assertion with a detailed canonic description of the relationship of parts within the human body: the canon includes the famous statement about the human body inside the square and the circle, which has so often been illustrated by artists. What is more, in all the surviving examples, the ancients used the orders, and in particular in temples. And the very common dimensions, such as the foot and inch and ell, are derived from the human body, as the number ten, whose perfection Plato had pointed out, is taken from the fingers of the two hands. There follows a little Pythagorean discussion about the relative perfections of the number ten and the number six, with the inevitable commendation of sixteen.

At any rate, after this disquisition on numerology, Vitruvius goes on to discuss the number of columns, the distances between them and their relation to the walls of the temple front as a standard for their classification. It is when he comes to the Corinthian order, in his third book, that he analyzes the detailed relation of the Doric order to the male, the Ionic to the female body, while the Corinthian he derives from a legend about the recent past of which I have already written elsewhere.[4] He then passes on to the details: referring back to the story of the primitive hut, he goes on to describe the "carpenter's work" of which the upper part of every temple consists. He describes the superstructure in detail and concludes: "Because of all these things, and because of the nature of carpenters' work, craftsmen imitated this way of building by carving it in stone and marble when they built temples, and thought that these devices should be closely followed."[5]

The two arguments about the nature of the primitive huts, built of wood and reeds, and of the human body as the positive source of the whole numerical structure of understanding, and of which the orders are one instance, is summed up in this phrase of Vitruvius. He closes this section with an admonition. A cornice, he points out, should never be so arranged that dentils are placed *below* mutules. Since dentils represent battens, which in the original timber construction would have lain on top of the rafters on which the mutules are modeled, the ornament would be unfaithful to its timber origins. And the ancients—here Vitruvius clearly approves—"thought that what could not have happened in reality would not have any certain justification when represented in the image."

The next section opens with a recapitulation: "For they handed on by custom in the excellence of their works all they had drawn from certain fitness and the truths of nature, and accepted all that in an argument could be shown to be justified by reality."

I have left this essential text until this late stage of the essay since its exegesis has occupied architects in circumstances far removed from its original context; and I did not wish to diminish the achievements and originality of Laugier or Milizia by reducing their sometimes new and influential ideas to the status of a mere commentary: which in a sense they certainly were. Neither Milizia nor Laugier would have denied it. But then even Vitruvius's ideas bear all the marks of being received ones. The account is elliptical, and references are made to various other writings. The outline of the account, from the trauma of fire to the invention of language and of the arts as a social activity, the close development of the techniques from fragments of sensory impression, and the succession of logical steps which the impressions prompt in primitive men, until they achieve mastery of environment by observing external nature and by "realizing" their own bodies: all this smacks of Stoic doctrine tinged by peripatetic empiricism.

In his ninetieth moral epistle, Seneca also discusses the invention of the arts in the first age of humanity. He quotes the last great Hellenistic philosopher, Posidonius of Apamea, as saying: "When men were scattered over the earth, finding their shelter in dugouts or some fissured rock or hollow tree, philosophy taught them to raise up roofs."

Now as a Stoic purist, Seneca will not have this: philosophy could not have been responsible for such commonplace devices. The artificiality of story upon story, of societies jostling each other, could not have been due to philosophy, any more than philosophy could have produced the notions of property or elaborated the devices for titillating the glutton's palate. No, Seneca concludes, "believe me, it was a happy age before there were architects, before there were carpenters." And his condemnation is even more thorough than Rousseau's: "All this squaring of timbers and the sawing of beams exactly where the mark had previously been made, is born when luxury is born. The first men split their timbers with wedges."[6]

Seneca's conception of philosophy will not subsume techniques of any kind. Only the meanest of slaves would devote themselves to tasks like devising shorthand or inventing transparent windows or improving the heating in public baths. The wise man is concerned with the secrets of nature and the laws of life; he has found a way of assessing the truth of opinions and rejects all pleasures that are tainted with remorse. Above all, he knows that only he who is not seeking for happiness may be happy, only he who has mastered himself is powerful.

And here Seneca's ambivalent attitude (which he shares with many Stoics) to the golden age becomes apparent. The truths of philosophy were not evident—the Stoics thought—to the men who lived in the state of nature during the golden age: so it is only with the relative decadence implied by civilization that philosophy emerges.

There is another, more radical ambivalence implicit in all stories about the origins of techniques and civilization. Either culture is a consequence of man's need to survive, following a fault which deprives him of the benefits of grace and nature, as in the Book of Genesis; or the fall is itself the punishment for the theft of the divine secrets of the crafts, as in the legend of Prometheus. Vitruvius doesn't quite reach that far back. He is not a thoroughgoing Stoic like Seneca, but a rather omnivorous eclectic, depending on the encyclopedic works of Posidonius, of whom Seneca did not altogether approve. Like other philosophers who had considered this question, Theophrastus or Dicaearchus, for instance, but unlike Seneca, Posidonius held that it was philosophy and not necessity which taught humanity the arts. In Vitruvius's account of the origin of his own art he exemplified this belief in detail. A fire began as a result of trees rubbing against each other. It was the warmth of this accidental fire which caused men to reflect on its comforting influence, even before they had the use of speech. The natural catastrophe provides Vitruvius's humanity with the civilizing trauma: as in the legend of Prometheus, the Hephaestean element stimulated humanity. Again, in the form in which this legend appears in Vitruvius, it is likely to have originated with Posidonius, who believed that the whole universe was sustained by the *vis vitalis*, a warming breath which originated in the sun. What follows looks something like a Posidonian recasting of earlier ideas, those of Protagoras, for instance, as recorded in Xenophon's *memorabilia*.

It is interesting that the careful buildup of the history of architecture in terms of gradual improvement through competition and imitation justifies the practice of transferring the details of one form of construction into another as a coherent ornamental system; interesting too that this justification, though perfunctorily acceded to by most of the commentators on Vitruvius, does not become a cardinal point of architectural theory again until the eighteenth century, when indeed the intellectual climate had something in common, in its Stoic, empirical coloring, with that in which Vitruvius's book was written. I am almost tempted to conclude that Locke was to Laugier what Zeno was to Vitruvius.

Still, a Cynic theory of architecture would really be a contradiction in terms (witness Diogenes); an Epicurean theory might be reconstructable, but it certainly does not show in the greatest of all Epicurean documents to deal with the origins of the arts, the fifth book of Lucretius's *De rerum natura*. Although Lucretius also associates the invention of fire with the first buildings, he says very little about them. He speaks of how in their savage state men occupied "the well-known woodland haunts of the nymphs," and that "when they did not yet know how to use fire for their purposes . . . would live in woods and mountain caves and forests to shelter their rough limbs in the brushwood when the blows of rain and wind buffeted them. . . ."[7]

When lightning, or the swaying branches, as in Vitruvius's account, had produced a manageable fire, and the sun's heat had shown them how to cook food, then came building, though we learn nothing about details from Lucretius.[8] He does, however, talk about the beginnings of music: it was the clear notes of birds, and the whistling of Zephyrus through the reeds, that taught men to sing and to play music. This kind of imitating of animate and inanimate nature had of course appeared in other prehistories. Diodorus Siculus preserves fragments of that cosmogony of Democritus which Hecataeus of Abdera condenses: according to him, men learned the arts by imitating animals, they learned spinning from the spider, building from the swallow, and singing from the swan and the nightingale[9] — though he also points out elsewhere that music is a young art, to which need did not give birth.[10] Hecataeus embroiders on this, in suggesting that there were three stages of devising the arts; the first is the consciousness of need, the second is the example of animals and the consequent invention of the art, the third is the invention of arts which rely on the surplus left when needs have been satisfied, such as the art of music.[11] This laicization of prehistory does not really dispose of the mythographers, or of popular beliefs, but it was to become the principal source for the speculations of both Epicureans and Stoics in later centuries.

Vitruvius, as I have noted, adheres to a central Stoic position. It is not necessity, but reflection, that teaches men to turn the natural elements to their advantage. And Vitruvius is the one writer on the theory of architecture whom later theorists cannot bypass. To Vitruvius, as to all his literate contemporaries, the notion of origins had cardinal speculative importance. His whole theory of architecture flowed from it.

In spite of the odd medieval précis, Vitruvius was not widely read in the Middle Ages and had no real successor. He became popular in the ninth century and again in the fourteenth. Unfortunately, it would be far from the point if I were to say much about the use Boccaccio made of his book—indeed, of the very part of it I have been discussing —with reference to the legend of Vulcan, or of Sidonius Apollinaris's belief that Vitruvius was the inventor of the plumbline,[12] or the epitome compiled by Peter the Deacon, or Einhardt's possible interpretation of the *"obscura verba."* It is really in the fifteenth century, after Poggio's so-called discovery of the texts, that Vitruvius assumes a new importance, and the passage about the origin of architecture becomes a new matter for speculation.

To my mind, the first important commentary on this text is not a verbal but a pictorial one: the cycle of paintings which Piero di Cosimo executed for the house of a rich Florentine wool merchant, Francesco del Pugliesi. For all the recorded peculiarities both patron and artist displayed, we do not know enough of the pictures to reconstruct the whole cycle; as it is, the identification of the various pieces, which are dispersed among several museums, is still questioned by some. But there is little doubt that the cycle shows human and animal life before the invention of the arts. And the effect of the forest fire which Vitruvius and Lucretius had described is reinforced by the lesson Vulcan is teaching men. While the New York panels show the state of barbarism before the invention of language and the formation of institutions, the Oxford panel shows the fire itself. Of the two larger pictures, the Wadsworth Athenaeum one shows the fall of Vulcan among the nymphs of Lemnos—illustrating a charming misreading of Servius's commentary on Virgil[13]—while the Ottawa one shows Vulcan and Actus teaching mankind the arts, with the primitive hut as a familiar piece of apparatus prominently in the background.[14]

Fire, however, is the most prominent feature of these paintings. Vasari makes it quite clear that Piero's attitude to fire was not at all usual; Vasari obviously thought him an admirable if a very rum fellow. He comments, for instance, on the habit Piero had of cooking "not six or eight eggs at a time, but some fifty"; these he would put in the pot when boiling up glue "so as to economize on fire." He then kept them in a basket, eating when he felt like it. There were other indicative signs of Piero's state of mind which Vasari notes: his intense pleasure at rain, and terror of lightning (he used to veil his head if there was a storm), and so on. Piero saw himself—it seems—at times as being in some way of the race of the first men. He worshiped nature to the extent of being unwilling to have his fruit trees pruned or even grafted. He would not have the grass in his garden trimmed; presumably in the myth he painted, and which he had constructed out of the fragments in Vitruvius and Lucretius, he saw an artificial vision of a renewed, totally fresh, wholly authentic society, untouched by the artificialities and pettiness of his own time. Here, in a sense, is the quintessential renaissance: a passion of themes of birth and rebirth, displayed in a renewal of themes lost or misunderstood since antiquity.

The first writer to comment on Vitruvius in Italian, Cesare Cesariano, is obviously impressed by this section of his text. Cesariano already knows the comparative material about the origins of humanity and the golden age in Vitruvius, Juvenal and Ovid; he is less sure of himself with Greek authors: Hesiod and Diodorus Siculus. But his

House of the ancients according to the idea of Palladio, after Barbaro

commentary is not entirely bookish. He records, for instance, a forest
fire in the *"nemori Canturiensi,"* the fief "of our Milanese citizens of
the family of the Gayani" in the 1480s, a forest fire of which marvel
there was still a witness living. What is more, in 1513, there appeared
a portent, a great flame in the air, "as if from the moon . . . and the
people all went out of their houses and this same flame did no harm to
anything in this world that has been heard of. It seems to me that I
have said enough for the unlearned, and here I place for you a picture
showing the above event as a supplement." And Cesariano does in fact
show two pictures of the archetypal fire, one supplemented with the
aerial flame of the previous paragraph. ("For it is fire," he thought,
"which not only comforts many animals (and especially humankind)

The invention of fire, after Fra Giocondo

but it also moves them to speaking and then they are content and keep each other company.). . ."[15]

Of all the commentators perhaps the most distinguished — both as a scholar and as a social figure — was Daniele Barbaro (1514–1567), Palladio's friend and co-patron, with his brother, of the villa at Maser. In his notes on the same passage in Vitruvius's second book he notes — in the usual way — the discrepancy between Vitruvius's account and that of Scripture and he commends the pagan writer for having such a close knowledge of "natural" origins even if ignorant of the true revealed story of divine creation. For the rest, he follows Philander's Latin commentary in large measure, although he does mention the odd forms of primitive huts made of strange materials which were seen "in our own day on the island Hispaniola and those parts of the world discovered by the moderns." And when commenting on the primitive Phrygian earth mounds he notes, "I have seen similar huts in some parts of Germany: they seemed natural objects rather than man-made [*non enim factae, sed natae videntur casae*]." This in itself would be unremarkable; but the illustrations for Barbaro's edition were prepared by Palladio; in the third chapter of the sixth book, in which Vitruvius deals with the planning of private houses, Palladio shows a two-story, roughly built, "primitive" house with Corinthian temple-portico frontispiece. He was of course familiar with my Vitruvian texts, and sums it up himself in the preface to the first of his "Four books" to explain why he is going to deal with private houses first: "... since they suggested the method for designing public buildings; since it is most probable that men first lived in isolation, and later seeing that there were advantages in getting the help of other men to obtain those things which might make him happy (if there is any happiness to be found here below) he naturally came to desire and love the company of other men. So groups of houses became villages, and groups of villages towns, and in them [there were built] the public places and buildings. And so, since no part of architecture is more necessary for man, nor is it practiced more than any part of architecture, I will first treat of private houses, and then of public buildings. . . ."

Palladio believes therefore that the private house is not only historically but logically the first kind of building. And he deduces the form of the vanished primitive house of antiquity from the evidence of existing public buildings. Hence the temple frontispiece in his Vitruvius illustration, and hence too those insistent pedimented porticoes which grace even his most modest villas dotted about the Vincentino. The Palladian villa is therefore another variant of the primitive ancient house restored; and even the layout of his treatise bears the mark of Vitruvian "anthropology." To Palladio the conflict between the evidence of Scripture and the testimony of the ancients seemed less dramatic than to other commentators. Barbaro, too, with his devotion to Aristotle, did not feel the conflict oversharply. In a way the more naive Cesariano was more worried by it. Although he indulges in comparisons of primitive habitations: there are the caves of the Troglodytes that Pliny talks about; there are huts in the north of Europe; he has heard of some on the newly found isles of Taprobana (Ceylon?) or in Calcutta. But even if he admires and respects these "primitive" efforts and appears to accept Vitruvius's suppositions about the origin of building, yet he cannot refrain from the comment, "But the origins of our humanity cannot otherwise be known except through the sayings of our holy scriptures. . . ."

Walter Hermann Riff or Rivius, the translator and commentator of

Adam sheltering from the first rain, after Filarete

Vitruuio:
Adam:

Vitruvius Teutsch, is more explicit and even gives a little account of sacred history in his commentary, without using it to illuminate the text.[16] Such an attempt, if not a very sophisticated one, is made by Filarete. Near the beginning of his general treatise, Filarete supposes that "it must be believed that when Adam was driven out of Paradise, it was raining. Since he had no readier shelter, he put his hands up to his head, to defend himself from the water. And since he was forced by necessity to find food so as to go on living, so dwelling was a skill [he discovered] to defend himself from ill weather and from water. Some have said that there was no rain before the flood. I believe the contrary, since if the earth was to produce fruit, it was necessary that it should rain. As feeding and dwelling are skills necessary for living, it must therefore be believed that Adam, having made himself a roof with his two hands, considering the need for making a living, he reflected and exercised himself to make himself some habitation to defend himself from these rains, as well as from the heat of the sun. . . . If that is how things happened, then Adam must have been the first."[17] Filarete uses this very charming and original idea to introduce a chapter dealing with the analogy between architecture and the human body — the argument is from Vitruvius, but Filarete gives it his own very particular slant.

No such teaching may be found in Alberti's *De re aedificatoria.* He toys with the argument of origins for a moment. The art of architecture, he says, originated in Asia, went on to Greece and reached its full maturity on Italian soil.[18] As for its origins, he is prepared only to assert that "when men in the beginning were looking for a place where they could rest safely . . . not wanting however that all the individual and domestic functions should be carried out in the same room, but that the place for sleeping should be separated from that where the fireplace was, and at the same time that each room should have its proper function, then he began to design a roof, to protect himself from the rain and the sun. For this end walls were built lengthwise to keep the roof up . . . such was, in my opinion, building in its first beginnings and its original ordering. It does not matter who first thought of it: whether it was Vesta the daughter of Saturn, or the brothers Euralyus and Hyperbius . . ."[19] and so on; there follows a list of names from a corrupt manuscript of Pliny. Although he is so careless of origins, Alberti is most explicit and original about various matters, such as the orders. The analogy to nature in Alberti takes quite another form.[20] To him the building is really an analogy to a body, to an animal body in particular, which he believes to be ordered according to a Pythagorean proportional scheme.[21]

The third founding father of the Italian *trattato,* Francesco di Giorgio Martini, takes the argument about the primitive hut from yet another point.[22] He is concerned primarily to defend magnificence in building against the advocates of evangelic poverty, who also appealed to antiquity, particularly to such examples of ancient virtue as Cincinnatus, to condemn great expense on building. Obsessed with a notion of providing an image of cosmic order in building, Martini dismisses this argument as an irrelevance; moreover, he went further than Alberti in the use of the animal analogy. To him the city, the individual building, both in plan and elevation, and even parts of it, such as columns and cornices, were all designed on the analogy of the human body, which — being the summit of divine creation — was the ultimate origin and exemplar of architecture. Alberti believed (as Martini also seems to suggest) that the capitals of different orders evolved from simple brackets on top of the timber post which held up the beam. But neither is concerned to trace the detailed forms to all the mythical origins, nor to take the organic analogy too far.[23] They were both too reasonable to make the dotty but imaginative step to which the inferior mind of Filarete jumped: the poetic image of Adam sheltering his head from the extra-paradisal by pitching his hands as the origin of the displuviate, the double-pitched roof.

The primitive hut recurs in other treatises in various guises: in Serlio's it is simply part of the backcloth for satyr plays; Scamozzi refers to it obliquely but respectfully. He speaks of God the great architect having created the marvelous mechanism of the world, made man to be its master.[24] Man's intellect and thirst for knowledge give birth to architecture together with the other arts. Its great antiquity and enormous prestige are therefore beyond question, "since it had its origins in the times of our first fathers and great patriarchs, to whom it supplied against the need for a dwelling: as the sacred scriptures witness, confirmed by Vitruvius." Because Vitruvius and Alberti were the only writers on architecture printed before 1500, if one excepts Francesco Maria Grapaldi's architectural dictionary of 1494, manuscript literature is very scarce: Martini's manuals, as well as Filarete's book, had the limited circulation a few manuscripts suggest. Even the first commentaries on Vitruvius — and such commentaries were to become one of the principal vehicles of architectural theory for three hundred years — belong to the beginning of the sixteenth century.

However, in building practice, even at the height of the greatest excitement which the "discovery" of ancient models caused, certain medieval themes had not been forgotten; moreover, the antiquity which at that time was considered by many as the fittest precedent for a Christian architecture was not the timeless antiquity of myth, but the more specific "style" of the earliest Christian architecture, as it was exhibited by Constantinian models: Alberti's Easter Sepulcher in San Pancrazio, in Florence, is a precious memento of that idea.

The way in which such quotations, such references to the holy places, were used throughout the Middle Ages has been dealt with by many authors. So have the themes derived from the Cross — the cruciform church plan is the most obvious instance — and its correlative, the perfect, crucified manhood of the Savior. These are grafted onto ideas about the human body as a condensed universe, a microcosm: and variants connecting the Cross, the Savior's body and the cosmic temple are common in medieval speculation about building. Such teachings were most probably echoed in the verbal teaching of medieval Masonic lodges; they appear explicitly in the writings of theologians — of Abelard or the Victorine monks — or visionaries, such as Opicimus de Castris or Hildegard von Bingen. The problem was complicated by the existence, in Scripture, of "revealed" specifications for three ideal exemplars for architects: Noah's ark, the tabernacle in the desert and the Temple in Jerusalem — the only permanent sacred building Scripture describes in detail. And yet the Temple is specified under the conflicting forms of Solomon's actual building, its two later rebuildings and the vision of the prophet Ezekiel.

It was assumed in the excitement of the first renewal of the antique, of the first rereading of Vitruvius, that the concordance of the text and magnificent remains of ancient work might provide all the elements necessary for an architecture which would accord both with reason and with nature, and would therefore be undisputed, the only true architecture. A further assumption was commonly made: that the Temple in Jerusalem was also built in this manner, with the same magnificence as could be reconstructed from the ruins of classical antiquity. And this conferred upon the style the authority of scriptural precept, of divine command, even. The account which Vitruvius gives, in his extended asides, of the origin of building provided an ulterior justification for the modalities he proscribed, and the ruins of classical buildings illustrated. These modalities were invoked to transform an existing building tradition, and to absorb extraneous elements, such as the Orientalisms imported by Byzantine expatriates. But once the transformation was accomplished, a new problem arose.

The architecture of the sixteenth century could not simply make its appeal to nature and reason, or base its procedure on the operations of reason prompted by philosophy; in the sixteenth century rules which had to be invoked constantly, such as those of the orders, had to have the sanction of grace, had to be derived from, guaranteed by divine revelation; although revelation did not in any way contradict the operations of reason, but rather sanctified, elevated them. This belief was expressly enjoined on all Christians by Pope Leo X in his Bull *Apostolici Regiminus*, dated December 19, 1513. Such an attitude suggests a return to certain medieval themes; only the seven liberal arts had, however, been properly discussed in these terms during the Middle Ages. The so-called mechanical arts had less interest for theological and quasi-theological speculation. The fifteenth- and sixteenth-century writers who wished to give the activities of the visual artists that fully "literate" dignity they had not recently enjoyed turned to mystical and pseudo-mystical writing for theoretical justification; hence the large-scale pirating of Agrippa of Nettesheim by Pietro Lomazzo, or the absolute devotion to the teaching of Ramón Lull, the Catalan *Doctor Illuminatus*, shown by Juan de Herrera, the architect of the Escorial. Herrera is a puzzling personage: the strange part which he played in the life of Philip II of Spain is not limited to his being the architect—the second and more important—of the Escorial; he was also on very close personal terms with the king. There is little doubt that he owed this honor to something else beyond his ability as an architect: most probably to the devotion which he and the king shared to the teaching of Lull. Herrera was one of the most prominent Lullists of his time. And it seems that the building of the Escorial was held both by him and by the king to be a complex, extended spiritual exercise on a vast corporeal scale.

The palace-monastery was conceived as a result of a vow Philip II made before the Battle of St. Quentin, on August 10, 1557; a battle which ended with a decisive defeat of the French. The exact date was important for the project; the church was orientated on the axis of the sunset on August 10, St. Lawrence's Day in the church calendar, and the general grid-iron plan was intended to recall the instrument of St. Lawrence's martyrdom. The whole building history of the palace is punctuated by such astrological and church-calendar references.

But this kind of symbolism is only superficial. More complex notions are involved. I should like to illustrate them by reference to a rather neglected episode in architectural history, the reconstruction of the Solomonic Temple (as modified by Ezekiel's vision) by Juan Bautista Villalpanda.

This reconstruction—and its detailed justification—takes up the bulk of the second of the three great volumes in which Villalpanda, together with a fellow Jesuit of Cordoba, Jeronimo Prado, set out his commentary on the Book of Ezekiel; it was published in Rome between 1596 and 1604. The two Jesuits had gone from Spain to Rome (where Prado died before the book was finished) at the expense of Philip II, who had financed and generally protected their researches up to date. The first volume is dedicated to him, who "already resembled David in piety, Solomon in greatness of soul and wisdom as in building the most magnificent and truly royal works of St. Lawrence of the Escorial"; and Philip will now further come to be like "Ezekiel for holy ardor and zeal. For what his times made it necessary to wrap in the obscurity of dark words, that you will have illuminated, as if the veils of darkness were thrown back, with God's help. Who daily, increasingly illuminates his church."[25]

Villalpanda's enthusiasm carries him to greater heights, and he compares his detailed exegesis of the Temple (and the Escorial by implication) to shining with the light of truth like a great sun, which only those who connive with the obscurity of night cannot behold.

The comparison to Solomon is not just a conventional piece of court flattery. Philip II gloried in this parallel. One of his titles was King of Jerusalem, and this gave him a functional affinity to the king of the Jews. Other affinities were claimed for him: wisdom, prudence, piety and the familiarity with hidden mysteries attributed to Solomon by legend, which Philip II sought to reach through following the teaching of Lull, and finally that building of the church-monastery-palace of the Escorial, which was to be the crowning glory of his reign, much like the building of the Temple with its priests' residences and the palace in Jerusalem had crowned that of King Solomon.

This parallel to Solomon is one of the great commonplaces of the medieval iconography of kingship. Justinian already—or so Codimus has it—cried on entering the restored Santa Sophia, "Solomon, I have outdone you," and Charlemagne, according to one of his chroniclers (the anonymous monk of St. Gall), built his churches and palaces to accommodate all the dignitaries of his court "following the example of Solomon."[26] As David was the type of pious warrior, so Solomon was the type of wise builder: Philip II aimed to identify himself with his archetype. Moreover, in revealing the mysterious nature of his enterprise, he added yet a third archetype to his spiritual ancestry: the inspired prophet Ezekiel, who, in another way from Solomon, had had the vast secrets of universal harmony revealed to him under the guise of a description of the Temple.

Though even the close imitation of the Temple at Jerusalem was not a wholly new idea. The Sistine Chapel, built a century earlier than the Escorial, is in a medieval way modeled explicitly on the Temple building by repeating its dimensions. Although this precedent was not very often invoked during the Middle Ages, Durandus had explicitly stated, in the Rationale I quoted earlier, that the material form of the church derives both from the Temple in Jerusalem and the tabernacle in the desert. From Abelard onwards, this idea of the Temple as an image of universal harmony was ever-present to medieval builders, reiterated not only by philosophers and mystical writers, but by the hymn writers of the liturgy.

Villalpanda was therefore calling on a strong body of precedent, with which Philip II and Herrera were also familiar. We know from Villalpanda's own words that Herrera was his master, and that he was closely acquainted with the details of the reconstruction. What Villalpanda meant by referring to Herrera as his master is not really known. If it referred to architecture, then Villalpanda's architectural achievement is surprisingly modest: collaboration with a minor plateresque master, Alfonso Barba, on the interior of the Cathedral of Baeza, near Cordoba; the bas-relief of the Nativity over its doorway is attributed to Jeronimo Prado, Villalpanda's collaborator on the commentary. Prado, however, was well known to his contemporaries not as an architect, but as a biblical scholar, and it was in this discipline that he had trained Villalpanda, who besides the vast bulk of the Ezekiel commentary has another scholarly work to his credit, the edition of a medieval commentary on St. Paul's Epistles attributed to St. Rémy.

In spite of his very modest achievements in the field, Villalpanda speaks of architecture with enormous authority, and familiarity. He also appears to be a competent Hebraist, though that is not unexpected in a follower of Lull.

The commentary on the Book of Ezekiel and the restoration of the Jerusalem Temple it contained seems to have consumed the bulk of his energy. He was not, of course, the first to attempt such a commentary, but he felt—as he makes quite clear—that he was the first who was properly qualified for it.

He rebukes many of his predecessors, such as Richard of St. Victor, for their ignorance of Oriental languages; but when, like Nicholas of Lyra (whose commentary, with woodcut illustrations following the manuscript illuminations, was printed in 1489 and again in 1588), they were familiar with Hebrew, Villalpanda argues that they had the misfortune to be living when all Europe was bemused by "Langobardic fantasies" and therefore designed buildings like monsters or portents, and showed no knowledge of the laws of architecture.[27] For the only architecture which is consonant with reason, the only architecture worthy of the name, is that codified by Vitruvius; and it is familiarity with this architecture which an interpreter of Ezekiel must have. This notion is explicit throughout Villalpanda's book. Revelation cannot contradict reason: Vitruvian architecture, being the only *reasonable* architecture, was also the only possible architecture of divine revelation. Villalpanda therefore has no hesitation in constructing parallels (sometimes rather far-fetched) between Vitruvian rules and the revealed specifications found in Scripture.[28] He even in one case corrects a Vitruvian commentary by reference to the Book of Kings.[29]

The great antiquity of the Jews, their dignity as God's people, the wide empire which Scripture seems to ascribe to them, the great international authority of King Solomon, all this seemed to Villalpanda to justify the assumption that classical architecture was derived from Jewish models, and in particular from the Temple in Jerusalem, its archetype. The three canonic classical orders, with all their differences, did not exist in the Temple. The Temple had one complex order, whose ornaments and proportions were of divine origin, and from which the three orders described by Vitruvius were derived. This Temple order consisted of a modified Corinthian column carrying a Doric trabeation. The guarantee for this reconstruction lay partly in the

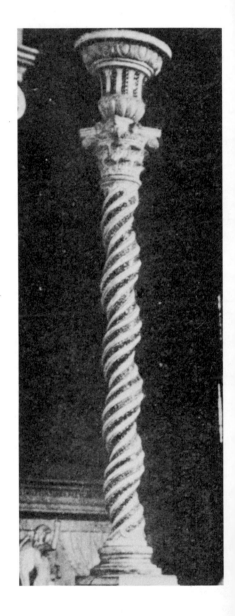

The Colonna Santa in the Pietà chapel,
St. Peter's Rome; the octagonal surround
is 15th-century; after Alinari

Paschal candlestick,
S. Lorenzo Fuori le Mura,
13th-century

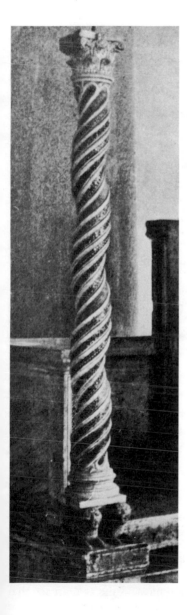

Paschal candlestick,
Santa Maria in Cosmedin,
Rome

Bernini: Two columns of the Baldacchino,
St. Peter's, Rome

Raphael: St. Peter and St. John in the Temple. Cartoon for tapestry.
Victoria and Albert Museum, London

assumption of the Jewish origin of classical architecture, partly in the statement Josephus makes in the *Antiquities* that the capitals of the Temple porticoes were Corinthian[30]; and since Josephus in the same place also writes that Herod heightened the Temple building to conform with Solomonic proportions, this confirmed Villalpanda's idea that Herod's Temple was a faithful reproduction of the divinely inspired original.[31]

But his assurance seems to have been inspired also by some very strong conviction external to the direct evidence, and to which he only alludes. Evidently the vast scale of his publication presupposes some years of preparation; he claims to have conceived the reconstruction sixteen years before the first volume was published — which would have been in 1580.[32] He makes it clear in the same place that Herrera was familiar with the reconstruction, and that seeing the drawings, had said that a building of such beauty could only have come directly from God. There is an air of mystification about this assertion, which suggests that there was something of a private revelation about the whole thing. Villalpanda never clearly says with whom the original inspiration lay: whether with himself or with Herrera. At any rate, Herrera possessed among his books a manuscript about Ezekiel's Temple, which, since he died in 1597 before the publication of Villalpanda's second volume containing the reconstruction, could not have depended on the printed book.

The appearance of the Jerusalem Temple had long been an inevitable part of Christian iconography. Throughout the Middle Ages the Temple was simply assimilated to a contemporary church; but during the fifteenth century only "antique" architecture could provide a model for a "grand" building. At a time when even medieval scenes, such as the *Vision of St. Bernard* (Perugino, Munich; Filippino Lippi, The Badia, Florence) took place against a "Vitruvian" background, or even a known Gothic setting was "improved" by antique importations (Vecchietta's *San Bernardino Preaching*, Liverpool, or the Ghirlandaio St. Francis frescoes at the Santa Trinità), the Temple itself could only be conceived in classical terms. And speculations on these lines began before Villalpanda. Philibert de L'Orme, Herrera's junior by a few years, proposed to add to his *Premier tome d'architecture*, which appeared in 1567, a second volume "of our architecture, which will be about divine proportions and measures of the first and ancient architecture of the Old Testament fathers, adapted to modern architecture. . . ." It is not certain whether de L'Orme intended to include a restoration of the Temple in this second book of his. Certainly no drawing in this connection survives. In spite of the many printed representations of the Temple, in spite of the numerological and cosmological speculations of visionaries and alchemists, there are very few precise or architectural reconstructions of the Temple building before Villalpanda.

That is why, perhaps, Villalpanda seems so sure of the inspired character of his own drawings, as he was that they corresponded to the divinely inspired original drawings for the Temple; he was convinced that there was a set of such original drawings, drawn by the hand of God Himself (as the tables of the law were inscribed by Him),[33] or else by a hand (David's?) guided by direct divine inspiration, as indeed the Book of Chronicles seems to imply.[34]

The imperious claims had already been made before the publication of the book and had raised theological objections; hence the journey of the two Jesuits to Rome, as Herrera had already had a brush with the Inquisition; but there had also been scholarly criticism, even in Philip II's immediate circle. The most persuasive and learned of the objectors was Benito Arias Montano, the first librarian of the Escorial, who had been a theologian of the Council of Trent, but is chiefly known as the editor of the vast Antwerp polyglot Bible, in the seventh volume of which (published in 1572) he included the "Exemplar, sive de Sacris Fabricis Liber," setting out his own rather more sober, though still wholly classical, reconstruction of the Solomonic Temple. Montano

TEMPLI CVM PORTICV ET CELLIS ABSOLVTA ORTHOGRAPHIA ex deſcriptione Bened. Ariæ Montani . Conuenit orthographia cum lenographiæ menſioris ad Vnguem . Membra omnia reſpondent Architecturæ Iſraelitanum

Montano: Restoration of the Temple in Jerusalem

denied, incidentally, that the Temple of Ezekiel's vision corresponded to Solomon's actual building.[35] Villalpanda found that this reconstruction "did not follow the specification of the holy prophecy, not even in part." Montano had committed the mistake, fatal according to Villalpanda, of reconstructing the Solomonic Temple without consulting Ezekiel, or Vitruvius and Euclid: so showing himself also "ignorant of the methods and the rules of art." Villalpanda, assured by supernatural guarantee and familiarity with the laws of architecture, staked an overwhelming claim on the theme, and certainly none of his successors or opponents, no one dealing with the matter of Solomon's Temple henceforth, could altogether bypass him. Not even when, like the baranabite friar Agostino Torinelli (whose *Annales sacri et profani* were popular for over two centuries), they were dismissive. And there were many other writers on the theme. In 1642 Rabbi Jacob Jehudah Leon published his version, which had already been much admired in the form of a wooden model he had made and exhibited in the Low Countries. John Lightfoot published his book on *The Temple, Espe-*

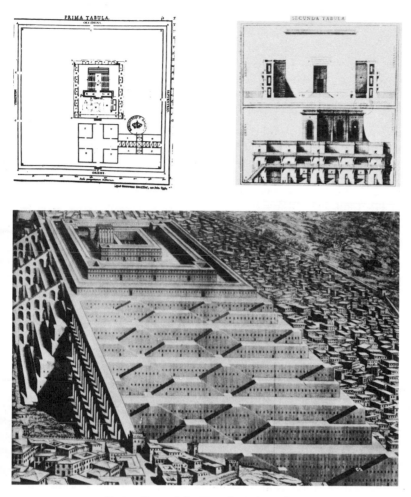

Restorations of the Temple in Jerusalem
above: Claude Perrault; *below:* Lamy

cially as it Stood in the Dayes of Our Saviour in 1650; and in 1657 the
first volume of the London polyglot Bible, edited by Brian Walton,
appeared; it contained a long paper, chiefly about Villalpanda's reconstruction, by the French Hebraist Louis Coppel. All these designs
were more or less grandiose: Lightfoot's perhaps a little down-at-heel,
but none as modest and as unclassical as the one Charles Perrault, the
demythologizer of the classical orders, devised for the Latin edition
of Maimonides's *Mishneh Torah*, which the French Hebraist Louis
Compiègne de Veil published in 1678; then in 1721 there appeared the
French oratorian Bernard Lamy's thick folio, devoted solely to the
Temple and to Jerusalem — a very elegantly illustrated book, which
seems to combine Perrault's basic reconstruction with some of
Villalpanda's grandiose ideas.

In spite of the bulky hostile literature, and in spite of all the justified
skepticism of distinguished biblical scholars (and even architectural
writers: Perrault, for instance, went out of his way to be scathing about
Villalpanda), the sumptuous plates of Villalpanda's book had an enor-

mous attraction. A number of architectural theorists allude to them: Guarino Guarini, for instance, includes the Temple order in a rather bowdlerized form among his fancy capitals and confesses that he used it to much effect. Fréart de Chambray, who wrote perhaps the most learned and popular manuals of parallel orders (first published in 1650), included Villalpanda's Temple order among his Corinthian columns; however, considering that he calls this "the flower of architecture, and the order of orders," Fréart is somewhat halfhearted in his recommendations. "For instance," he says, "suppose one were to build churches and altars in memory of those generous virgins who from their tender age vanquished the cruelty of tyrants . . . surmounting all sorts of torments in their constancy: what could we imagine more expressive and suitable to their courage than this divine order?"[36]

It is clear that the mixture of Corinthian and Doric went against Fréart's academic grain. In the special case iconographic reasons suggest that it may be used "with that address and reason as will not only render it excusable, but very judicious."

The influence of the plates was not limited to this imitating of the Temple order. Villalpanda's Solomonic Temple appears in scriptural commentaries, in illustrated Bibles or editions of Josephus, in travel books. But above all it becomes a touchstone of architectural literature; for instance, Nicolaus Goldmann, the mathematician who also devoted his attention to civil and military architecture, constructed a proportional system upon a modified version of the Villalpanda reconstruction. It was amplified and published, firstly as a commentary on the Temple, and then as a section devoted to harmonic proportion (*Die unentbärliche Regel der Symmetrie oder: Des Ebenmasses, Wie sie zuförderst an dem herrlichsten Exempel des göttlichen Tempels von Solomone erbauet wahrzune(h)men . . .*). René Ouvrard's speculations on the universal validity of harmonic proportions, which appeared in 1679, are clearly dependent on such ideas. When Fischer von Erlach published the first general history of architecture, *Entwurf einer historischen Architektur,* in 1721, he showed the Temple in Jerusalem according to Villalpanda's reconstruction. The disputes were given new currency in the 1740s when much pro and anti (mostly anti) Villalpanda material was published in the eighth and ninth volumes of Biagio Ugolino's *Thesaurus Antiquitatum Sacrarum.*

Villalpanda's general ideas about the origins of the orders were to inspire one of the oddest books in English architectural literature: *The Origin of Building, or, the Plagiarism of the Heathens detected,* by John Wood the Elder, the architect of Bath, which appeared in 1741.

Wood's idea was that the "secret" of the orders was directly revealed by God to Moses; the command of God to erect the tabernacle is, according to Wood, the true origin of a formal art of building. And the construction which Scripture described meant that the old business

Restoration of the Temple in Jerusalem according to Villalpanda,
after Fischer von Erlach

of planting forked branches in the ground to support a roof, described
by Vitruvius and Lucretius, had to be abandoned. "The trees or poles
of which the pillars were made, became deprived of that base, in this
structure the sticking them up in the earth, which former buildings
gave them. Therefore, this defect GOD supplied, by the assistance of art
which he had REVEALED, in giving them another sort of base, so broad
as to make a sufficient base to keep them upright. . . . Moreover, GOD
was graciously pleased in those pillars to direct how we should supply
our necessities in building, with the materials of the earth, and even
reconcile Art with Nature . . . to which purpose, as the pillars imitated
trees, so they were made with a base at the bottom, to answer the root
end and with a capital at the top to represent the head of the tree: God
shewing us, in the very same structure, how we ought to apply the
imitation of natural things. . . ."[37]

I will not, here, recount the fanciful chronology according to which
the details of Mosaic revelation were transmitted to the Greeks; the
orders were, according to Wood, traditionally attributed to the Greeks
because "being a people naturally inclined to fiction, they so dressed
up their story of the origin of the orders that the Romans very readily
had given the invention of these beautiful parts to them, as appears by
the writings of Vitruvius. . . ." Wood's chronology was of course dependent on Archbishop Ussher's and Isaac Newton's, though with re-
visions. Some years after *The Origin of Building*, he amplified it in a
little guide to Bath and also in a work on Stonehenge, the Druids and
the mythical British king Bladud, founder of Bath (*Choir Gaure, Vul-*

above and opposite:
Reconstruction of the Temple in Jerusalem according to Villalpanda.
Wooden model by J. J. Erasmus

garly Called Stonehenge, etc.), in which the British were, among other things, credited with the building of the Delphic Temple of Apollo.[38] Wood was a nationalist, in an eighteenth-century vein, but he was also an evangelical of Wesleyan leanings. Although not directly familiar with Villalpanda's book, or much of the literature in Italian, Spanish, German or Latin – the works he quotes are mostly English – he would presumably have seen the vast model of the Villalpandian Temple which the Hamburg architect Johann Jakob Erasmus finished in 1694, and had exhibited in Britain before 1720 (it may still be seen in the Museum für Hamburgische Geschichte), or at any rate heard of it. His own Palladian practice was animated by his belief, oddly parallel to that of Philip II two centuries earlier, that in following Vitruvian precept he was performing a work of piety. It is strange to find this belief so vigorous at a time when the extra-temporal, mythical character of the orders was being questioned by the earliest theorists of neoclassicism and the Vitruvian rules flippantly defied by the rococo masters.

Whatever the weaknesses and exaggerations of Villalpanda's reconstruction of the Temple and its ornaments, there can be no doubt that his work contributed to a revitalizing of the classical orders. In the fifteenth century classical architecture had provided the only repertory of themes for the reinterpretation of the traditional programs of sacred as well as public secular architecture. The evocation of ancient greatness was after all *the* great theme of Quattrocento rhetoric. Moreover, the reference to Constantinian building provided classical architecture with the added guarantee of a reference back to the first Christian architecture. But as architectural literature proliferated, the specific architectural references (republican in Florence, imperial in

133

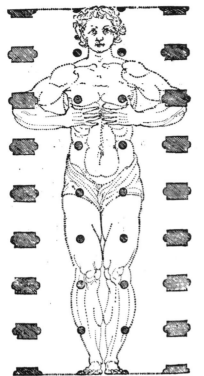

The sanctuary of the Temple
in Jerusalem and the perfect body,
after Prado and Villalpanda

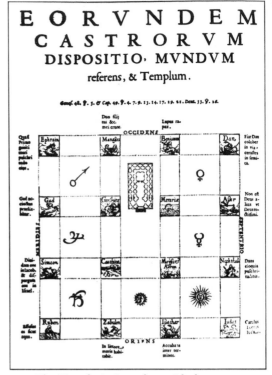

The Temple in Jerusalem with the courts
attributed to the planets, the porches of the
tribes to the signs of the zodiac,
after Prado and Villalpanda

Milan) of a politicized classicism to some definite past were dissolved
into an indefinite archaic and mythical time, and the architecture of
classical antiquity came to be seen as an absolute, timeless architecture whose justification did not lie in any precedent but in reason
itself. So the appeal of the sacred, Constantinian precedent also
weakened.

Villalpanda took the absolute nature of classical architecture for
granted. But reason — for him — was not a sufficient guarantee of such
absolute rightness, nor would he believe that unaided reason could
have arrived at the perfection of the faith. It is worth remembering
here that Villalpanda was not an architectural theorist, but a biblical
scholar and a theologian who justified the building enterprises of his
master, Philip II, as spiritual exercises unusual only because of their
vast corporeal manifestations: and even in scale they seemed to reflect those of King Solomon, who was the type of the wise ruler.

Villalpanda was one of the few writers concerned about other
matters who yet made a direct and important impact on five or six
generations of working architects. It was incidental to his main purpose to raise architecture above reason and above myth: to give it direct divine authority, while not denying its historical context. The
newly experienced need for such authority was perhaps even more
powerful than Villalpanda himself reckoned. At any rate, it was a
consequence of his work which turned the classical orders into the

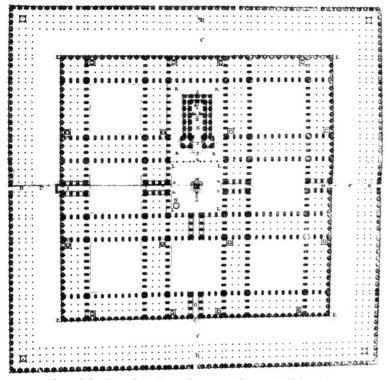

Plan of the Temple in Jerusalem according to Villalpanda,
after Prado and Villalpanda

inevitable archetype for an architecture of grace. As an archetype, the
Temple itself incorporated its predecessors: Noah's ark and the tabernacle in the desert; indeed, the Temple's ornament was based on that
of the tabernacle. This translation of timber forms into stone echoes
the theories of Vitruvius about the origin of the orders in timber building. The very layout of the Villalpanda Temple, with its twelve pavilions, imitated in disposition the tribes around the desert tabernacle;
but it also represented the twelve zodiacal houses, while the seven
courts represented the planets. The antique derivation of the canonic
proportional system from the human body is again very important for
Villalpanda, though it is given a new and almost medieval formulation. The proportions of the Temple are based on the perfect human
body, which is the body of the Savior, who, being in a special sense
the temple of the Holy Spirit, is anagogically prefigured in Jerusalem
by the presence of the Temple "built with hands." I suspect that even
skeptics among architectural theorists adopted an indulgent tone
towards Villalpanda because they found his underlying reasoning acceptable, if they rejected his scriptural interpretations and his detailed reconstructions.

One writer who structured his book on such notions was the garru-
lous and roguish bishop of Vigevano, Juan Caramuel de Lobkowitz.
His treatise on architecture (one of his many publications) was even
called *Templum Solomonis in Jerusalem, Rectam et Obliquam exhi-*

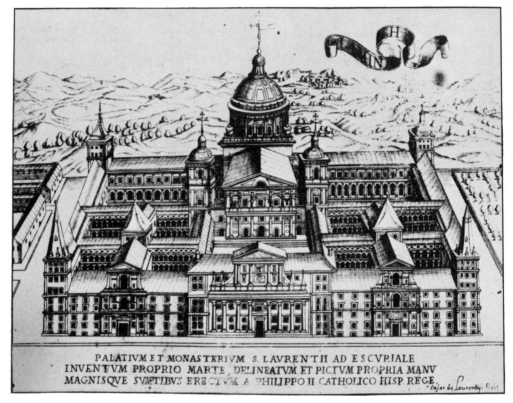

The Escorial, after Caramuel de Lobkowitz

bens, and lengthily subtitled in Spanish (the language of the text) — I give an extract only — *Architectura civil Recta y Obliqua, Considerada y Debuxada en el Templo de Jerusalem . . . Promovida a summa Perfection en el Templo y Palacio de D. Lorenco cerca del Escorial.* Lobkowitz published this through his own diocesan printer in 1678. Although his own illustrations of the Temple owe more to Rabbi Jehudah Leon than to Villalpanda, nevertheless Lobkowitz quotes the latter with great respect; and in any case, the basic notion underlying the whole argument is obviously derived from Villalpanda. Again, Lobkowitz is convinced of the divinely inspired character of both temple designs, yet he is very insistent on the timber origin of all stone architectural ornament and indeed construction, which, he says (quoting yet another and earlier theorist, Fr. Pierre de Chales), is "the true and common teaching" about architectural origins. Lobkowitz is familiar with the argument about the origin of architecture in huts and caves, as it was set out by ancient writers, particularly of course Vitruvius, and amplified by his commentators. But he is also one of the first to make extensive references to the dwellings of American Indians, of Eskimos (the lawless and troglodyte Scriningeri — he does not seem to have heard of igloos), and he is familiar with Malay houseboats and with African tree dwellings. He gathers material from popular missionary and travel literature, though curiously enough he notes seeing a hammock at the house of an Antwerp merchant and comments on the good sense of Amerindian sleeping habits.[39]

With all this, Lobkowitz, who loves paradox and logic-chopping, argues that military architecture is more ancient than civil: he recalls that although man was created perfect, he sinned, was put out of Paradise, and the walls which kept him out were the first architecture, guarded by the first soldiers, angels with flaming swords. This prototype is the product of Lobkowitz's idiosyncratic reasoning and has no direct connection with the less tortuous deductions of mainstream theorists. The vast ashlar walls guarded by the shining celestial knights recall the barrage of the "earthly paradise" which medieval fabulists and voyagers described. Nevertheless, Lobkowitz does not develop this idea. By contrast, he devotes an unusually extensive part of his book to describing primitive dwellings of various kinds; he is particularly insistent, as I have already pointed out, on those of the American Indians, whose personal dignity, ordered life, generosity and good looks were to make them the ideal candidates for that part of the noble savages a later age was to find so fascinating. To take one instance, Lobkowitz dwells in great detail on the wood-and-pisé "palace" of a cacique of Hispaniola (i.e., Haiti) and describes the court, the porticoes and pillars in terms he might have used of a classical building. He does not mention the much more advanced stone architecture of Peru or Mexico anywhere in the book; either he doesn't know it, or he doesn't care about it. After all, he is not concerned to provide an analytical or comparative description of world architecture, but to justify the derivation of *all* architecture from the "rational" procedure of the ancients and the intervention of divine providence, to culminate in the only possible architecture, that of classical antiquity; and this (as the title of his book indicates) is finally brought to perfection in the building of the Escorial, the successor of the Temple in Jerusalem.

Classical architecture stems, "es la doctrina verdadera y comun," from timber building, and ultimately from huts built of wood and rushes; and since Lobkowitz demonstrates their existence everywhere in the world (together with the caves and tree dwellings which Vitruvius also mentions), classical architecture, as the only properly rational "deduction" from primitive construction, *must* have universal validity. I have already suggested the ground for this assurance.

Huts in Hispaniola, after Caramuel de Lobkowitz

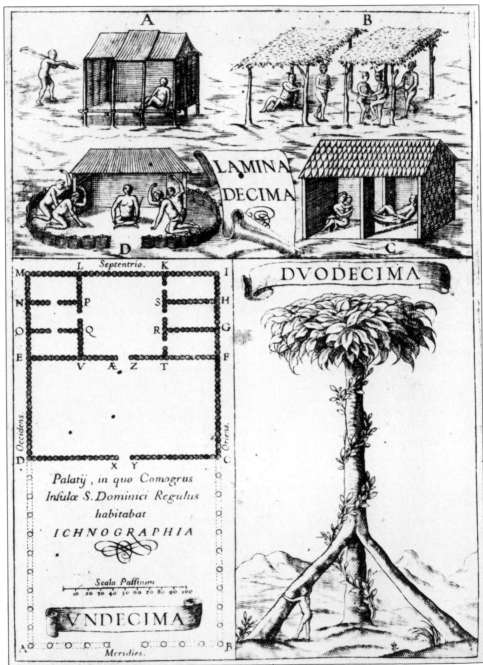

Palace of the king in S. Domingo, after Caramuel de Lobkowitz

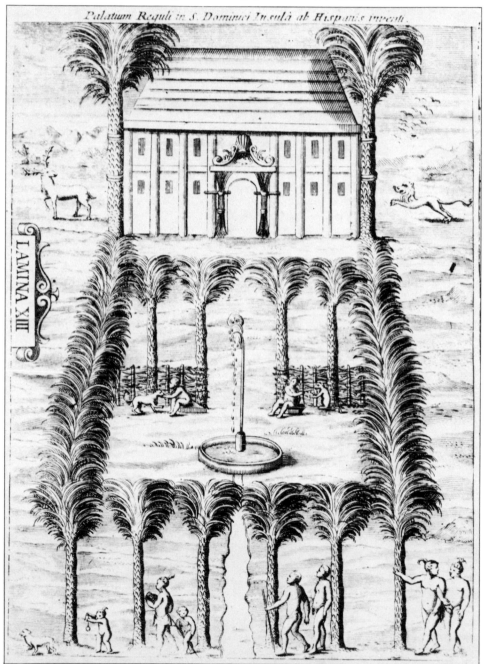

Palatium Reguli in S. Dominici Insula ab Hispanis inventa.

LAMINA XII

And yet in the matter of origins, there is a distinction worth mentioning. Scripture isolates the invention of language as the first properly human activity — whatever else may be implied in the first chapters of Genesis about Adam. It is the first indication of his spontaneous activity. Building in the communal sense is properly the activity of Cain; while the pagan authors I have quoted associate the origin of language with that of building in the first human grouping, the first truly human form of association. And this association has obviously fascinated all Western writers on architecture — to an obsessive degree in the eighteenth century, when problems of the origin of language became one of the staple concerns of speculation.

In one sense, the Vitruvian text is a dead end; no earlier architectural writings survive and my theme might therefore seem exhausted. Scriptural commentators (it is true) provide some consolation in treating of Noah's ark, of the tabernacle and the Temple, even of the Tower of Babel. And yet the first building *implied* by Scripture among fallen man is even earlier than all these archetypes: "And Cain knew his wife, and she conceived, and bore Enoch: and he builded a city and called the name of the city after the name of his son, Enoch."[40] But then Scripture says little of the slight matter of my inquiry. On the other hand, myth and popular legend — above all, ritual — show something of the many beliefs that surround the invention of building, and of the passage from friable, perishable materials to stable and hard ones.

There is a vast array of building rituals in all cultures; but it is not those which deal with building private houses, or temples and palaces, or even whole towns which concern me: I am chiefly interested in the "other" house. This may be a house which had once existed, before heroic or divine intervention turned it to stone; it may involve a hut still standing, which had "in the first days" been inhabited by god or hero; most commonly it is a rite of building huts which in some way resembled or commemorated those which ancestors or heroes had built at some remote and important time in the life of the tribe. In every case they are "other" than the normal dwellings of the time and place. And in every case they incarnate some shadow or memory of that perfect building which was before time began: when man was quite at home in his house, and his house as right as nature itself.

Chapter 6: THE RITES

IN THE EIGHTH BOOK OF THE *METAMORPHOSES*, OVID TELLS THE STORY OF Philemon and Baucis, who, as a reward for their generous hospitality, had their house changed into a temple by Zeus and Hermes; its wooden posts became marble columns and the thatched roof turned to gilt bronze. And when the two old people reached their appointed time, they did not die but were transformed, he into an oak, she into a linden tree, standing side by side.[1] This charming story of happiness in poverty, of generosity and fidelity rewarded, incidentally shows two features I find interesting. One is the incarnation of human beings in trees, the other is the transformation of the hut into a stone temple.

The two faithful spouses were not "simple" people, of course: the two trees in which they were enclosed by the gods were offered the kind of worship which was usual at a hero shrine. The story has something in common with tales in which human beings are changed into plants, like Hyacinth or Narcissus, though the subclass of changes into trees has somewhat different connotations, particularly as regards ritual. The story of Apollo and Daphne, which comes first in Ovid's *Metamorphoses*, is the most familiar and appealing of all these legends.[2] The laurel tree had a very important part in the cult of Apollo. In his description of the greatest and most famous of all Apollonian shrines, the Delphic Temple, Pausanias includes the mythical building history of the main building. "It is said," he reports, "that the most ancient temple of Apollo was made of laurel-wood and that the boughs were brought from Tempe. This temple must therefore have been in the form of a hut. The Delphians think that the second was made of wax and feathers and that it was sent by Apollo to the Hyperboreans." (Here Pausanias inserts an excursus about the punning myth of the man Pteron—*pteros*, fern—and a possible fern-leaf temple, which does not really concern me.) "As for the third temple," says Pausanias, "it is not surprising that it was built of bronze."[3] However, as to the rest of the legend, I do not believe that it was built by Hephaestus, nor the story of the golden songsters which the poet Pindar mentions when speaking of this particular temple:

> And from above the gable
> Sang charmers all of gold.[4]

Here, it seems to me, Pindar merely imitated Homer's description of the sirens. Again, as to the way in which the temple vanished, I found the accounts differed. Some say it fell into a chasm in the earth, others that it was melted down by fire.

"The fourth temple was built by Trophonius and Agamedes, and the tradition says it was built of stone. But it burned down . . . and the present temple was built . . . by the Amphictyons." Even as it stands in Pausanias, the legend must be given some credit. The original shrine is described as being a hut of laurel boughs: this clearly has bearing on my principal argument, and I will return to the theme. But the story about the second and third temples also contains certain references to some Delphic beliefs. In Delphi the three fateful sisters, the Thriae, were known as Bees; and if I understand the Homeric Hymn aright, lived in a cleft of Parnassus and busied themselves making wax.[5] Their divining could only be relied on when they could feed on "the sweet food of the gods"; if honey was denied them, they lost direction and would not speak the truth. Of course, Delphi was not the only place where bees and honey were worshiped. At Ephesus there was a bee sisterhood, Melissae, who belonged to the cult of Artemis, and there were priestesses of Demeter who bore the same name. The nymph Melissa and the she-goat Amalthea were the twin nurses of the baby Zeus in Crete.[6] Commentators have noted in this connection that when Canaan was promised to the Jews it was described as a land "flowing with milk and honey," and that the Jews had a prophetess who was called a bee-Deborah,[7] who in turn was identified with another Deborah, the nurse of Rebecca.[8]

Honey is identified with childhood and nursing, and with prophecy in the form of mead. Honey was also known to be a preservative, and hence — or simply by association with nursing children — one of the substances to be offered to the dead. The souls of the dead were themselves sometimes called bees.[9] Wax too was a preservative: it shared many of the properties of honey with which it was found. The color and translucency of honey associate fairly obviously with amber; amber was associated too, obviously enough, with gold, and seems to have been deposited in tombs in a similar way to the incorrupt jade deposited in Chinese graves, as gold was. And amber came, so legend had it, from the river Eridanus, in the land of the Hyperboreans,[10] a legendary northern country which Apollo visits in his winter absence from Delphi, and with which it had other mythical links. Does the gift of the wax, god-built temple celebrate the transmission of casting techniques to some northern people? Perhaps. The Hyperboreans are represented in legend as guileless and gentle savages, dwelling in an ideal land: an exalted version of the eighteenth-century noble savage.[11]

The succession of shrines is completed by the stone temple, built by two hero-builders with the assistance of the god himself. Trophonius was, according to some legends, Apollo's son; but he was also related to Agamedes (his stepson? his brother?), and they were the heroes of other building legends, some with curious Egyptian echoes. But he was most famous as the deity of the great Boetian divinatory shrine at Lebadia — a shrine of the incubatory type and of an obviously chthonic character.[12]

If legend is to be believed, this also was the character of the Delphic shrine when it belonged to Ge, the earth-mother, and was

Apollo killing the python at the tripod.
Coin of Hierapolis. British Museum, London

guarded by her son, Pytho, the monstrous snake whom Apollo killed
before he himself took over the patronage of the oracle.

And yet there is something ambiguous about the killing of Pytho.
It was not, as the deaths of monsters so often seem in fairy tales, a
ridding the world of some awful curse; it was an act which required
expiation, and not the simple expiation that may accompany the
killing of an animal, even a sacred animal.[13] It was an expiation which
required submission to complex ordeals, and a journey. This journey
to the Valley of Tempe, between Olympus and Ossa, had a permanent
ritual connection with Delphi. In every eighth year (every ninth
year, says Pausanias) a festival called the Septentrion, from the seven-
year interval, was celebrated at Delphi. What happened at it is told

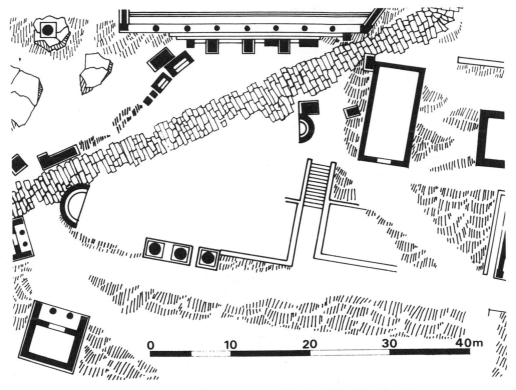

The Delphic temple site. Drawing showing "threshing floor"

rather confusedly by several writers. "The Septentrion," says Plutarch, "seems to be a representation of Apollo's flight to Tempe and the pursuit that followed that flight. Some will have it that Apollo fled because he desired purification . . . others that he was following the wounded python. The Septentrion is therefore a representation of these matters . . ."[14] and here unfortunately Plutarch breaks off to discuss the other Delphic festivals. But he returns to the Septentrion in another book, where he puts a somewhat different emphasis on his account, which he attributes to one of the interlocutors, Cleombatus of Sparta, who is discussing the matter of the decline of oracles.

"For the wooden cabin which is put up for the threshing floor," says Cleombatus, "is not like the nest, the lair of a serpent, but is the copy of the house of some despot or king, and the silent aggression on it through the place called the Dolonia [text defective?] . . . then the torchlight procession which brings the youth, both of whose

West central Greece showing Delphi
and the valley of Tempe

parents must still be living, and when they have set fire to the hut
and overturned the table, without looking back they fly by the gates
of the shrine. And finally the errant wanderings and servitude of the
boy, and the purification which takes place at Tempe, make one suspect some great antiquity, some daring deed." Cleombatus dismisses
the etiological myth: "For it is ridiculous to claim that having killed
the savage beast, he had to flee to the other end of Greece to be purified. . . ." While the events described by Cleombatus took place in
the course of a night, he implies further rituals, and considering that
Tempe is a good hundred miles from Delphi, they obviously took
much more time. The ritual at Delphi was very public. Cleombatus
calls it "the rites connected with the oracle, those to whose celebration recently the [Delphic] oracle invited all the Greeks living
between Tempe and Thermopylae. . . ."[15]

The layout of the ritual itself suggests that the etiological myth
(in spite of Cleombatus) had some elements relevant to its possible

interpretation, for the threshing floor on which the hut was built faced (across the sacred way) some of the mementos of the archaic shrine: the outcrop of stone known as the Sybil's Rock, which is reputed to have been the Pythia's original divining spot hard by the supposed location of the fuming chasm, or alternatively the site of the sanctuary of Ge, near which Pytho lived.

It is clear that Cleombatus would have taken some piled-up faggots or tree branches to be the serpent's lair which legend led him to expect. But the rite demanded something more elaborate; and yet not quite as substantial as a proto-Hellenic ruler's palace [Priam's?] either – so the context seems to imply.[16] Whatever it was, it had to be fairly inflammable and only large enough to have one notable object within it, a single table, which is upset in the rite. I take it that it was some single-chambered structure: the word *oikesis* is generalized enough to allow for almost any interpretation. But since the whole area called the threshing floor is triangular, with the shorter sides of some 20 meters each, and there would have to be room for maneuver, the size itself provides a parameter.

It is worth remembering that Plutarch was familiar with just such an anachronism of a royal dwelling, the reputed hut of Romulus on the Palatine in Rome.[17] I take it that is what he had in mind here: a rough "megaron" set up at the last turn of the Sacred Way, in a theater formed of the temple platform, the Athenian portico, and the ground rising and falling around the "threshing floor." Here, after nightfall, some sort of ceremonial attack involving the overturning of a table, presumably within the structure, took place. The group had its principal actor, Cleombatus's *kouros amphithalis*, who was accompanied by the torchbearers. It is not clear who else took part in the procession, but the action certainly involved the boy's flight, implying that he is followed. Now flights of this nature are common enough in Greek, and indeed much primitive, ritual. Here the text seems to suggest that according to the ritual, the principal actor will be or will allow himself to be caught: the point about the ritual chase is too complex for me to consider in greater detail here. But I take it that is what the words about servitude imply. Plutarch is, however, very uninformative about the subsequent action, and unfortunately the author whose account provides further information about this festival, Aelian, takes the rite up at a somewhat later point. In describing the Valley of Tempe, he ends his description like this: "And it was here, according to the Thessalians, Pythian Apollo was by Zeus's order purified, when he had shot the serpent Pytho who had guarded Delphi when the earth had still the oracle there. So when Apollo made himself a wreath of this Tempe laurel, and taking a laurel branch in his right hand, the son of Zeus and Leto returned to Delphi and took charge of the oracle. There is an altar in the very

Delphic Apollo, enthroned and holding a laurel branch.
Detail from a volute crater by the Cleophon Master (ca. 430 B.C.).
Museo Archeologico di Spina, Ferrara

place where he crowned himself and took the branch. And even now
every ninth year the Delphians send some noble youths there, and
one of them is the *architheros*, the leader of the procession. When
these have reached Tempe and performed a splendid sacrifice there,
they return, having plaited themselves wreaths from [branches of]
that tree from which the lover-god [text defective?] had taken his
wreath. And they followed the road which is called Pythian. . . .
They [the people through whose territory the road passed] accompany the boys with veneration and honors . . . it is customary to crown
the victors of the Pythian games with wreaths from the same laurels."[18]

I have already referred to Daphne, and the laurel's mythical connection with Apollo. At Delphi there were more occasions for the
laurel to appear. In the historical period a laurel tree, possibly cast
in metal, stood in the temple building[19]; the Sibyl chewed laurel
leaves and drank the spring water of Castalia before entering into
her trance, or (as another source has it) shook the sacred tree in
imitation of Apollo.[20] Also, those who had consulted the oracle went
home wearing laurel wreaths, which rendered them sacrosanct, even
if they were slaves.

A cluster of themes seems connected with Delphi; blood-guilt and its redemption, Apollonian myth, a kind of initiation, and the laurel: Daphne transformed, and Apollo's special tree. But the Delphian Septentrion was not the only town to have a festival procession carrying laurel branches. At Thebes there was a "May" festival, the Daphnophoria, in honor of Apollo Ismaeos. The principal priest of this cult, who was again a presentable young man of good family, both of whose parents were still alive, was appointed for the year, and again the festival was probably celebrated every ninth year. The trophy round which it was centered was a piece of olive wood, decorated with laurel leaves, with wool and various baubles, to which a second-century writer ascribed a cosmological significance[21]; it was carried in procession by the priest's nearest male relative. The priest himself, crowned with a gold wreath and wearing long (perhaps female?) garments, carried a laurel branch, as his name suggests. The female choir which accompanied him also carried boughs, and all the young men of the town wore laurel wreaths and carried laurel boughs on the day.

At Athens, too, there were festivals involving laurel and olive branches, called *eiresione*. They were featured in two festivals, the Thargelia (May) and the Pyanepsia (October). Plutarch provides an etiological myth of the Oschophoria—a part of the Pyanepsia—in which he explains, by reference to Theseus's arrival from Crete after he had killed the Minotaur, the various ceremonies, including the procession of the *eiresione*, which was after the procession fixed to the doors of the Temple of Apollo (*patroos*?).[22] But there was also an *eiresione* fixed at the door of every Athenian house, and it may be that the *eiresione* were ceremonially burned.[23] There were many other Greek ceremonies involving boughs. The expulsion of the Pharamakoi at the Thargelia belongs to a large group of rites in which victims or participants are beaten with green boughs; much has been written about this. There were other rites, more relevant to my theme. At the Panathenaia boughs were carried. On Samos there were bough-carrying ceremonies every night of the new moon. There were a number of names for the ceremonial green bough, usually of laurel or olive: *aisakos*, *bakhos*, *thylla*, or even just *hygeia*, health.[24] Magical, powerful tree branches are familiar enough in myth. An obvious instance is the juniper bough with which Medea charmed the dragon guarding the Golden Fleece—a curious echo of Kadmeian Thebes.[25] Both Jason and Kadmos had sown dragon's teeth from which warriors arose; as Deucalion had, at Dodona, sown stones, the bones of his mother, the earth. Kadmos had moreover gone into slavery to Ares for killing the same serpent whose teeth he had sown.[26]

Modern commentators have seen etiologies of initiation rites in accounts of struggles with daemons, involving sometimes the hero's death in the dragon's jaws, and his subsequent resurrection. The dragons of myth they usually consider a form of the earth-demon, sometimes (as Pausanias considered Pytho) as a son of the great mother or even her consort. The defeat of the dragon, his killing, or simply his spewing up of the hero (paralleled to the killing of the Minotaur by Theseus, and his return from the interstices of the Labyrinth) seems connected with a nine-year cycle of initiation. Such myths have an inevitable connection with the underworld, for the matter of death and the life after death are an essential *materia* of all initiatory and "mystery" teaching. Hence the connection between the epic poem and the journey back to the underworld, such as those of Odysseus and Aeneas, and that of Gilgamesh, who searches after the undersea tree of eternal youth, which is stolen from him, as he sleeps, by a serpent: upon seizing it the serpent instantly sloughs its skin and gains immortality.

In another legend connected with Gilgamesh, the god-hero kills a serpent "who knows no charm," and who prevents (together with the *Imdugud* bird who nests in its branches, and Lilith who builds her house in its trunk) the goddess Inanna from cutting down the *huluppu* (willow?) tree she had planted and making a chair out of it.[27] When the guardian serpent died, the *Imdugud* bird flew away, and Lilith fled from her house. Gilgamesh made a drum out of a piece of the trunk and drumsticks out of the branches. In the Sumerian poem, the drum and sticks fall into the underworld. The text of the poem is defective so that we do not know quite how or why this happens, and the final part of the poem is concerned with how the precious objects are retrieved. Much of this myth recalls the practices of certain northern and even Amerindian shamans.

This epic may remind the reader of the connection between the theme of my present essay and the vast literary area of underworld descents, through the powerful image of the living bough whose power saves the hero from the dangers that beset him, or opens doors to him that appear otherwise to be closed for ever. The image also evokes the continued power of the sacred wood, transformed into a cultic object. Unfortunately, it would be really beyond the scope of this essay to explore the ramifications of this imagery. But the deeds of Gilgamesh are worth recalling here, if only to serve as a reminder that these themes are not limited to classical mythology. The theme of the spirit-devouring monster, whether male or female, sometimes seen as a mother-and-son couple, is common in many cultures throughout the world. It is therefore the business of many initiatory practices to equip the initiate for his journey to the land of the blessed dead by avoiding the wiles of these monsters. In this trial the spirits of the dead ancestors are at hand to help the initiate: there may even be an account of the route and its dangers left by the hero-ancestor who first made the journey. Such a description may be in the form of an epic, or even of a dramatic, representation.

Quite often this drama is performed or the epic sung in initiation rites, either in those of secret societies or simply in tribal puberty rituals; whether in Australia, America or in the Asian steppe, they involve also the seclusion of the postulant/initiates in a hut or tent.[28] In this temporary dwelling they have to submit to a variety of ordeals, some of which may be dangerous and even have fatal results on occasions. It is common enough for this to be accounted for by saying that the monster has "swallowed" the unsuccessful initiands —who in any case are often treated as being ritually dead and are almost always unclean—while it disgorged the successful ones. There are many varieties of the initiation drama and correspondingly many etiologies to account for them.[29] Consequently, even in the remotest derivatives of such etiologies, which children's fairy stories sometimes provide, such incidents provide an essential ingredient. Any account of folk literature will inevitably contain a great many references to them.[30]

In New Guinea circumcision is often performed in a hut which is identified with a monster—it is always described as having a belly and a tail; some tribes build it with two entrances, the large one representing its mouth, the small one the anus. The presence of the initiand in the monster's belly is often equated with a return to the womb, and the initiation then becomes a new birth. The rather fragile hut of leaves or raffia which represents the monster refers me back to the Delphic festival.[31] In this the etiological myth may have had the essential doctrine in a form nearer the ritual "truth" than Cleombatus's enlightened skepticism allows, for if the hut built on the Delphic threshing floor was not the dragon's lair, but the dragon itself, then its destruction by burning may well be a representation of the death of Pytho at the hand of Apollo after the initiation was finished and the initiates had been disgorged. At Delphi the custom of building the hut celebrated a kind of Delphic "great year," and was accompanied by other ceremonies. The laurel brought back from Delphi was used for the coronation of the victors at the Pythian games, granting them something of Apollo's divinity, at least for a time. But the custom of building such huts more frequently survived from earliest times elsewhere in Greece. Pausanias, again, tells of a festival celebrated in honor of Tithorean Isis, "one of the oldest sanctuaries of the Egyptian goddess built by Greeks." The festival was held twice a year, once in spring and again in autumn. Three days before the feast, "those who were allowed to enter the sanctuary purge it in a secret way of all the things remaining from the victims of the previous feast, and they carry it all in one place and bury it. . . . The next day the traders put up booths of reed or some other material to hand. On the last of the three days there is a fair, at which slaves and all sorts of cattle are sold, as well as clothing, gold and silver. They turn to worship in the hour after midday. Bulls and deer are sacrificed by the richer people; the poorer sacrifice geese and chickens; swine are not permitted sacrifice, nor are sheep or goats. . . . The manner of this worship is Egyptian: while all the sacrifices are offered in procession, and when they have been received in the inner sanctuary, some who remain outside set fire to the huts and depart hastily. . . ."[32]

These market booths share the usage of burning and hasty retreat with the more solemn hut at Delphi. Tithorea was about twelve miles from Delphi, and it is not clear how much of the Tithorean ritual Isis inherited from some older deity who had a shrine there, rather than bringing it with her from Egypt. There were other analogous customs, not so well known: at a sanctuary of the Dioscuri at Elatea, also in Phocis, those who made sacrifices erected huts into which women were not allowed to go.[33] The Dioscuri — the Anakes, as they were called in their Athenian cult — were initiatory gods, and had their festival during the Thargelion. There appears to have been another cult which involved the erection of booths during the Thargelion: it was celebrated during Pyanepsion in honor of Demeter and Persephone, and here men were excluded.[34] Moreover, the Laconians celebrated in the midsummer Karneia yet another festival involving a pharmakos and some form of initiation: and also dedicated to Apollo — indeed it was the Laconian version of the Apollonian epiphany, much as the Daphnophoria was the Phocean one.[35] The Karneia, then, lasted nine days, and during the festival the participants seem to have feasted, divided into nine phratries under tents or canopies called skiades, and obeyed a strict quasi-military ritual. Some of the participants wore crowns of palm leaves; Plutarch seems to imply that huts roofed with palm leaves bound with ivy were a normal part of the Bacchanalia.[36]

There were no doubt other festivals at which such customs obtained; we are not acquainted with all Greek ritual, by any means. These examples ensure, however, that the building of leaf and reed huts may be seen as a commonplace of Greek religious practice, whether Phocean, Doric or Attic.

In Italy the custom also appears, rather ambiguously and in a context in which one might expect it: the acts of the Arval brothers, an initiatory phratry, who celebrated at the center of their festivals a banquet in huts.[37] The apparatus of the brotherhood's ritual consists of secret dances, of games, of torches and masks, and of ceremonies with dry and green wheat carried out by priests in wheat wreaths and white bandlets; and their duties include year-renewal ceremonies at the Saturnalia. A much clearer evidence of the custom is provided by the plebeian feast of Neptunalia, celebrated on July 23. The first lexicographer, Festus, explains the word *umbrae* as referring to the leafy huts that are put up as shelters (*tabernacula*) on Neptune's feast day.[38] It would be much easier to comment on this if anything was known about the Italic deity of waters, who is in fact totally overshadowed in mythological writing by his Olympian opposite number, Poseidon.[39] Much more is known about another deity, Anna Perenna, in whose honor the Romans, and more particularly the Roman *plebs*, celebrated a tipsy festival on the Ides of March.

Here again, a number of puzzles remain. We are not even sure how the goddess was worshiped in the state cult. Macrobius suggests that as part of the New Year festival a Flamen was sacrificed to the goddess both publicly and privately so that the year might be completely fortunate: "*ut annare perannareque commode liceat.*"[40] Apart from the state cult, there was the popular celebration, which Ovid describes as an eyewitness. "On the Ides is the jolly festival of Anna Perenna, not far from your banks, you Tiber, you who come from strange lands; the people crowd together and sit about the green grass, each with his mate, drinking. Some stay in the open air, some pitch tents, and there are those who build their huts of leafy branches, others set up dry reeds for columns, and stretch their togas over them. Now they are warm with sun and wine, and pray for as many years as they will drink cups, and count as they drink. You will meet the man here who has outdrunk Nestor's years, or the woman who, to judge by her cups, should equal the Sybil's age. . . ." The next few lines of the poem describe the drunken dances. Ovid goes on to his witnessing a "procession" surrounded by a crowd: a drunken old hag dragging a drunk old man behind her.[41]

Tibullus, without specifying any particular date or deity, mentions a festival in similar huts, lashed together with ropes.[42] Since he had been talking earlier in the same passage of the *Parilia*, another March holiday, he may be referring to Anna Perenna's Day[43]; elsewhere he speaks of some summer festival, or so it seems, during which slaves build huts by bonfires. Horace mentions huts of twigs and leaves as a children's game.[44] Obviously in Rome, as in Greece, this custom was equally familiar.

Since it is Anna Perenna who provided the Roman populace, or at any rate a section of it, with the opportunity to indulge in it, I would like to examine the enigmatic goddess more closely. Divine rhyming names, like Mutunus Tutunus or Mamurius Veturius, occur occasionally in Roman mythology, more particularly in the context of the family. Indeed, Mamurius Veturius had a strange connection with Anna Perenna, and it is worth looking at him first.

On March 14, the day before her feast, Mamurius Veturius was a *pharmakos*, a scapegoat. I must omit any discussion of the calendar curiosities of the two feasts here. At any rate Mamurius (as Lydus, who is the only one to describe the ceremony exactly, calls him), who for the purpose of the rite was a man dressed in animal skins, was "beaten" out of the town with peeled twigs, and abused. Hence the saying "to play the Mamurius" for "getting a beating." The legend says, according to Lydus, that Mamurius the smith was beaten out of the city when the shields he had substituted for the ones that fell from heaven brought bad luck on Rome.[45]

This etiology does not square with more ancient forms of myth about Mamurius. He appears as an artist in Propertius's monologue of Vertumnus[46]; in a myth apparently more ancient and more important for the state religion of the city, Mamurius appears as a metalsmith. The Salian brotherhood was instituted to guard the sacred shield, *ancile*, which had either been found in the house of Numa or had fallen from heaven on March 1.[47] Such sacred objects are well known to folklore and mythology. It is curious, here, that while the Arval brothers were the twelve adopted brothers of Romulus, so the *ancilia* of the Salian brothers' chapel on the Palatine were the twelve companions of the heaven-sent shield. At any rate the brilliant smith seems to have some curious connection with the god. Mars was of course the patron of the Salian brothers, and he was called "Mamurius Veturius" in the ritual *carmen* of the brotherhood.[48] This appears to have identified him both with the smith of legend and with the old year.

There is another myth connecting Anna and Mars, which, according to Ovid, was the subject of indecent songs sung by girls on that day. The legend had it that Mars, in love with Minerva, asked Anna, who had a share in his month, to act as go-between. But the go-between insinuated herself into the bridal chamber as a veiled bride, to the god's rage and the entertainment of Venus.[49] All these stories indicate Anna Perenna's status clearly. Her name shows it, in any case. She is the ring (*annus*) of the completed year. It is proper that Mars, who rules over the New Year and its protective feasts, should court her. He himself rules over the fortnight from the beginning of the religious year, on his Kalends, and she has the Ides of the same month. These two new years reconcile (presumably) the archaic lunar and solar calendars.[50] It is perhaps inevitable that the old calendar deity, Anna, should be identified with the moon. There are some other etiologies: since fresh bread is used in the rite, Anna is identified with an old woman of Bovillae, and with an Egyptian, both of whom figure in legends connected with bread.[51] But most interesting to me is the identification with Anna, the sister of Dido, queen of Carthage.[52] Ovid offers a number of legendary explanations for the worship of the Phoenician princess even in Italy, and of her transformation into a river nymph. It is difficult to believe that they are his or his contemporaries' inventions, however learned they may have been. The Punic Wars were already far away, it is true; yet although the Romans had a vivid memory of the two centuries of conflict, they had a way of taking over the deities they defeated.

The curious thing is that the Dido and Anna of legend are not quite the separate characters they appear in the *Aeneid*. According to Servius, Virgil himself suspected that it was Anna, not Dido, who loved Aeneas.[53] In some versions of the legend it was both sisters — not Dido alone — who committed suicide, to attain the deification which Phoenician religion promised the self-immolating hero or heroine.[54] Dido herself, outside the *Aeneid*, is not simply the tragic queen of the epic. Her original name, according to legend, was Elissa, which suggests that she was a goddess first, and queen only secondarily[55]; that she was the founding and patronal deity of Carthage.[56] It is conjectured that she is identified with Ta'anit, the Phoenician queen of heaven.[57] Two perfectly convincing derivations of her Latin name from western Semitic roots (from $\sqrt{\text{IDD}}$ — to love strongly, and $\sqrt{\text{NDD}}$ — to move to and fro, i.e., like the moon) have been given. But neither explains the curious Semitic echoes of this very archaic feast.[58]

It is difficult to go very far towards such an explanation. There is no literary account of the Phoenician calendar, except a strange Hellenistic fake compiled by Philon of Byblos, who purports to provide a Phoenician cosmogony including an account of the origins of communities and of building — not unlike the one I quoted from Vitruvius and Lucretius — and which we know through Eusebius's evangelic parallel.[59] The heroic civilizing figure in this protohistory, Hypsouranios, first builds huts of reeds and papyrus. He quarrels with his hunter-brother, Ousoos, who first invents clothing of animal skins. It is difficult to say whether Philon is here echoing some Egyptian legend, or simply taking his Egyptian information from Diodorus Siculus; whether he is familiar with the story of Jacob and Esau from the Book of Genesis, or whether he knows it indirectly; there may even be some genuine Phoenician source for the story.

At any rate, the parallel scriptural passage is interesting. After his quarrel with Esau, "Jacob journeyed to Succot, and built himself a house; and he made booths for his cattle. Therefore the name of the place is called Succot."[60]

Succot — booths — is also the Hebrew name for the feast of tabernacles, perhaps the most evident continuation of a ritual in which huts are built of green plants until our own time. It is an autumn festival, one of the three great temple feasts (with Passover, and the feast of weeks, Pentecost) and has several features relevant to my argument. The first of course is the building of the booths themselves. This is already prescribed in the Mosaic ritual commands. "On the

A modern cloth *huppah* at a Jewish wedding, after "Art Sacré"

fifteenth day of the seventh month is the feast of tabernacles for seven days unto the Lord . . . and ye shall take you on the first day the fruit of godly trees, and branches of palm trees and boughs of thick trees and willows of the brook and ye shall rejoice before the Lord seven days. . . . Ye shall dwell in booths; all that are born in Israel shall dwell in booths. So that your generation shall know that I made the children of Israel to dwell in booths, when I brought them out of the land of Egypt: I am the Lord your God. . . ."[61]

The feast of tabernacles was, with Passover and Pentecost, one of the three great seasonal festivals of the priestly code. As in the other Jewish festivals, its "action" is a popular action: the building of tabernacles, and the procession carrying palm branches, is a command for all Israel.[62] As Passover and Pentecost are joined cultically by the seven-week "counting of the Omer,"[63] so the feast of tabernacles is assimilated to another celebration, rather different in character: the New Year and the Day of Atonement. The two festivals of Passover and Tabernacles have other symmetrical features.[64] Passover occurs on the first full moon of the year, on the fifteenth of Nisan, while Tabernacles is celebrated on the seventh, the "sabbatical," full moon, on the fifteenth of Tishri. There is something odd about the New Year being celebrated on the first day of the *seventh* month, while the first of Nisan, the first New Moon of the year, does not call for any more commemoration—either in Scripture or in contemporary religious practice—than any other New Moon. Nevertheless, the Mishnah recognizes the anomaly: "There are four 'New Year' days: on the first of Nisan is the new year for kings and feasts; on the first of Elul is the new year for cattle tithes . . ." and so on. In the next paragraph: "At four times in the year is the world judged: at Passover through grain; at Pentecost through the fruit of the tree; on New Year's Day all that come into the world pass before Him like legions . . . and at the feast [of Tabernacles] they are judged through water. . . ."[65]

These two seasons of judgment are closely related to other spring and autumn "passage rites." All the neighbors of Israel seem to have had the same ambiguous features in their sacred calendars, and it may well be that there were changes of emphasis in the Jewish, as well as in other Near Eastern calendars.[66] The Mishnah, which is a second-century edition of much earlier verbal traditions, follows Scripture, and calls the feast of tabernacles simply "The Feast," much as its closest neighbor in the Jewish calendar, the Day of Atonement, is still called "The Day" by pious Jews.[67] The Day of Atonement is the tenth and last of the "Terrible Days," the judgment days of the Jewish calendar, which start on New Year's Day, the first day—and therefore the New Moon—of the month of Tishri. Scripture prescribes priestly rather than popular activities for this period. The people participated by fasting: the mournful character of the post-exilic festival is absent from the scriptural accounts of the celebration, and even from the rabbinic lore; the essential rites were the expiatory sacrifices, which renewed the purity of the temple and of the people.[68] Besides other sacrifices, two goats were led before the high priest. At the door of the tabernacle he was to cast lots on them, and one goat was to be sacrificed as a sin offering to God. The other goat was for an unknown power called Azazel and was the "scape-goat." "And Aaron shall lay both his hands on the head of the live goat, and confess over him all the iniquities of the children of Israel . . . and shall send him away into the wilderness by the hand of a fit man. And the goat shall bear upon him all their iniquities unto a land not inhabited. . . . And he that let go the goat for Azazel shall wash his clothes, and wash his flesh in water, and afterwards come into the camp."[69]

These rites are a major and public analogue to private ones for cleansing and curing a leper.[70] Their purifying function is very evident and must have been very clear to the people before whom they were performed.[71] The festival of tabernacles was therefore the feast of a cleansed people, who, as the historical etiology of the feast made clear, were celebrating their incorporation. In the Pentateuch it is often called the feast of Asaph, and the word suggests the double meaning—*gatherings*, as of the harvest, and *assembly*, as of people.[72]

It is generally assumed by modern commentators that the festival of tabernacles is the ancient Canaanite, or even generally western Semitic vintage and New Year festival, adapted by the nomadic, pastoral Israelites on their settlement in the Land of Promise.[73] The Mosaic Law gave it the essential etiological placing in the sacred history of the nation.

Passover—the trial by grain, the festival of the barley harvest—was marked by the sacrifice of firstlings, their blood marking the doorposts, and the hastily eaten ritual meal in the house. So Tabernacles, with its scapegoat and the leafy, frail image of the nation's forty years of precarious, nomadic life, represented the trial by destiny and by water: inevitably more public, with the people forced out of their usual permanent habitations into booths on rooftops or on the open ground.

To a stranger the booths were not the most obvious features of the celebration of the feast. One of the interlocutors in Plutarch's *Symposium* remarks that "the solemn festival of the Jews fits in perfectly, both as far as season and ceremonial are concerned, with rites of Dionysius. That which they call 'The Feast' they celebrate at the height of the vintage by displaying tables on which are set all kinds of fruit; and they feast in booths specially put together of palms and ivy, calling the day before the feast 'Tabernacles,' *skinion*. Some days later they celebrate a feast which is not secretly dedicated to Dionysius, but publicly. For they have a solemn celebration of *Kradhirephoria*, in which they agitate palm branches, and *Thyrsophoria*, in which they enter the temple carrying *thyrses*. What they do once they have gone in I do not know. But it is natural to suppose that these festivities were in honor of Dionysius."[74]

The identification of the Old Testament God (sometimes called *iao* in Greek, therefore assimilated to *iakhos*) with Dionysius was much favored by some gnostic writers. In this particular case Plutarch has apparently taken the Day of Atonement and Tabernacles as one feast, and separated the Hoshanah procession, a daily feature of the ritual of Tabernacles, into a separate celebration.[75] The mention of the two kinds of bough, the derivation, a little later in the same passage, of the word *Levite* from *Lysias*, rather suggests that Plutarch is here using hearsay as evidence. Nevertheless, it is interesting that to his understanding the rites of the Day of Atonement and the feast of tabernacles are sufficiently similar to those of the Athenian Pyanepsion festivals (or perhaps he is thinking of the Athenian Haloa, which occurred at the same season as the Jewish Hanukkah?) for such a close parallel to suggest itself as obvious. The booths, therefore, and the boughs carried must have seemed very familiar to an uninitiated Greek observer. Jewish ritual practice is insistently precise about them. The Mishnah, though written a century and a half

Menorah, Etrog, Lulab. Detail of wall painting
over the Torah shrine of the synagogue
in Doura-Europos, after Goodenough

after Plutarch's death, codifies practice current long before. The
booth is required to be of a certain size, self-supporting, not so
thickly roofed that the sky cannot be seen, and built afresh for each
festival.[76] Of the boughs to be used in the procession, the Mishnah
is also explicit: "R. Ishmael says that three myrtle branches are needed
and two willow branches and one palm branch, and one citron. . . .
R. Akiba says: as one palm branch and one citron only are needed, so
also one myrtle and one willow.[77] The rabbis may disagree about how
many boughs are ritually correct, or what material may be used to tie
them together, and other such details, but they are quite clearly
unanimous about the species of plant to be used for the *Lulab*.

Lulab is the branch that is shaken in the procession, held in the
right hand, while the citrus fruit, *Etrog*, is held in the left. The *Lulab*
is shaken rhythmically during certain psalms. Processions of men
carrying *Lulab* and *Etrog* went round the temple altar. On the seventh
day, called Hoshana Raba, the procession went round seven times,
and it is perhaps this custom which misled Plutarch. But there were
other temple ceremonials, not specifically ordained in Scripture,

but of which the Mishnah gives details: a libation of wine with water from the pool of Siloam; this water was drawn ceremonially on each day of the feast.[78] There was also the ceremonial lighting of a huge candelabrum on the court of women: "and there was not a courtyard in Jerusalem that did not reflect the light of the Bet Ha-She'ubah."[79] Bet Ha-She'ubah, the house, the place, perhaps the time of water drawing, is also associated with a torch dance: "Men of piety and good works used to dance before [the candelabrum] with burning torches in their hands, singing songs and praises. And countless Levites [played] on harps, cymbals, lyres and trumpets. . . ." So the passage goes on to enumerate the various musical instruments. But the general atmosphere of the festival is best conveyed by a sentence which the Mishnah does not attribute to any particular rabbi: "And they have said, 'He that has never seen the joy of Bet Ha-She'ubah has never in his life seen real joy.' "[80]

Allowing for the conventional hyperbole, clearly it was a very memorable time of year. It is hardly surprising that it was during the feast of tabernacles that King Solomon chose to consecrate the Temple.[81] When Jeroboam set up a rival shrine, he ordained a feast analogous to Tabernacles and consecrated his sanctuary during it.[82]

Nehemiah held the solemn reading of the newly discovered Book of Laws on the first of Tishri, and celebrated the feast of tabernacles as a new "incorporation" of the people.[83] When Judas Maccabeus celebrated the victory over Antiochus Epiphanes by purifying the Temple, he did so with a procession of boughs and palms, and the lighting of a candelabrum, remembering how at another time "they had spent the feast of tabernacles hidden in the mountains and in caves like wild beasts."[84]

There is, finally, a rabbinical tradition that God created the world in the beginning of the month of Tishri: the creation is also variously associated with Mount Moriah. And Jesus chose to open his mission in Jerusalem, the mission that was to end on that fatal Passover, on the feast of tabernacles.[85]

There was therefore an intimate connection between the feast of tabernacles and the Temple; as there was between the Temple and the desert tabernacles tent, both reflecting on the identity of the people of Israel. There is something of an ambiguity in the scriptural command to commemorate Israel's explicitly tent-sheltered wandering in the desert by building huts of fresh leafage, the command presupposing fertile, well-wooded land. The Greek *skene* and the Roman *umbrae* were made indifferently of cloth stretched over reeds and of fresh boughs: it may well be that this indifference goes back to a more archaic tradition, which Jewish rigorism could not tolerate.[86] Although this is perhaps more readily explicable by the assimilation of an agricultural custom to the structure of a historical etiology.

Marduk kills Ti'amat. Babylonian cylinder seal.
British Museum, London

In the Diaspora, the Pentateuch reading — which had been high solemnity in the Temple, reserved for feasts of tabernacles of the seventh, Sabbatical, year in pre-exile times — was divided among all the Saturdays and festivals of the year for reading, the day on which the last chapter of Deuteronomy and the first chapter of Genesis were also read.[87] I shall risk stretching a point a little and suggest that this reading seems a pale echo of the recitation which occurred in such a prominent place in the New Year festivities in Mesopotamia — the Enuma Eliŝ.

"Enuma Eliŝ" are the first words of a creation epic, "When on High." It tells of the creation of all things in the three gods Apsu, Ti'amat and the nebulous Mummu. It was recited twice every New Year's Day in Babylon before the image of Marduk. Marduk, according to the epic, created the world as we know it by killing the monster Ti'amat, the dragon of darkness and deep waters. Marduk first netted Ti'amat; as she opened her hell-mouth to swallow him, he sent in the winds to keep it open, and then shot an arrow which pierced her heart. Her allies fled, and Marduk captured her consort Kingu, from whom he took an important ritual object, the "tablets of destiny," which became one of his royal insignia.[88]

Marduk then crushed Ti'amat's skull with his mace, and opened her arteries. Her blood was carried away by the winds, and Marduk cut her gigantic body in half "like a leather bag" (or "like a mussel," shellfish?); he made the earth of the lower half and raised the upper half to make the sky. He measured the sky with a rod, and built his dwellings in it. Later, Kingu was judged and executed, and from his blood the first men were made. The gods, who had given the young Marduk all the power they had in their giving, celebrated this victory with a great banquet, which is the protocelebration of the Babylonian New Year.[89]

In the course of the New Year celebrations in the city of Babylon, the long epic was recited twice. On the fourth of Nisan—the principal New Year celebration was in spring—in the evening, the urigallu, the chief priest of Marduk's temple, had to recite it with his hands raised "from the beginning to the end."[90] On the fifth day, there occurred purifications, of which we know very little, though one of them was a curious "scape-sheep" or kupurra ceremony, in which the carcase of a decapitated sheep was rubbed all over one of the temples, and the magus (amil maŝmaŝu) had to throw the carcase into the Euphrates, facing West, while the sacrificial swordbearer did the same with the head.[91] These two functionaries became ritually impure until the end of the feast; the urigallu himself became impure if he saw any part of the rite. While the purified temple of Nabu (Marduk's son and avenger) was freshly decked out, in the great temple Esagil nearby the king gave up his insignia to the urigallu, who took them into the sanctuary before the statue of Marduk. Then he went out to the king and slapped his face; he took him into the sanctuary and "pulled his ears and made him bow to the ground." The king made a general confession and was absolved by the urigallu, who gave him back his insignia and led him out of the sanctuary. "Then he shall slap the king's cheek," says the ritual text; "when he has struck his cheek / if tears come, then Bel is well [disposed] / if tears do not come, Bel is angry / the enemy shall come and cause his fall." While the purification and the king's humiliation were taking place in the temple, the city was in disorder. Marduk, the patron of Babylon, was not among the living. He was not exactly dead, he was imprisoned "in the mountain." Somewhere in the city of Babylon there was an actual building or place that was known as his tomb. He was mourned and sought by the people. His chariot drove to the Bit Akitu, the festival building outside the city, empty. On the sixth day of Nisan the god Nabu arrived by boat from Borsippa; other gods also assembled from the towns they patronized. After they had been welcomed, some kind of battle was enacted to release Marduk, and on the eighth of Nisan a great coming together of the gods was celebrated, in Marduk's temple. Absolute power was conferred on Marduk prior to his fight with Ti'amat. This is the first "determination of destiny," a phrase so important in Mesopotamian theology, and so enigmatic.[92]

On the ninth of Nisan there was a solemn procession to the Bit Akitu, in the course of which there seems to have been some kind of a ritual acting out of the Enuma Eliŝ: the king smashed a jar, which represented Ti'amat. In an Assyrian account, a bird, who represented Ti'amat, was cut in two; a sacrificial ram was made to represent Kingu, and so on.

The same night Marduk returned to Babylon, and his holy marriage was celebrated. Various forms of "hieros gamos" were so common, and have been discussed so frequently, that I will only point out that the chamber in which it was mimed or celebrated was known as gigunu, which strangely enough was also the name of the "tomb" in which Marduk was imprisoned.[93] It is difficult to say whether this implies a temporary structure in both cases, or whether there was a chamber in the ziggurat which could serve both purposes. It was, apparently, decorated with green boughs when it served for the hieros gamos. The morning after the hieros gamos there followed another, again enigmatic, "determination of destiny" for the year, and the gods returned to their temples.[94]

The Enuma Eliŝ, the central ritual document of all these doings, is inevitably a syncratic one. Within the epic itself the fight between Bel Marduk, who is the protector of the city of Babylon, and hence king of the Babylonian pantheon, is doubled by the victory of Ea-Enki, the ruler over the ancient center of Eridu, over Apsu, the male god of sweet waters. Ea established his dwelling in the body of Apsu, much as Marduk did in the body of Ti'amat. Later, in Assyria, Assur, the patronal god of Nineveh, was to supplant Marduk in the epic and in the festival; while in earlier, analogous poems, Nibbu fights Labbu, Ninurtu, the demon Asag; and in the most famous of all Sumerian texts, Gilgamesh destroys the demon Humbaba.[95] Akitu festivals were presumably celebrated in all parts of Mesopotamia long before the Enuma Eliŝ had taken its final form some time about the middle of the second millennium B.C.[96] But there had always been, presumably, epic accounts of the struggle of creation recited in the course of New Year celebrations, and analogous rites performed.

I have described the Akitu festival (and called it by its later, Akkadian name, though it was also known by its older Sumerian name, Zagmuk) as it was performed in the city of Babylon early in the first millennium B.C., since it happens to be the best documented. There it was celebrated at the beginning of Nisan, at the time of the spring rains. But it was also sometimes done in the autumn season, at the beginning of Tishri, as in Israel. It is quite clear that insofar as the rites were described, there are precise indications for some of the doings of the king and of certain prominent priests; while the rubric often simply asked that things should be done "as is customary." The part played by the people is only alluded to. Hence, even if there had been a firm tradition about building huts by the people, there would not necessarily have been an indication of it in the description of the rituals. As it is, there are curious allusions to some such practices: the decoration of the gigunu, the pigsties built of reeds which Marduk's son Nabu had to inspect on his entry into Babylon, pigs which represented Ti'amat's allies. There appears also to have been a prisoner in-

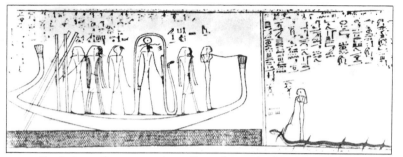

Ra destroys the serpent Apsu, from the tomb of Seti I in Thebes
(ruled ca. 1320 B.C.)

carcerated there, who was beheaded. And finally, a curious ceremony, which the Babylonian ritual puts just after the humiliation of the king, "The *Urigallu* shall gather 40 reeds, each one three cubits high / neither cut nor bent nor broken / but straight, which he shall bind together with a palm branch / In the exalted court a ditch shall be dug / in this ditch he shall place [the reeds] and honey and cream and best quality oil . . . / . . . he shall put in there and a white bull he [shall place before the ditch?] / The king [shall set fire] to this with a burning reed [into the ditch] / The king and the *Urigallu* shall say this prayer. . . ." Of the prayer only a line and a half survive: the words make the color of the bull and the fire the matter of the invocation: "O heavenly bull bright light who [illuminates darkness] / Burning bull of Anu . . . / O Gibil. . . ."[97] Here the tablet literally breaks off. What survives shows that the white bull was offered to the sky-god, Anu, in some way associated with his oldest son, Gibil, the god of fire.

Gods of wind and storm separate sky and earth in some myths: like Enlil, or the Egyptian wind-and-air god, Shu, who holds up the belly of the sky as a cow; or supports it in the form of a woman over Geb, the male earth. But creation is also the tearing, the impregnation of the chaotic dark by the light. It is the light which God saw was good, which was celebrated in the torch dances and the great candelabrum of the Jerusalem feast of tabernacles. Light was the arrow which struck the heart of Ti'amat, and also of her double, Pytho; the light of Apollo, who, like Marduk, was the "fixer of destinies"; and in Egyptian mythology it is the light of Re which destroys Apophis the serpent of darkness as he rises over the horizon: "The great sun disc at your forehead punishes the evil dragon / It cuts his spine / The flame destroys him / The heat devours him. . . ."[98] The destruction of Apophis was reenacted daily in some Egyptian temples, but the complexities of the victory of Re over Apophis are not my concern here, nor are the further parallels to battles between serpents of darkness and gods of light.[99] Though I note that the particular defeat of Apophis, the defeat which figures in the Egyptian coronation ceremonial against the Pharaoh's enemies—"and they shall be as Apophis the serpent on the morning of the New Year"—coincides with the calendar victory of Marduk over Ti'amat.[100]

I wish, however, to reconsider the use of reeds in the *Akitu* rituals. Reeds are the archetypal building material of Mesopotamia, predating leather tents and mud bricks, or so one of the Sumerian creation epics teaches: ". . . Before the divine Tag-tug had been born, when he had not yet donned the crown . . . / Men who were created for the light of day / Were not able to find any food / The clothing-which-gives-rest [tents?] they did not yet know / The people performed their devotions in reed huts / They made a noise like sheep, they fed on grass. . . ."[101]

In another epic poem the god Enki speaks to Nintud, the mother of Sumer, about the coming disaster, the Flood, which he has decided to inflict on the world: ". . . He opened his mind in the temple / he declared his revelation in the house of reeds as his decisions. . . ."[102] In the epic, reed houses are the dwellings of both the antediluvian men and the gods. The Sumerian mother goddess Inana herself was represented in ritual by a reed bundle. This is suggested both by the pictograph of her name, and by the two earliest important Sumerian works of pictorial representation, the tall vessel and the "trough" from Warka.[103] The second has been generally assumed to have been provided for animals at the shrine of the goddess, but the first has been interpreted as a representation of the *Akitu* festival in its earliest form, in which the death and resurrection of Dumuzi/Enlil may have played a more important part than in the rituals I have described. The goddess is shown standing before the upright reed bundles which so often accompany her. Inevitably the reed bundles recall another representation of a mother goddess: the bundle of papyrus called the *Djed* pillar, which represented Hathor pregnant with Osiris in the Egyptian mystery play of the death and resurrection of the god celebrated during the coronation ceremonies, and in which the raising of the pillar represented the resurrection of the dead Pharaoh. The manipulation of the pillar was associated with mock fights, in which papyrus reed became a ritual weapon.[104]

The *Djed* also appears very early in an architectural context, in the so-called southern tomb of the third-dynasty Pharaoh Djoser. Here it is part of the brightly glazed wall decoration, which generally reproduces a slight wooden frame covered, tented, with reed mats.[105] This form of construction was common enough in Egypt from the earliest times. Reed shelters, so common in the southern Sudan, among the Nuer and the Dinka, are even occasionally used by Egyptian peasants, with a form of "hut" consisting of a hard, oval floor, sunk below ground level, surrounded by a dwarf wall. The image of

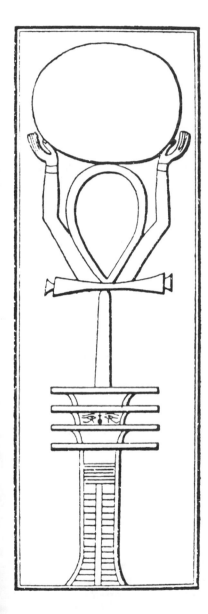

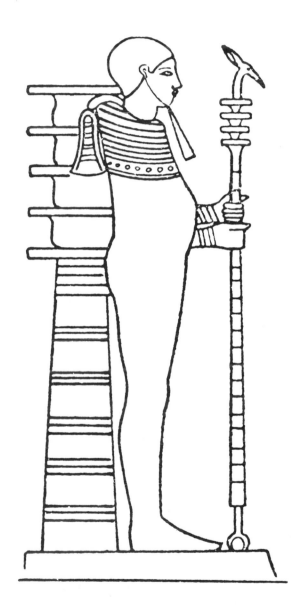

The sun raised by an Ankh
out of the Osiris-Djed pillar,
after Budge

The god Ptah of Memphis, the creator earth god,
standing by a *djed* pillar and leaning on
his scepter-measuring rod, after Budge

the floor and the dwarf wall survives in the hieroglyphic signs for "threshing floor," "hut," "fireplace" and "horizon."[106]

The whole of Egypt was often imagined as a house. In particular, the Egyptian temple, a series of colonnaded spaces surrounded by a high wall, was often conceived as a shorthand image of Egypt, the land of inundations; the image is of high walls of rock among which the river flowed, and in which the sun rose and set between two mountains, since the rock face is fissured by innumerable small tributaries of the Nile, both to east and west. The columns — generally — recalled another cosmic image: that of the table-top sky supported on tree legs, which had its "animated" echo in the myth of the goddess Nut, whose body sprawled over the earth in the form of the sky; or of the sky as the underbelly of Hathor, the cosmic cow.[107]

The ornamental scheme of the Egyptian columns was practically always vegetal and referred to yet another mythical model, that of the creation-landscape. The three forms which are most frequent are the palm, the lotus and the papyrus bundle, squashed out at the capital and at the foot (an entirely different form, this last, from the *Djed* pillar, whose sides are straight, and whose capital is a triple crown assimilated to a head). Such columns supported a ceiling which practically always carried some reference to the sky (a blue ground with stars; the falcon with the sun disk; astronomical expositions), and they were echoed outside the temple walls by a "sacred landscape": an artificial lake set among palms and surrounded by clumps of papyrus reed, with lotus rising from the pool.[108] Again, the usual central path of the temple, which represented the Nile for processional purposes, was clerestoried, and flanked by lotus rather than reed pillars. It rose to the highest point of the temple floor, which represented the primeval hillock which first arose from the chaotic mud of uncreation. This reference was of the greatest importance in the Egyptian theology; it was reinforced by such echoes as the pyramidal roof usual in divine shrines, which in turn referred to a sky-given relic, the sacred pyramidon preserved at Hierakonpolis.[109]

The plan I have described here is only a topological scheme, of course, on which temple architects could play variations. The symbolism is only documented once in full, in the Ptolemaic and unfinished temple of Khnum, at Esna. Nevertheless, the iconographic scheme is sufficiently general, the departures from it sufficiently consistent, and references to it scattered through Egyptian literature; so that it is quite clearly familiar to the lettered Egyptian, and presumably to the lay as well.

Although the temple was among other things a stone model of the creation-landscape, the orders of columns were not designed to be read as direct representations of plant life, but rather as stone reproductions of idealized landscape features, which seem first to have

Capital of a palmiform column. The ornamental band
below the string course *djed* pillars, after Perrot and Chipiez.

Model of the reconstruction of Djoser's pyramid complex at Saqqara,
detail, after J. P. Lauer

been produced in less durable materials. Even the common palmiform
column, already fully developed in the fifth dynasty (as in the tomb of
Sahu-rê at Abusir) and used constantly for more than two millennia
(it last appears in the Ptolemaic Horus temple at Edfu), does not show
a date palm tree carrying the weight of the roof on its crown of
leaves.[110] It is made up of a circular column, which might indeed be
the trunk of a palm tree, and which carries the weight directly (as do
the polygonal columns at Medinet-Habu and Deir el-Bahri), but with
its top section ornamented with palm leaves, tied in a crown round the
column. They are held fast by a thong, clearly shown in the stone columns, its end firmly tucked in for security. Features like this one
could be found in many other details of Egyptian ornament.

The first consistent use of such ornament in stone which has survived is in the complex of buildings connected with the pyramid of
Djoser. Although the palmiform columns are of a rather rudimentary
type, and the reed bundles are simply straight-sided shafts, the thin
lotus column is already fully developed. It appears both as a column
proper and as a column ornament in many paintings and reliefs, where
it is presumably a metal or wooden feature.[111]

Again, the reed-bundle columns of the entrance colonnade do not
represent a reed *fasces* carrying the simulated wood-log roof, but
rather a wooden post, decorated with reeds tied to it, or even the reed-
covered *anta* of a brick wall.[112] The ornamental features of a stone

building with no precedents are more likely to follow or idealize a similar constructional procedure as a system, rather than take over willfully individual features of such construction, particularly (as is most likely) if this form of building already has a system of literary and theological associations.

The reed and wood column of Djoser's temples again recalls the *Djed* pillar, which—as I have pointed out earlier—was figured in one of the "apartments" under Djoser's pyramid. The enigmatic courtyard to the south of the building has been explained as being a stone version, for the Pharaoh's use after his death, of the booths built for the *Sed* festival. Djoser is shown running the course on the two stelae of the pyramid grave, as well as on one found in the "southern" tomb of the complex.[113] The *heb-sed* was a festival which remained important throughout the three millennia of the Pharaonic monarchy.[114] Since it involved a renewal and confirmation of the king, it was not celebrated often; although the proscribed period seems to have been thirty years after the coronation, it is known to have been celebrated much more frequently. Like the coronation, it was associated with a New Year's Day—not necessarily the solar one. And like the *Akitu*, it was a lengthy affair.

The opening was celebrated by great night-time illuminations of the temple and court selected for its celebration. The *Djed* pillar was raised in the chosen place; gods arrived by boat, to be welcomed by the king; there were declarations of loyalty; gifts were presented; and, most spectacularly, the king "dedicated" the field of the festival, running, or perhaps even dancing, its length and breadth four times, and so taking possession of it as a divine gift. A number of buildings were required for the festival, and whatever their actual construction, the ritual texts claimed for them the nature of prehistoric buildings: "The hall of King Unas is plaited of reeds."[115] Djoser's complex had a series of such pavilions (whose decoration I have described earlier) which, in reproducing the reed plaiting of the *Sed* pavilions in stone, may well have been intended as a raising of the frail, temporary pavilions of Djoser's *Sed* festival to a lithic eternity.

The *Sed* pavilions are the nearest the Egyptian texts record to compare with the Isaiac festival of Thithorea in Greece, whose practices were originally Egyptian, according to Pausanias.[116] But although, apart from a curious reference in Theocritus, the texts do not say much about such rites, nevertheless innumerable Egyptian paintings and reliefs show impermanent, leafy or painted shrines erected for festivals, often on boats: these are the earliest representations of such shrines, in the pre-dynastic tomb paintings at Hierakonpolis and on Garzean pottery.[117]

But there is another feature of early Egyptian architecture which I wish to consider here: the recessed brick wall, so common in the

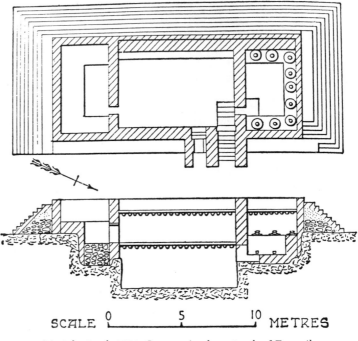

SCALE 0 5 10 METRES

Mastaba tomb 3038, Saqqara (perhaps tomb of Ennezib,
6th Pharaoh of the 1st dynasty), first stage,
showing the incipient pyramid form of the structure

mastabas of early royalty and grandees, so grand and monumental
when translated into stone for the *enceinte* wall of Djoser's complex.
The feature seems to have been taken by the Egyptians from Mesopotamia, together with the use of brick construction with which it is first
associated. In Mesopotamia, "monumental" buildings with recessed
sides appear in the lower strata of Tepe Gawra and Abou Sharein;
more impressive, the battered sides of the platform from which the
white temple at Warka, itself faced with recessed walls, rose, appears
to have been incised with just such brickwork panels, and to have
represented a mountain.[118] Little is known of the antecedents of such
proto-literate buildings in Mesopotamia, though there are one or two
obviously earlier remains, in which the recessions of the exterior wall
are connected with interior buttresses, and therefore presumably with
a system of beams. This connection is not carried through to the more
monumental buildings of the Uruk period, but the recessions went on
being used and they were a most obvious feature of the artificial holy
mountains, the Ziggurats, those huge heaps of brick which now litter
the Mesopotamian plain. The Egyptians seem to have taken over the
meaning and the technique together: as Djoser's pyramid city represents all Egypt, so its outside walls seem to represent the rock face of
the mountains which line the Nile Valley. However, although by the
time of Djoser's reign Egyptian is written, the short inscriptions which
survive are still too laconic to say much about such things as the symbolism of the pyramid. Yet inspecting its precedents does suggest an
approach. The recessed wall of the Djoser *enceinte* is, it has been suggested, analogous to the recessed walls of the much more modest

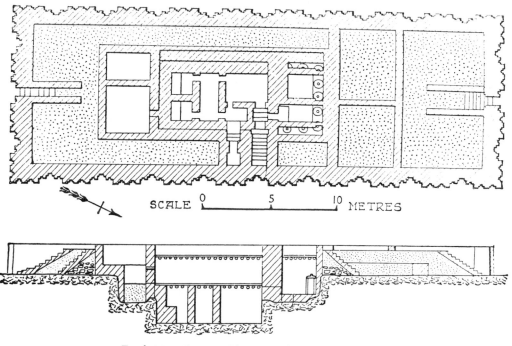

SCALE 0 5 10 METRES

Tomb 3038, Saqqara. The original truncated pyramid
enclosed by the more usual recessed walls

mastabas.[119] More painstaking recent excavations have shown that the
core of the mastabas was rather more complex than had hitherto been
thought. In several cases an independent structure has been found
over the burial chamber, which was later embedded in the whole
mastaba. It begins, apparently, as a modest earth tumulus covered
with a brick casing, as in the tomb said to be of Queen Her-nit, built
early in the first dynasty, and by the end of the dynasty develops
into a miniature step pyramid, which occupies half the area of the
mastaba that encloses it.[120] The conflation of the two forms of the
southern monument-burial mound (which becomes a pyramid) and
the northern palace or house façade (which becomes enclosure wall)
is a by-product of the union of the two kingdoms, borne out in terms
of funerary custom.[121]

The wooden house/palace sarcophagus, in which both contracted
(womb-position) and extended bodies were buried during the early
dynastic period, was the successor of much rougher terra-cotta and
wooden boxes, of the small brick vaulted or roofed chamber of the last
predynastic period; this in turn replaced the even earlier rush mats or
oval jars enclosing the flexed corpses — flexed burial was almost universal in chalcolithic and neolithic Egypt. The house sarcophagus was
itself replaced by the familiar body-fitting mummy case.[122] These developments represented, as far as is known, a continuous economic
and technical improvement: it is unlikely that they correspond to
violent theological revolutions.

The co-existence of different forms of burial in a single culture is
sufficiently common not to require comment here.[123] Moreover, the

Ceremonial bronze vase, Yu type, Shang period, North China.
Freer Art Gallery, Washington, D.C.

particular co-existence of womb-shaped pots containing flexed burials,
the body shaped in cloth cerements and the house urn is found among
several Andean subcultures. There is no possibility of any direct historical contact between Egypt and Peru, of course. At an intermediate
point, in China, such practices were developed with great subtlety
and documented rather better than in many other cultures. The association of the dead with habitations is witnessed by the elaboration of
the timber construction details in the great Shang Dynasty bronzes
(ca. 1500–1027? B.C.), particularly in the Fang-I and Yü types. The
form of timber construction details which these vases depict was not,
as far as is known, the echoing of the current palatial building, for
which pisé was used much more commonly in the Shang period to
which such bronzes belong. Indeed, the existence of round huts, which
recent excavation has finally proved for the neolithic period, was first
deduced from the form of the Yü vase.[124] The commoner Chia and
Chüoh ritual bronzes are decorated with an abbreviated form of the ancestral spirit dwelling: a small house, either square or circular in plan,
recalling perhaps indifferently a tent or a hut of reed or wood.[125] An
analogous form of decoration is found on the funerary urn, on the

Chalcolithic house urns, from Kusdeirah,
ca. 3400 B.C. Jerusalem Museum

ossuaries, to be more precise, of a somewhat later culture in Europe,
that of the "Villanovan" peoples (a name given to the inhabitants of
northern and central Italy round the turn of the first millennium B.C.).
The basic biconic urn, used for cremation burial, was common to
many of the neolithic peoples of Europe.[126] It underwent a very elaborate transformation in Italy, and by the beginning of the millennium
a great variety of types existed, particularly in central Italy. The
biconic ossuary was sometimes crowned with a cup, as with a roof;
in other urns the capping was a bronze helmet. In addition, the decoration of the urn was sometimes anthropomorphic. Sometimes there was
a hemispherical cap, which might be decorated with thatch ends, suggesting a normal roof. It is this kind of hemispherical capping which
occasionally has small projecting houses as decoration. Quite early in
this period these people came to use the small house model, usually
about one foot high, as an ossuary instead of the urn. The vast majority
of these ossuaries are of a dark terra cotta, though occasionally both
house and biconic urns are of stone, and a very few, towards the end
of the prehistoric period, after the turn of the millennium, are of
bronze.

The Hut of Romulus, reconstructed by Giacomo Boni, ca. 1900, on the Palatine Hill, near the Villa Mills

If one is to believe the present state of archeological evidence, the people who buried their dead in the round huts inhabited, when living, oblong, almost rectangular ones.[127] It is tempting to assume that the circular huts represent an earlier form of dwelling, particularly as rectangular house-shaped ossuaries do appear at the beginning of the Etruscan period. But it may well be that the ossuaries represented an "abbreviated" and sacral type of dwelling. Later, the Etruscans — who were very much concerned with afterlife — gave these ideas an elaborate development. Sarcophagi, both of cremated and inhumating funerals, commonly took the form of a building with a pitched roof, with the dead person depicted on the roof; and the sarcophagi in turn stood within tombs sculptured to imitate timber-built houses. This may be seen illustrated in exhaustive abundance in the great Etruscan necropoles of Tarquinia and Chiusi.

Yet in Rome itself there seem to have been two "true" replicas of the kind of hut the urns represented. The first was on the Palatine, the second on the Capitol. The Palatine hut stood at the western end of the hill, close to a group of antiquities which were connected with the mythical origin of the city and had a corresponding place in the more archaic rites of the state religion: the Lupercal, to which the chest containing the infant Romulus and Remus was carried by the floodwaters, and in which the she-wolf that suckled them lived, and the fig tree, *Ficus Ruminalis*, beside which the shepherd Faustulus, who was to bring them up, found them. Since he had first lived in that Palatine hut, it was also known as the *Tugurium Faustuli*.[128] Varro lists it as one of the sights of the Palatine. Dio Cassius rather enigmatically records among the bad omens for the year 38 B.C. the destruction of the hut by fire "as a result of some ritual which the *Pontifices* were performing there."[129] We know nothing of these rituals, but the hut was clearly restored at once, because Dio Cassius records that it was burned down again in 12 B.C., as one of the portents of Agrippa's death. This time, because "crows dropped burning chunks of meat picked off some altar" on the thatch roof.[130] It was restored again. Moralists refer to it as a demonstration of the humble origins of Roman glory.[131] It was still recorded by travelers well into the Christian era, which means that it must have been kept in fairly good repair.[132]

The Capitoline hut is less known, though Vitruvius explicitly says that it was thatched with straw.[133] He couples this reference with another one to an archaic building: the clay-roofed Athenian Areopagus. The Areopagus is the bare outcrop of rock under the Acropolis and was chiefly famous as the place of meeting of the most exalted Athenian law court. Round it were clustered several other shrines, with which the fate of the city was connected, such as the temples of Ares and of the Furies, and the Tomb of Oedipus. The court, however, judged cases in the open air, and therefore did not, presumably, need

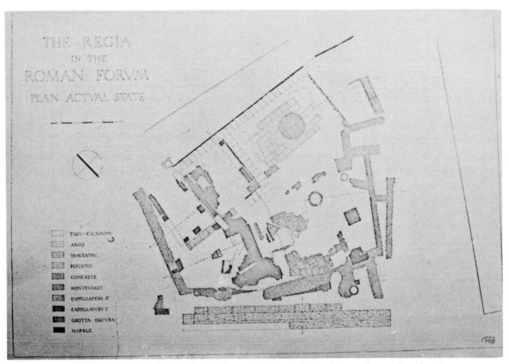

Plan of the Regia of the Roman Forum. The circle in the southern chamber is
the great hearth of the shrine, after F. E. Brown

a court house. Certainly Pausanias does not mention one, nor does he
notice any particularly archaic roof on any of the other buildings.[134]
He does, however, remark on the anachronism of the curiously primitive terra-cotta acroteria of the roof on the Royal Stoa of the Athenian
agora, in which the Areopagus sometimes met.[135]

The Royal Stoa was called that because it was where the *Archon
Basileus* officiated: he was a republican official who continued to
carry out those religious duties of the state religion which had been
the king's prerogative. Rome too had such an officer, the *Rex sacrorum.*
His functions were also connected with an archaic building, the Regia
on the Roman Forum, hard by the more famous Temple of Vesta.

The Regia became the headquarters of the pontifical college generally, but its holiness is due to the tradition that it was the home of
the "other" great king of Rome, Numa.[136] Like all the buildings of central Rome it suffered a number of fires and destructions; and although
the definitive form in which it survived was due to Domitius Calvinus,
a contemporary of Augustus, yet even that restoration, and whatever
work may have been done there later, respected the archaic and ac-
curately orientated building.[137] Moreover, over the centuries of the
building's existence, the hearth in its main chamber, a disk made of
eight *capelaccio* slabs, retained its shape and its size since a period
prior to the conventional dating of the republic: to the time of the
legendary kings.[138]

By historic times the Regia was never used as a dwelling. It was a
shrine, associated with such archaic rites as the sacrifice of the Oc-

tober horse, and it was the chief reliquary of the Roman state, where the lances, which represented Mars as protector of Rome, were kept, as well as those holy *ancillae* associated with Mamurius Veturius on which the safety of the state depended.[139]

While the hut of Romulus was maintained as a whole fabric, so that its walls and roof remained of the same rustic stuff as the original building, the Forum shrines retained the basic form of the archaic buildings, but enriched the material. "Where you now see bronze, you would once have seen thatch / and walls plaited with the tough willow. . . ." writes Ovid of the Temple of Vesta, which "faced the great palace of unshaven Numa."[140] But then on the Forum the buildings were reliquaries: on the Capitol and the Palatine the buildings were themselves relics.

Here I can adduce an analogy which is contemporary, in the sense that the buildings are still renewed according to ancient practice, though it is very distant culturally and geographically; buildings which in a sense are both reliquary and relic. This is the shrine of Ise in the Mie Prefecture, perhaps the best known of Japanese religious buildings.

Ise consists of two groups of varied buildings: the outer shrine, "Geku," and the inner one, "Naiku." Each is composed of a number of buildings, ancillary shrines, storehouses, workshops, and so on, and each has an inner precinct with a main sanctuary and two attendant shrines, a number of treasuries, fences and gates. In each precinct the buildings are of the same proportion, though different in size; and in each case they are totally rebuilt on an adjoining site every twenty years. The empty site keeps its sacrality: it is strewn with large marble pebbles. The only building on it is a small hut, inside which is a post, about seven feet high, known as *shin-no-mi-hashira* (literally, "the august column of the heart"). The new shrine will be erected over this post, which is the principal *sacrum* of the temple. The worship, however, concentrates on a bronze (or copper) mirror, which represents *Ama-terasu-omikami*, the sun goddess, who is also the ancestor of the Imperial family. The mirror is kept in a number of silk and wooden containers, on a boat-shaped stand directly over, and also substituting for, the sacred central post. The removal of the stand with the mirror on it is the central act of the consecration of the new temple. The old buildings are then pulled down, and sacred wooden members broken into small sticks which pilgrims take away with them as a memento of the pilgrimage.

Although the last Naiku rebuilding was in 1953, there is little doubt that it reproduces faithfully the temple the Empress Jito first ceremonially rebuilt in A.D. 692, a temple which had originally been set up twenty years earlier by her husband, the first Mikado to rule over a united Japan, the Emperor Temmu (673–686).[141] Temmu's building

A *takayuka* house. Engraving on a bronze plaque,
1st or 2nd century A.D., Yayo period, after Drexler

of Ise was the fulfillment of a vow: the site was already venerable
when the ceremonial rebuilding was instituted. Ise is not alone among
Shintō shrines to be rebuilt ceremonially, though it is the most famous, a shrine to which every Japanese should make a pilgrimage at
least once in his life, and the only one which is known to have retained its primitive shape over such a long period of time.

The most curious feature, perhaps, of the construction at Ise is the
way in which the roof is carried. The chambers of the shrines are
raised on timber piles analogous to the central sacred one. The walls
are of sizable boards, and in most cases framed, though in some of the
smaller buildings they are notched into each other in the way in which
the primitive shrine may be presumed to have been built. The oddest
feature is that the roof is not supported on the walls.[142] The rafters do
indeed rest on purlins, but the ridge beam is independently carried by
two large columns at either end, which go directly into the ground.

Sparse remains of primitive Japanese houses showing such construction survive. Most of them, however, if one is to judge by the
scanty fragments and the funerary models, were either thatched
dwellings on a rudimentary framework (mostly in the north and west),
or perhaps pile dwellings elsewhere. A building so built, and with

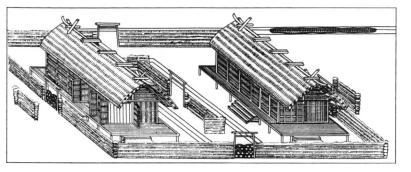

The Daijo-kyu, central shrine of the Japanese coronation enclosure,
after Tange and Kawazoe

the Ise feature of the ridge pole on independent columns, appears
in a drawing which decorates one of the panels of a bronze *Yayoi*
(660 B.C.–A.D. 97), a bell-shaped object of uncertain use, though its
general ornamental scheme suggests some kind of ritual purpose.[143]

It may well be that the building represented is not a house but a
granary: there is an old association between granaries and Imperial
buildings. But, in any case, there are too many pile-dwelling villages
round Southeast Asia for this kind of construction in a prehistoric
Japanese context to need special pleading.[144] Moreover, there are
records of another kind of ceremonial rebuilding in Japan. The ancient
enthronement ceremony of the Mikado took place in a temporary en-
campment, the *Daijo-Kyu*, which is described in the *Jogan Kyakushiki*.[145] There were some hundred pavilions altogether, surrounded
by a *sakuki* fence, built without foundations, of logs from which the
bark was not stripped, and thatched with fresh, green grass. The two
central pavilions were long, narrow structures, and the Emperor, as
part of the main rite, the *Ononike*, ate a meal in each one of them of
food supplied by the eastern and western provinces respectively.
Through the consumption of these meals he came to "incarnate" the
two parts of the country, as the pavilions "represented" them. The
Jogan Kyakushiki was composed in the Heian period (A.D. 794–893)
and describes a contemporary celebration, though it speaks of rites
which were already venerable. Moreover, later commentators have
written a great deal about this rite, and they don't always agree. By
the Heian era, even the act of construction was already ritualized, and
the monopoly of a family guild of craftsmen. Until much later, the
construction of temporary shrines, built ad hoc for specific occasions, was a commonplace in Japan. All this means that before Mikado
Temmu made his bow to the Ise shrine across the bay on setting off
for the rebellious eastern provinces, such practices were already

Ise shrine, the Geka or outer shrine, from an 18th-century print

familiar there. His victory marked the "establishment" of Ise as the principal cult shrine of Imperial Japan, but the site itself, and the cryptomeria tree that grew on it, were already holy before then.

The Japanese cypress (cryptomeria) is the tree associated with the Shintō shrines, even if the sacred plant of Shintō, the *sakaki*, is a shrub related to the tea bush. The *shin-no-mi-hashira* is taken to represent a *sakaki* branch stuck upright in the ground. There is a prophecy associated with the Empress Jingo-Kogo (201–269), which speaks of a *sakaki* branch at Ise, and the maiden that flies down from heaven. The prophecy is interpreted as referring to the sacred central post of the temple and the reflection of the sun in the mirror associated with it. Which, in turn, refers back again to another association of a *sakaki* branch, mirror, and the sun maiden. This is one of the most important of the Japanese, or at any rate Shintō, creation myths. It tells of the anger of the sun goddess Amaterasu, the ancestress of the Imperial dynasty, who, infuriated by the misdeeds of her brother, the thunder god Susa-no-wo, withdrew into a cave and plunged the whole world in darkness. The eight myriad gods gathered round the cave entrance. Uzume, the goddess of laughter and of dancing, performed an obscene dance at the entrance to the cave on an overturned wooden tub, and all the millions of gods laughed. Amaterasu, intrigued by their laughter, peeped out, and seeing herself in a mirror which had been placed on a *sakaki* tree at the cave's mouth, was pulled out and persuaded not to withdraw again.

The Ise mirror is one of the essential cult objects of the Shintō religion and regalia of the Mikado; another is the sword of Susa-no-wo, which is kept in the Izumi shrine at Kitsuki, also a building of willfully archaic aspect.[146] The building of this temple was itself mythical; the chronicle tells how the temple pillars "were made firm in the nethermost ground, and its crossbeams raised to the plain of high heaven."

Ise shrine, the Naiku or inner shrine, from an 18th-century print

The middle pillar of Ise, too, is both the *sakaki* branch and the pillar "confirmed in the nethermost ground," like the heaven-tree of so many legends. At Ise this column is echoed by the two outermost pillars, while at Izumi the ridge pole rests in a thick central pillar and the central posts of the outside walls are given no special emphasis. Isumi is an eighteenth-century rebuilding. The reconstructions show a shrine of much stranger proportions, which, however, do not materially alter its iconographic implications. It is assumed by architectural historians that the Shintō shrines had a "primitive" stage, before the construction was ritualized. And yet it may well be that they incarnate building rituals which are older than the establishment of cults at Ise or Kitsuki, and Shintō commentators insist on the derivation of the style of early shrines from primitive dwelling huts. At any rate, the "pure Shintō" manner of building, the *shinmei-zukuri*, is a formalization of the *kuroki-zukuri* style of the temporary Imperial coronation enthronement pavilions. At Ise, and at shrines which emulate it, the rustic technique of an age before there was a fixed manner of building is displayed as an exemplar: when there was a Shintō revival in the later half of the eighteenth century, it was to the style of Ise that its protagonists turned for a model of religious architecture, and later accretions were destroyed on many shrines, which were brought back to a *shinmei-zukuri* style.

The living divinity of the Mikado was a rather different institution from Augustus's immortality. Romulus was not an ancestor of an Imperial house: he was the founder of the city and the deviser of its institutions. His house was therefore a guarantee of their antiquity and a witness to their authenticity; a witness, too, to the dynamic movement of history, which had brought a state ruled from a hut like Romulus's to the glory of housing its rulers in the vast marble complexities of the Palatine. Ise, on the other hand, showed the once-for-all, the never-to-be-surpassed achievement of the god-sired and god-guided emperors in the mythical past.

I have presented rites practiced by a number of peoples: Greeks, Romans, Jews, Egyptians, Japanese, in all of which a "primitive" hut has either been built ritually — and at seasonal intervals — or deliberately in a "primitive" state for analogous ritual purposes. They are all rites of urbanized, or at any rate semi-urbanized peoples, implying a more permanent, more elaborate form of building against which the "primitive" hut provides a memento of origins. The procedures are analogous, and no doubt many more such procedures could be found among ancient, as well as among modern, "closed" societies. The return to origins is a well-known ritual procedure. The particular variant of building and inhabiting a hut like those of the earliest ancestors (as in the case of the Jews and Japanese) suggests a cosmogonic attempt to renew time by reinstituting the conditions "which were in the beginning"; in addition, the Japanese example suggests an identity between the house and the land. So the rite not only renews time for the occupant of the hut but for all those who inhabit the land which the hut represents. The Roman custom is more summary, the Mesopotamian much more circumstantial; the fairy tales tell rites already forgotten by history, but deeply embedded in the folk memory. All of them contain some variation on the ideas of renewal and transition; analogy between hut, land and world on the one hand, and hut and body on the other. The range of meaning attached to these rites is limited, however many the variations of theme. And its extraordinary persistence, on which I have already remarked, suggests that these procedures and the ideas which attach to them have an unalterable value, and therefore a permanent relevance: which I would like, in conclusion, to examine in a rather different context.

Chapter 7: A HOUSE FOR THE SOUL

After all, the penis is only a phallic symbol.
— attributed to C. G. Jung

TO CONCLUDE: MY THEME HAS BEEN THE CONSTANT INTEREST IN THE PRIMITIVE hut. It seems to have been displayed by practically all peoples at all times, and the meaning given to this elaborate figure does not appear to have shifted much from place to place, from time to time. I should like to suggest that this meaning will persist into the future and that it will have permanent and unavoidable implications for the relationship between any building and its user.

The writers on architectural theory I have quoted in this essay acknowledged the relevance of the primitive hut directly or indirectly, since it has provided so many of them with a point of reference for all speculation on the essentials of building. These speculations intensify when the need is felt for a renewal of architecture. Nor is this interest limited to speculation: various theorists have attempted to reconstruct such a hut in three dimensions and show the "natural" form of the building; natural, rational or divinely revealed according to their lights. Some are content to show this hut in drawings and engravings; but none attempt to suggest where such an original may be found and excavated, since it was built in some remote and primal scene, which we call Paradise, whose location cannot be found on any map.

Moreover, the idea of reconstructing the original form of all building "as it had been in the beginning," or as it was "revealed" by God or by some divinized ancestor, is an important constituent of the religious life of many peoples, so that it seems practically universal. In rituals, huts of this kind are built seasonally. They have elaborate and varied connotations; often an identification with a body, whether the human body or some perfect supranatural one, with affinities to the land it is in, to the whole universe. And the building of the primitive huts seems particularly associated with festivals of renewal (New Year, coronation), as well as the passage rites of initiation and marriage. I would like to show that a concern with the future, with projection, is endemic to the theme itself by another look at the feast of tabernacles.

Both in rabbinic and in Christian — particularly patristic — tradition, the feast has a "projective" character, since it is intimately and inextricably involved both with ideas of immortality and with messianic hopes. This traditional association is summed up in the interpretation of Psalm 118 (117), which closed the *Hallel* procession — the most conspicuous part of the tabernacles celebration — and even carried a direct reference to the customs with which I have been concerned: "Order the festival procession with boughs, even unto the horns of the altar."[1] In the liturgy of the synagogue it has remained in the place which it occupied in the temple service.

As the Midrash recognized, this was traditionally a processional psalm.[2] The wording and structure clearly refer to a procession through the Jerusalem Temple, even if the exact topography is not absolutely clear.[3] But the wording has overtones of messianic promise, for all its local, earthbound references: "The Lord is my strength and my song; the voice of rejoicing and salvation is in the tabernacle of the righteous. . . . Open me the gates of righteousness: I will go unto them, and I will praise the Lord. This gate of the Lord into which the righteous shall enter. . . . The stone which the builders rejected is become the headstone of the corner. . . . Blessed is he that cometh in the name of the Lord: we have blessed you in the name of the Lord. . . ."[4]

The tabernacles of the righteous, both Christian and Jewish, tradition recognizes as the dwelling of the redeemed in the messianic kingdom, but also as having the form of the festal *sukkah*.[5] Writing in the fourth century, St. Methodius of Olympia takes up the rabbinic tradition and turns it to his own ends: "I also come out of the Egypt of this life, I come first to the resurrection, the first Tabernacle feast. There, having built my beautiful hut on the first day of the feast, that of the judgement, I celebrate the feast with Christ during the millennium of rest, called the seven days, the true Sabbaths. Then, following Jesus, who has crossed the heavens, I start my journey again, as they [the Jews in the wilderness] after the rest of the feast of Tabernacles, journeyed toward the land of promise, the heavens, not waiting any longer in tabernacles that is to say, my tabernacle not remaining any longer the same but, after the millennium, having passed from a corruptible human form to an angelic grandeur and beauty. . . ." Methodius identifies his own body with the tabernacle; the tabernacle with the temple; and the temple with Paradise and Christ.[6]

This association builds on Christ's own words as reported in the Gospels; and Peter, during his first examination in Jerusalem, identifies Christ as the rejected stone of the psalm.[7] The association of the feast has a further sanction from the Gospels. When Christ was transfigured on Mount Tabor, and the disciples saw Elijah and Moses speaking with him, Peter thinks in his confusion of building three tabernacles: "Lord, it is good for us to be here: if Thou wilt, let us make here three tabernacles; one for thee, and one for Moses and one for Elias." "Not knowing what he said," adds Luke.[8] This has suggested to many commentators that the event is situated during the feast: indeed Luke's reading suggests that it happened on *Hoshana Rabba.*

The *Hoshana* procession, perhaps out of season, recurs in the Gospel account of Christ's entry into Jerusalem: as He rode into the city on an ass the palm-bearing crowd which accompanied Him sang the two verses from Psalm 118: "Blessed is he that cometh . . ." etc., so signifying their acceptance that the great prayer for salvation of the *Hoshana* litany was answered by the coming of the Messiah.[9]

The grandest reference to the customs of the feast in Scripture is St. John's description of the cosmic liturgy which the justified perform before the Lamb: "A great multitude, which no man could number, of all nations and kindred and peoples and tongues stood before the throne and before the Lamb, clothed in white robes and with palms in their hands . . . and he that sitteth on the throne hath his tabernacle [skenosei] among them . . . the Lamb . . . shall lead them to living fountains of waters."[10]

The triple function of the festival is clearly marked by St. John — the "tabernacle," the procession waving palms, the "trial by water." And the skena, the tabernacle, recurs several times in the Apocalypse[11]; the prophet associated with the eschaton — as the palms of the waving Lulab, the palms of the Hoshana procession were associated with messianic hope and with immortality. The Lulab and Etrog are a reminder of the messianic condition in rabbinic symbolism, and a frequent token of immortality on Jewish grave stelae.[12] The moralizing interpretation of the Midrashim and the eschatological vision of St. John show the extreme spiritualization of my theme. And yet in the mind of St. Methodius the theme is restated in anagogical linking of the festival custom to the history of Israel, which in turn is identified with the incidents of the life of Christ and back again to the personal initiation of the believer into immortality.

By contrast, I would like to inspect an extreme somatization of it, since this presents the theme in such a context as to bring out yet another aspect: I wondered how this complex of actions and ideas is dealt with by a people who have no building techniques at all, such as the aborigine tribes of central Australia.

If they build at all, very little is known of their techniques or their ideas about the matter. They are semi-nomadic food gatherers, and they seem to have no permanent buildings at all except churringa houses, the platforms on which the sacred bull-roarers of stone or wood are preserved. Otherwise their buildings are lean-tos against some rock face, and in the north huts of withies with wood-bark covering (as a protection against mosquitoes) and of plain wood bark (as an extended umbrella).[13] It appears that the aborigines use wood-bark sheets as umbrellas, holding them bent over their heads — as Filarete's Adam sheltered his head with his displuviate hands — and they sometimes set the same sheets of bark over tree trunks so that there is an immediate identity between the "objectified" shelter and the hand-held, makeshift extension of the body.[14]

But central Australian tribes, such as the Aranda who live in the basin of the Finke river, right in the center of the continent, do not even appear to have use for this kind of rudimentary building. The only shelters they put up for their own use are windbreaks of bush and scrub which are made by weeding and trimming as much as by piling up. They sleep out in the open, sheltered by these breaks, with small fires to warm them in cold seasons. These breaks also play an important part in the "construction" of their ceremonial grounds.

In their rituals they use wood or stone bull-roarers, which they treat as treasures, like most other Australian tribes; they paint their bodies elaborately and decorate them with fur and birds' feathers; and like most of them, they also make ceremonial objects which are destroyed after one use. There are roughly two classes of these objects: nurtunja and waninga. The first of these are bundles of grass, usually rein-forced with a spear or stick running through the middle, bound to-gether with human hair or opossum-fur "string"; they are decorated according to the totem and occasion. There is a related class of objects, ceremonial poles, which various tribes use in their rites.

The waninga are more immediately interesting. They consist of one long stick — usually a spear — and one or two cross-sticks, lashed to it at right angles. On this framework string is wound in dense parallel lines, so that the whole object appears as a rectangle with a triangle at each of its short ends. As in the nurtunja the string is mostly human hair, though some animal-fur string is usually also used. It is decorated with ocher, pipe clay, blood, feathers, and down.

Small waninga and nurtunja were sometimes carried on the heads of some officiants as part of their ritual costume; more often, particu-larly in the case of the waninga, they were independent objects which were carried about and which formed the center of most initiation ceremonials of whatever totem.

Like the nurtunja, the waninga represents the totemic animal or object; its different parts and decorative treatment are associated with different aspects of the totem. But its general form also represents some constellations. The Milky Way, the place where the ancestors live forever, is interpreted as a fence made up of waningas; and finally, the waninga represents the coupling of the ancestral pair.[15]

The waninga is carried about in dances and processions; it is also planted in the earth and used as a "taxonomic" map to explain the totemic myths as well as their connection with natural phenomena to the initiates. At a crucial point in many initiations the postulant em-braces the waninga itself after its mysteries have been explained to him.

The geometrically rigid construction of the waninga may remind some readers of the passage from Corbusier's Vers une architecture quoted at the beginning of this essay: the Australian aborigines who produce them are — in terms of the conventional cultural stratification — savages; not even barbarians. And yet even they manufacture rudi-mentary objects of a strict geometrical regularity, which seem in a sense to antedate any notion of building. I must disclaim here any in-tention of presenting the aborigines as an Urvolk, transmitting down to our times the unchanged procedures of our paleolithic ancestors. On the contrary, such information as is available at present has led some writers to suppose that the aborigines are a people who degen-

Kana-Kana of the Mantuntara tribe
with the big *waninga*, after Roheim

erated from a higher stage of material culture at the time of the arrival of the European colonizers.[16] The Australian evidence seems interesting to me for a different reason: in that it provides an instance of a people without building invoking a similar nexus of primal notions to the ones I have been tracing throughout this essay. And in this instance they are exhibited in an abstract form, through an object which has no further physical end than this exhibition; once this is performed, it is destroyed, as the elaborate body painting also used in these rites is washed off immediately after the rites are finished.

The *waninga* is treated in the same way as the body drawings. But as against the other sacred drawings (on the *churringa*, on boomerangs, on cave walls, etc.) it shares a certain feature with the initiatory hut: it is a coherent, formally self-contained "map"; and it refers to the initiate's body — he identifies himself with it when he embraces it — to sacred history, the hierogamos and the cosmic order.

But the articulation of the *waninga*, the naming of its parts, recalls yet another complex of ideas: the house, and particularly the house of the immortalized initiates, as a complex of living beings. In the Egyptian Book of the Dead, the dead man is instructed in the various procedures he must follow in order to achieve "salvation" (I use the term in the sense of well-being in life-after-death). The text provides him with an elaborate description of Osiris's Hall of Judgment in which he is finally to be judged. "Homage to you, O gods who dwell in your hall of double Maati," he is to say, "I, even I know you, and I know your names. Let me not fall under your slaughtering knives, and bring not forward my wickedness to the god in whose train you are. . . ." He then protests his innocence of many sins, and justifies his doings, moral and ritual, ending with a reference to specific rites he has performed. "Come then [they say] and enter in through the door of this hall of double Maati, for you know us.

"We will not let you enter through us, say the bolts of this door, unless you tell us our names: Tongue of the Balance of the place of right and truth is your name. I will not let you come in by me, says the right lintel of this door, unless you tell me my name. Balance of the support of right and truth is your name. . . ." And so on through the right lintel, the threshold, the latch, the doorleaf, the floor, etc.: the dialogue is a long one.[17]

There are other rites in which the tomb is identified with the universe, and its parts given the character of living beings, like the curious ritual in which four celebrants assume the character of the four pillars of Horus (the world supports) by the names written on their shoulders.[18] This identification of building elements of the holy house or the tomb with human figures is common enough. Franz Boas reported a northwest Indian myth in which the hero, whose father is the sun, descends to earth, and having married a woman of the earth, builds a house. The myth tells how the columns are all men, and gives them different names. The fore columns supported a serpent beam, the rear ones supported a wolf-and-serpent one. The door is hung on high hinges, so that anyone who does not come in quickly is killed by it. "And when he had finished his house, he gave a great feast and the columns and beams came alive, and the men-columns who stood in the further part of the house warned him when a wicked person came in. And the serpents killed that person at once."[19]

The parts of the hut had individual names and suggest some rite such as the Egyptian one I have just described. The power of the name ("open, Sesame") is so familiar a mythological and ritual trope that I need no more than mention it here. But the living, individualized parts of the hut, of the building, refer me back to the Australian *waninga*. Of course, the *waninga* is not a building in any sense, but it exhibits the features which the initiatory hut incarnates without actually enclosing space. Whether this Australian object represents a decadent stage of material civilization—and therefore may be taken as an abstraction from the huts of an earlier and richer period—or whether it may be taken as a logical (if not temporal) predecessor of building—on the assumption that the Australian aborigines never knew building at all—I am not sure. I incline, on the current archeological evidence, to the second supposition. But in either case it seems to me remarkable that a people who only adopt an excruciatingly uncomfortable form of enclosure as a temporary expedient, devise this extraordinary construction and endow it with all the majesty of a hope which the Apocalypse was to glorify.

The *waninga* shares its temporary nature with the booths and huts of many rituals. And although it is idle to ask whether the initiation rites precede the *waninga*, or the object developed as part of the rite, yet it appears to show that the ritual and mythological complex of which the primitive is a shell is not dependent on it; and that it must be of such hoary antiquity that it almost partakes of the biological nature of man.

As the *waninga* was the coupled primal pair, so the hut of boughs is met with as a "bridal chamber" in Mesopotamia and among the Blackfoot Indians, to take two widely separated instances.[20] And the Jews, too, had the custom of marrying the young couple under a canopy of boughs; this presumed to be a formalized abstraction of the chamber decorated with boughs and flowers in which the couple were originally bedded; and recalling too the *gigunu* of the Mesopotamian hierogamy.[21] In spite of the successive sumptuary prohibitions marking the various defeats of the Jewish nation, both cloth and trellised *huppahs* remained part of Jewish ceremonial until now.[22] Moreover, the Talmudic tradition saw a certain unity in these rites of building tabernacles. That is presumably why people involved in the marriage ceremony and the building of the huppah (ba'al huppah) are excused from the obligation of building a tabernacle.[23] (See p. 155.)

This identity suggests an answer to the puzzle I set myself at the beginning of the essay. Not that the Talmud actually asserts that Adam built a sukkah in Paradise. But a para-Talmudic legend records a tradition about the wedding of Adam and Eve: "The Holy One, Blessed be He, made ten wedding canopies for Adam in the Garden of Eden. They were all made of precious stones, pearls and gold. Is it not true that only one wedding canopy is made for a king . . . ?"[24]

This great love of God for Adam seems to make him a mirror image of the messianic king, to whom tradition also attributes the ten canopies.[25] Now the huppah of the Pirkê de Rabbi Eliezer – whenever that strange work may have been composed – is not the hut of boughs, but a vast construction of gold and precious stones, proper to a legend of this splendor. Whatever it was made of, clearly it was not meant to keep the weather out, or to perform any of the functions attributed to building, besides providing physical enclosure. The shelter provided by the huppah was notional. Although it was notional, it was nonetheless necessary. Its floor was the earth, its supports were living beings, its trellised roof was like a tiny sky of leaves and flowers: to the couple sheltering within it, it was both an image of their joined bodies and a pledge of the world's consent to their union. It was more; it provided them – at a critical moment – with a mediation between the intimate sensations of their own bodies and the sense of the great unexplored world around. It was therefore both an image of the occupants' bodies and a map, a model of the world's meaning. That, if at all, is why I must postulate a house for Adam in Paradise. Not as a shelter against the weather, but as a volume which he could interpret in terms of his own body and which yet was an exposition of the paradisal plan, and therefore established him at the center of it.

To many readers such a claim, made on behalf of innumerable couples – illiterate or semi-literate, often unattractive and certainly unable to articulate such ideas in conscious terms – might seem exaggerated or even absurd. But an awareness of quite complex matters of this kind does not necessarily imply an ability to articulate them, or even to hold them in a half-conscious way. Somewhere in the minds of the people who practiced them through long millennia there was lodged a conviction of the necessity for these elaborate procedures, a conviction that was in no way magical – and which they acted out with their own bodies.

Whether in ritual, myth or architectural speculation, the primitive hut has appeared as a paradigm of building: as a standard by which other buildings must in some way be judged, since it is from such flimsy beginnings that they spring. These huts were always situated in an idealized past. Le Corbusier's ideal barbarians built so as to know that they thought; Loos's equally ideal peasants built well because they knew without taking thought, by obeying external necessity and innate ideas alone. Both Loos and Corbusier cite the engineer, uncluttered by cultural baggage and responding to necessity alone in the case of Loos, and reason in Corbusier's, as the true correlative of the early builder. Loos reflects earlier attitudes closely. He is heir to the idea that human nature is in no way discontinuous from animal creation, that right building should also in some way be continuous with nature: Ruskin's belief that the best buildings are an essential part of natural landscape is an instance of this. It has its obverse in Durand's writings, in which the extreme attenuation of eighteenth-century rationalism shades off into a utilitarian conventionalism. And yet in the nineteenth century there are other writers who recognize another drive in man's creative activities: that of echoing the essential rhythms of nature as the spur to the acquisition of all skills, which, in the case of Semper, makes the daisy chain into the archetype of all human activity. Corbusier may have owed something to this view, as well as to earlier ideas formulated before buildings were ideally situated in a continuous nature.

Eighteenth-century writers, so exercised about the origins of speech, had seen the origin of human achievement either in a peculiar kind of inference from the data of experience or, sometimes, as the by-product of the shock of terror. Which led them to discuss, when they came to consider the higher stages of civilization, what was positive and necessary, what arbitrary and capricious: what is implied in following nature and/or reason, and how far these two were continuous. These ideas echoed, transformed ancient themes. But before the notion of a departure from the "natural" model as a token of decadence had again been developed, the tension between nature and grace developed other aspects of the theme. It led to an obsession with the rules of a "revealed" architecture, an architecture whose rules would not be based on a sequence of deductions from natural origins, but could be firmly based on revelation. Hence a divinely inspired model had to be proposed for the all too imperfect human skills. Long before such speculations were enshrined in books, a return to the first known habitations became part of the powerful desire for renewal by a return to origins which seemed to be a staple of the human social condition.

Throughout these many transformations, my theme returns as a guarantee of renewal: not only as a token from the past but as a guide to the future. Its perennial quality has long been noted by psychologists. The passion for building enclosures, or for "adopting," for taking possession of an enclosed volume under a chair or table as a "cozy place" for making a "home," is one of the commonest of all children's games.[26] Even in this context we have the double parentage of the original house: the "found" volume of the cave and the "made" volume of the tent or bower in a radically reduced form. There is another thing about this phylogenetic "justification" of Vitruvius's hypothesis about origins: psychologists have often noted the social character of such games. They have associated them—their ambivalent terror/pleasures, their play on exclusion and inclusion—with the child's relation to its mother as it is focused in the fear and desire of the womb.[27]

The return to origins is a constant of human development and in this matter architecture conforms to all other human activities. The primitive hut—the home of the first man—is therefore no incidental concern of theorists, no casual ingredient of myth or ritual. The return to origins always implies a rethinking of what you do customarily, an attempt to renew the validity of your everyday actions, or simply a recall of the natural (or even divine) sanction for your repeating them for a season. In the present rethinking of why we build and what we build for, the primitive hut will, I suggest, retain its validity as a reminder of the original and therefore essential meaning of all building for people: that is, of architecture. It remains the underlying statement, the irreducible, intentional core, which I have attempted to show transformed through the tensions between various historical forces.

The desire for renewal is perennial and inescapable. The very continued existence of social and intellectual tensions guarantees its recurrence. And renewal was always sought for in the rituals of seasonal change and initiation, much as the reform of corrupt custom and practice was renewed by theorists in their appeal to a primitive hut. I believe, therefore, that it will continue to offer a pattern to anyone concerned with building, a primitive hut situated permanently perhaps beyond the reach of the historian or archeologist, in some place I must call Paradise. And Paradise is a promise as well as a memory.

NOTES

Chapter 1: THINKING AND DOING

1. Genesis 1:27.
2. Ibid., 2:9.
3. Le Corbusier, *Vers une architecture*, pp. 53–55.
4. Ibid.
5. Ibid., p. 55.
6. André Lurçat, *Architecture*, p. 39.
7. Frank Lloyd Wright, *The Living City*, pp. 23–24.
8. Ibid., p. 25.
9. Cf. Frank Lloyd Wright, *The Future of Architecture*, pp. 44–48.
10. Quoted in Philip C. Johnson, *Mies van der Rohe*, pp. 197–198.
11. Antonio Sant'Elia, "Manifesto of Futurist Architecture," *Controspazio*, p. 18.
12. André Lefèvre, *Les Merveilles de l'architecture*, p. 11.
13. Banister Fletcher and Banister F. Fletcher, *A History of Architecture*, p. 1.
14. André Leroi-Gourhan, *Le Geste et la parole*, vol. 2, pp. 139–140.
15. Auguste Choisy, *Histoire de l'architecture*, vol. 1, p. 2.
16. Gottfried Semper, *Der Stil in den technischen und tektonischen Kunsten oder praktische Aesthetik*, vol. 2, p. 298 n. 2.
17. Hans M. Wingler, *Das Bauhaus*, p. 39.
18. Ibid., pp. 62–63.
19. Konrad Wachsmann, *Holzhausbau*, pp. 30–33.
20. Josef Strzygowski, *Der Norden in der bildenden Kunst Westeuropas*, p. 100.
21. Josef Strzygowski, *Altai-Iran und Völkerwanderung*, pass.
22. K. I. Afanasev, V. Afanasev, and B. E. Chasanova, eds., *Iz Istorii Sovetskoy Arkhitekturi 1917–1925*, pp. 225–226, 229.
23. Adolf Loos, *Gesammelte Schriften*, pp. 302–303.
24. Ibid., p. 317.

Chapter 2: NECESSITY AND CONVENTION

1. Ernest Jones, *Sigmund Freud*, vol. 2, p. 60.
2. Gottfried Semper, *Der Stil in den technischen und tektonischen Kunsten oder praktische Aesthetik*, vol. 1, p. 7.
3. Ibid., p. 819.
4. Ibid., p. 113.
5. Ibid., p. 213.
6. Ibid., p. xxiv.
7. Ibid., pp. xxi–xxii.
8. Alois Riegl, *Stilfragen*, pp. 23–24.
9. Ibid., pp. 30–41.
10. Semper, vol. 1, p. xxii.
11. John Ruskin, *The Poetry of Architecture*, pass.

12. A. Welby Pugin, *The True Principles of Pointed or Christian Architecture*, p. 2.

13. Ruskin, p. 80.

14. Thomas Percy, *Reliques of Ancient English Poetry*, vol. 1, p. 2.

15. Antoine Chrysostome Quatremère de Quincy, *Dictionnaire historique de l'architecture*, s.v. "Architecture."

16. Eugène Viollet-le-Duc, *Histoire de l'habitation humaine*, p. 4.

17. Ibid., p. 5.

18. Ibid., p. 9.

19. Eugène Viollet-le-Duc, *Lectures on Architecture*, vol. 1, p. 7.

20. Jean-Nicolas-Louis Durand, *Précis des leçons d'architecture données à l'Ecole Royale Polytechnique*, vol. 1, p. 21.

21. Ibid., p. 9.

22. Ibid., p. 19.

23. Ruskin, p. 245.

24. Durand, vol. 1, pp. 90–91.

25. Ibid., p. 58.

Chapter 3: POSITIVE AND ARBITRARY

1. Jean-Nicolas-Louis Durand, *Précis des leçons d'architecture données à l'Ecole Royale Polytechnique*, vol. 1, p. 9.

2. Marc-Antoine Laugier, *Essai sur l'architecture*, p. 2.

3. Jean-Jacques Rousseau, *Discours sur l'origine et les fondements de l'inégalité parmi les hommes*, in *Oeuvres complètes*, vol. 4, pp. 134–135.

4. Rousseau, *Si le rétablissement des sciences et des arts a contribué à épurer les Moeurs*, in *Oeuvres complètes*, vol. 4, p. 22.

5. Immanuel Kant, *On the Critique of Judgement*, in *Works*, vol. 5, pp. 280–281.

6. Jean-Jacques Rousseau, *Essai sur l'origine des langues*, pp. 578–579.

7. Gianfranco Torcellan, *Una figura della Venezia settencentesca: Andrea Memmo*, p. 34.

8. Andrea Memmo, *Elementi d'architettura Lodoliana*, vol. 1, pp. 291–292.

9. Ibid., pp. 295–297.

10. J. J. Winckelmann, *Storia delle arti e del disegno presso gli antichi*, vol. 3, p. 178.

11. [P. Jacopo Belgrado], *Dell'architettura egiziana*, p. xxv.

12. Rousseau, *L'origine des langues*, p. 505.

13. Henri Focillon, *Giovanni-Battista Piranesi, 1720–1778*, pp. 80–81.

14. Giovanni Battista Piranesi, *Osservazioni di G. B. P. sopra le lettere di M. Mariette*, p. 10.

15. Athanasius Kircher, *Latium, id est Nova et Parallela Latii tum Veteris tum Novi Descriptio*, p. 40.

16. Giovanni Battista Vico, *La scienza nuova*, in *Opere*, vol. 5, p. 97.

17. Giovanni Battista Piranesi, *Diverse maniere di adornar i cammini ed ogni altre parte degli edifizi desunte dall'architettura egiziana, etrusca e greca,* p. 7.

18. Edmund Burke, *On the Sublime and Beautiful,* in *Works,* vol. 1, p. 24.

19. Memmo, vol. 2, p. 117.

20. Ibid., vol. 1, p. 275.

21. Ibid., pp. 84–85; cf. Massimo Petrocchi, *Razionalismo architettonico e razionalismo storiografico,* pp. 21–22.

22. Giovanni Poleni, *Exercitataiones Vitruvianae,* p. 120.

23. Claude Perrault, *Ordonnance des cinq espèces de colonnes selon la méthode des anciens,* p. vii.

24. Ibid., p. vii.

25. Ibid., p. viii.

26. Ibid., p. vi.

27. Ibid., p. xii.

28. Ibid., p. x.

29. Charles Perrault, *Parallèle des anciens et des modernes en ce qui regarde les arts et les sciences,* vol. 1, p. 128.

30. Ibid., p. 159.

31. Ibid., pp. 167–169.

32. Vico, vol. 5, p. 97.

33. Antoine Chrysostome Quatremère de Quincy, *De l'architecture égyptienne,* pp. 239–241.

34. Sir John Soane, *Lectures on Architecture, as Delivered to the Students of the Royal Academy from 1809 to 1836,* pp. 17–20.

35. Quatremère de Quincy, p. 241.

36. Francesco Algarotti, *Saggio sopra l'architettura,* in *Opere scelte,* vol. 1, p. 20.

37. Ibid., p. 37.

38. Jacques-François Blondel, *Cours d'architecture,* vol. 1, pp. 3–4.

39. Ibid., p. 5.

40. Francesco Milizia, *Memorie degli architetti antichi e moderni,* vol. 1, p. i.

41. Ibid., p. v.

42. Ibid., pp. xi–xii.

43. Ibid., p. xii.

44. Ibid., pp. xiii–xv.

45. Francesco Milizia, *Principii di architettura civile,* vol. 1, p. 34.

46. Ibid., p. 36.

47. Etienne-Louis Boullée, *The Treatise on Architecture,* pp. 27, 33–34.

48. Etienne-Louis Boullée, *L'Architecture, essai sur l'art,* p. 43.

49. Boullée, *Treatise,* p. 83.

50. Ibid., p. 35.

51. Boullée, *L'Architecture,* p. 60.

52. Ibid., p. 27.

53. Boullée, *Treatise*, p. 103.

54. Sir William Chambers, *A Treatise on the Decorative Part of Civil Architecture*, p. 103.

55. Ibid., p. 106.

56. Vitruvius, *Les Dix livres d'architecture de Vitruve corrigés et traduits nouvellement . . . par M. Claude Perrault*, fig. 5.

Chapter 4: NATURE AND REASON

1. Henry Home, Lord Kames, *Sketches of the History of Man*, vol. 1, pp. 77–79.

2. James Burnett, Lord Monboddo, *Ancient Metaphysics*, vol. 3, pp. 41–42; cf. Lois Whitney, *Primitivism and the Idea of Progress in English Popular Literature*, p. 282.

3. James Boswell, *Life of Johnson*, vol. 2, p. 224.

4. Ibid., vol. 3, p. 115.

5. Daniel Defoe, *The Life and Surprising Adventures of Robinson Crusoe of York, Mariner*, p. 37.

6. Ibid., p. 45.

7. Boswell, vol. 2, p. 169.

8. Siegfried Giedion, *Mechanization Takes Command*, p. 647.

9. M. Ribart de Chamoust, *L'Ordre François trouvé dans la nature*, p. 6.

10. Samuel Johnson, *A Dictionary of the English Language*, s.v. "National."

11. Sir James Hall, Bart., "On the Origin of Gothic Architecture," in *Transactions of the Royal Society of Arts and Sciences of Scotland*, Edinburgh, 1797, vol. 4, sec. 2, pp. 12–53.

12. Ibid., p. 16.

13. Ibid., p. 25.

14. Ibid., p. 4.

15. Friedrich von Schlegel, *Works*, vol. 5, p. 194.

16. Samuel Taylor Coleridge, *The Philosophical Lectures*, pp. 256–257.

17. Hall, p. 12 n.

18. Johann Wolfgang von Goethe, *Gedenkausgabe der Werke*, vol. 13, p. 20.

19. Ibid., pp. 19–20.

20. Ibid., vol. 10, pp. 392–393, 411, 455; cf. p. 896.

21. Alste Horn-Onken, *Uber das Schickliche*, pp. 9–28.

22. Goethe, vol. 11, pp. 486–488.

23. Georg Wilhelm Friedrich Hegel, *Aesthetik*, vol. 2, p. 75.

24. Ibid., p. 28.

25. Ibid., pp. 53–54.

26. Ibid., p. 23.

27. Ibid., p. 24.

28. Ibid., pp. 26–27.

29. Ibid., p. 29.

30. Georg Wilhelm Freidrich Hegel, *Sämtliche Werke*, vol. 11, pp. 56–57.

GOTHIC EXCURSUS

1. William Empson, *Seven Types of Ambiguity*, p. 2.

2. Alexander Pope, *The Works*, vol. 3, pp. 326–330.

3. Raffaello Sanzio, *Tutti gli scritti*, p. 57.

4. Philip of Cluver, *Germania Antiqua*, pp. 233–257.

5. Lucan *Pharsalia*, 3. 390.

6. Edmund Spenser, *The Poetical Works*, vol. 5, pp. 42–43.

7. Henry Home, Lord Kames, *Elements of Criticism*, Edinburgh, 1762, vol. 1, p. 183.

Chapter 5: REASON AND GRACE

1. Vitruvius (ed. and trans. Frank Granger) 2. 1. 2.

2. Ibid., 1. 4.

3. Ibid., 3. 1. 1.

4. J. Rykwert, "The Corinthian Order," *Domus*, 426 (May 1965), pp. 25–30.

5. Vitruvius 4. 2. 2.

6. Lucius Annaeus Seneca *Letteres a Lucilius* 90. 7–9.

7. Lucretius *De rerum natura* (trans. H. A. J. Munro) 5. 11. 1104.

8. Ibid., 11. 1091.

9. Hermann Diels, *Die Fragmente de Vorsokratiker*, v. Democritus 68. 154.

10. Ibid., 144.

11. Plutarch *Moralia: On the Tranquility of Spirit* Diod. Sic. 1. 8. 6.

12. Sidonius Apollinaris *Poems and Letters* 6. 3. 5.

13. Servius, in *Virgilii Maronis Opera*, Eclogue 4. 62.

14. Erwin Panofsky, *Studies in Iconology*, p. 33.

15. Vitruvius (ed. Cesare Cesariano), p. 31 recto.

16. *Vitruvius Teutsch*, pp. 57–62.

17. *Filarete's Treatise on Architecture* 1. 4. 5.

18. Alberti *De re aedificatoria* 4. 3.

19. Ibid., 1. 2.

20. Ibid., 1. 9; 7. 5; cf. 3. 12.

21. Ibid., 9. 5.

22. Francesco di Giorgio Martini, *Trattati di architettura ingegnerìa e arte militare*, pp. 325–326, 372–373.

23. Alberti 7. 6; Martini, pp. 57–58.

24. Vincenzo Scamozzi, *L'Idea dell'architettura universale*, p. 9.

25. Hieronymus Pradus and Ioannes Baptista Villalpandus, *In Ezechielem explanationes et apparatus Urbis ac Templi Hierosolymitani*, vol. 1, p. vii.

26. Julius von Schlosser, *Schriftquellen zur Geschichte der karolingischen Kunst*, p. 104.

27. Pradus and Villalpandus, vol. 2, pp. 20–21.

28. Ibid., pp. 426–427.

29. 2 Kings 7:20.

30. Josephus Flavius *Jewish Antiquities* 15. 2.

31. Pradus and Villalpandus, vol. 2, pp. 589–593.

32. Ibid., pp. 17–18.

33. 2 Paralipomenon 28:11.

34. Pradus and Villalpandus, vol. 2, p. 71.

35. Ibid., pp. 20–21.

36. Roland Fréart de Chambray, *A Parallel of the Ancient Architecture with the Modern*, p. 76.

37. John Wood, *The Origin of Building*, p. 70.

38. John Wood, *Choir Gaure*, p. 10.

39. Juan Caramuel de Lobkowitz, *Architectura civil recta y obliqua*, p. 77.

40. Genesis 4:17.

Chapter 6: THE RITES

1. Ovid *Metamorphoses* 8. 611–725.

2. Ibid., 1. 450–595.

3. Pausanias *Description of Greece* 10. 5. 5.

4. Pindar *Fragments*, paean 8, fr. 41: 70–71 (Pindar had spoken of six charmers).

5. Homer *Hymns: To Mercury* 551–563.

6. Callimachus *Fragments: Hymn to Apollo* 105; cf. Ovid 3. 27.

7. Judges 4:6.

8. Genesis 35:8.

9. Cicero *Tusculan Disputations* 1. 45.

10. Herodotus *Histories* 3. 112.

11. Alkaios *Fragments* 2. Apollonius Rhodius *Argonautica* 2. 674–682; 4. 611–615. Pliny *Natural History* 4. 12. 89. Cicero *De Natura Deorum* 3. 33. 57.

12. Pausanias 9. 39. 5.

13. Pausanias (trans. Sir James George Frazer), vol. 3, p. 53.

14. Plutarch *Moralia: Greek Questions* 12; cf. Ephorus, quoted in Strabo *Geography* 9. 422.

15. Plutarch *Moralia: On the Decline of Oracles* 15.

16. Joseph Fontenrose, *Python*, p. 400.

17. Plutarch *Lives: Romulus* 20. 8.

18. Aelian *Varia historia* 3. 1. 15.

19. H. W. Parke and D. E. W. Wormell, *The Delphic Oracle*, vol. 1, p. 26.

20. Aristophanes *Pluto* 213 and scholia.

21. Proclus, in Photius *Bibliothèque* 239, (321b). Cf. Albert Severyns, *La chrestomathie de Proclos*, vol. 2, p. 219.

22. Eustatius *Commentary on the Iliad* 22. 496; Plutarch *Lives: Theseus* 18.

23. Aristophanes *The Knights* 729 and scholia; idem, *Pluto* 1054 and scholia.

24. Hesychius *Lexicon*, s.v. "aisako, hygeia."

25. Apollonius Rhodius 4. 135.

26. Apollodorus *The Library* 3. 4. 2; Suidas *Lexicon*, s.v. "Kadmeia, Nike"; Apollonius Rhodius 3. 1165.

27. Samuel Noah Kramer, *Sumerian Mythology*, p. 271.

28. Mircéa Eliade, *Birth and Rebirth*, p. 35.

29. Stith Thompson, *Motif-Index of Folk-Literature*, vol. 1, sec. B11, pp. 2–11. 11; vol. 3, sec. G.

30. Vladimir J. Propp, *Le Radici storiche dei racconti di fate*, pp. 343–347, 391–402.

31. Eliade, pp. 35–41; cf. Margaret Mead, *Male and Female*, pp. 102–105.

32. Pausanias 10. 32. 17.

33. E. S. Roberts, *An Introduction to Greek Epigraphy*, vol. 1, no. 229 bis.

34. Aristophanes *Thesmophoria* 624, 658 and scholia.

35. Athenaeus *The Deipnosophists* 20. 141e, 635e; Hesychius *Lexicon*, s.v. "Karnetai, Stafilo-dromoi."

36. Plutarch *Moralia: Convivial Questions* 4. 6. 2; cf. Euripides *Bacchae*, pass.

37. Gaetano Marini, *Gli atti e monumenti de fratelli Arvali*, vol. 1, p. xxvi.

38. Festus *De Verborum significatu*, s.v. "umbrae" (M 377).

39. Georges Dumézil, *La Religion romaine archaïque*, p. 381.

40. Macrobius *Saturnalia* 2. 12. 6; cf. John Lydus *De Mensibus* 4. 36.

41. Ovid *Fasti* 3. 523–544.

42. Tibullus *Elegies* 2. 5. 89–112.

43. Ibid., 2. 1. 1–24.

44. Horace *Satires* 2. 3. 247–249.

45. Lydus 3. 29; 4. 36.

46. Propertius *Poems* 4. 2. 16.

47. Ovid *Fasti* 3. 351–408; Plutarch *Lives: Numa* 13; Dionysius of Halicarnassus *The Roman Antiquities* 2. 71.

48. Varro *On the Latin Language* 6. 49.

49. Ovid *Fasti* 3. 677–696.

50. Jean Bayet, *Histoire politique et psychologique de la religion romaine*, p. 106.

51. Ovid *Fasti* 3. 657–662; Plutarch *On the Fortune of Alexander* 28.

52. Ovid *Fasti* 3. 544–545.

53. Virgil *Aeneid* 4. 682; 5. 4. Cf. Silius Italicus *Punica* 8. 29–97.

54. Gilbert Charles-Picard, *Les Religions de l'Afrique antique*, pp. 28–29.

55. Felix Jacoby, *Die Fragmente der griechischen Historiker*, Justin, xviii, iv–vi.

56. Michael C. Astour, *Hellenosemitica*, p. 273.

57. Charles-Picard, p. 65.

58. Angelo Brelich, *Tre variazioni romane*, p. 65 n. 3.

59. Marie-Joseph Lagrange, *Etudes sur les religions sémitiques*, p. 416.

60. Gen. 33:17.

61. Leviticus 23:33–43; cf. Numbers 29:12–38 and Deuteronomy 16:13–15.

62. Yehezkel Kaufman, *The Religion of Israel*, p. 305; Hans-Joachim Kraus, *Gottesdienst in Israel*, pp. 79–82.

63. Lev. 24:15–16.

64. Kaufman, pp. 306–307.

65. *Mishnah*, Moed Rosh-Hashanah 1. 1–2.

66. Arnold van Gennep, *Rites of Passage*, pp. 178–181; Norman H. Snaith, *The Jewish New Year Festival*, pp. 29–30, 62.

67. 1 Kings 8:2; cf. John 7:2; *Mishnah*, Moed Ta'anith 1. 1; see also Josephus Flavius *Jewish Antiquities* 8. 4. 1.

68. Lev. 23:27–32; *Mishnah*, Moed Ta'anith 4. 8.

69. Lev. 16:7–10; 21–27.

70. Ibid., 14.

71. Geza Roheim, *The Riddle of the Sphinx*, pp. 362–365; Sir James George Frazer, *The Golden Bough*, vol. 9: *The Scapegoat*, p. 35.

72. Exodus 23:16, 34:22; Deut. 16:13–17.

73. E.g. Salomon Reinach, *Orpheus*, p. 195; cf. Kaufman, p. 179; Snaith, pp. 38–41.

74. Plutarch *Moralia: Symposium* 4b. 1; Tacitus *Histories* 5. 5.

75. Martin P. Nilsson, *Geschichte der griechischen Religion*, vol. 2, pp. 457–458.

76. *Mishnah*, Moed Sukkah 1, 2.

77. Ibid., 3. 4.

78. Ibid., 4. 9; cf. Lucian *On the Syrian Goddess* 13.

79. *Mishnah*, Moed Sukkah 5. 3.

80. Ibid., 5. 4; cf. 1 Kings 18.

81. 1 Kings 8:2.

82. Ibid., 7:32.

83. Nehemiah 8:2, 13–18.

84. 2 Maccabees 10:5–6.

85. R. J. McKelvey, *The New Temple*, pp. 59–60.

86. Kraus, pp. 81–82; Roland de Vaux, *Ancient Israel*, p. 495.

87. Deut. 31:9–13; de Vaux, p. 502.

88. James B. Pritchard, *Ancient Near Eastern Texts Relating to the Old Testament*, pp. 60–72.

89. Henri Frankfort and H. A. Groenewegen-Frankfort, eds., *Before Philosophy*, pp. 179–180.

90. François Thureau-Dangin, *Rituels accadiens*, pp. 136–139.

91. Pritchard, pp. 331–334.

92. Henri Frankfort, *Kingship and the Gods*, p. 321.

93. Svend Aage Pallis, *The Babylonian Akitu Festival*, p. 109; Frankfort, p. 331 and n. 78.

94. E. O. James, *The Ancient Gods*, London, 1960, p. 144; idem, *Seasonal Feasts and Festivals*, pp. 87, 136.

95. Pallis, p. 187.

96. Frankfort and Groenewegen-Frankfort, p. 183.

97. Frankfort, p. 324 and n. 41.

98. Ibid., p. 132.

99. Pritchard, p. 6; Fontenrose, pp. 186–188.

100. James, *Seasonal Feasts*, p. 75 (the reference there is mistaken).

101. Stephen Langdon, *Le Poème sumérian du paradis*, p. 140.

102. Ibid., p. 173.

103. Henri Frankfort, *The Art and Architecture of the Ancient Orient*, p. 10; H. A. Groenewegen-Frankfort, *Arrest and Movement*, pp. 151–153.

104. Frankfort, *Kingship*, pp. 129, 178–180; cf. Sir Ernest Alfred Thompson Wallis Budge, *From Fetish to God in Ancient Egypt*, pp. 12–13, 65–66; Erich Neumann, *The Great Mother*, pp. 242–244.

105. Jacques Vandier, *Manuel d'archéologie égyptienne*, vol. 2, pp. 884–891.

106. Ibid., vol. 1, p. 113.

107. Cf. Leo Frobenius, *Kulturgeschichte Afrikas*, p. 238.

108. Henri Frankfort, *Ancient Egyptian Religion*, pp. 153–156.

109. Pritchard, p. 3.

110. I. E. S. Edwards, *The Pyramids of Egypt*, pp. 179, 188.

111. Vandier, vol. 2, p. 928; Edwards, p. 63.

112. Vandier, vol. 2, pp. 907–909.

113. Ibid., pp. 888, 918.

114. Frankfort, *Kingship*, p. 79.

115. Ibid., p. 80.

116. Ibid., p. 197.

117. Vandier, vol. 1, pp. 334–341, 561–563.

118. Frankfort, *Art and Architecture*, p. 4.

119. Walter B. Emery, *Archaic Egypt*, pp. 144–146.

120. Edwards, pp. 42–45.

121. Emery, pp. 130–132.

122. Vandier, vol. 1, pp. 168–169, 192–193, 234–235; vol. 2, pp. 684–685, 800–801.

123. Carl Hentze, *Das Haus als Weltort der Seele*, pp. 69–71, 110–112.

124. William Watson, *China Before the Han Dynasty*, pp. 38–41.

125. Hentze, pp. 32–34.

126. V. Gordon Childe, *The Danube in Prehistory*, pp. 303–369.

127. Einar Gjerstad, *Early Rome*, vol. 4, pt. 1, pp. 45, 59.

128. Solinus *Collectanea rerum memorabilium* 1. 18; Zonaras *Annales* 7. 3. 9; Varro 5. 53.

129. Dio Cassius *Roman History* 48. 43. 4.

130. Ibid., 54. 29. 8.

131. Seneca *Letteres a Lucilius (ad Helvetium)* 9. 3; Valerius Maximus *Memorabilia* 2. 8.

132. Giuseppe Lugli, *Fontes ad topographiam veteris urbis Romae pertinentes*, vol. 8, pt. 19, Ia, 9–10; Marcus Annaeus Seneca *Controversiae* 2. 1. 4.

133. Vitruvius 2. 1. 5.

134. Pausanias 1. 28. 5–8.

135. Ibid., 1. 3. 1.

136. Solinus 1. 21; Festus 278.

137. Dio Cassius 48. 42. 4–6.

138. Frank E. Brown, *The Regia*; and verbal communication.

139. Plutarch *Moralia: Roman Questions* 97; Festus 295–296.

140. Ovid *Fasti* 6. 261.

141. Kenzo Tange and Noboru Kawazoe, *Ise*, p. 199.

142. Ibid., p. 191.

143. Robert Treat Paine and Alexander Soper, *The Art and Architecture of Japan*, pp. 162–163; J. Edward Kidder, *Early Japanese Art*, pp. 37–41.

144. Tange and Kawazoe, p. 199.

145. D. C. Holton, *The Japanese Enthronement Ceremonies*, pass.; Sir Ernest Saton, "Ancient Japanese Rituals," *Transactions of the Asiatic Society of Japan*, vol. 9, pass.

146. Basil Hall Chamberlain and W. B. Mason, *A Handbook for Travellers in Japan*, p. 428.

Chapter 7: A HOUSE FOR THE SOUL

1. Psalms 118:27.

2. *The Midrash on the Psalms*, vol. 2, pp. 244–245.

3. Franz Delitsch, *Biblical Commentary on the Psalms*, vol. 3, pp. 207–211; Sigmund Mowinckel, *The Psalms in Israel's Worship*, vol. 1, pp. 130–131.

4. Ps. 118:14–15, 19–20, 22, 26.

5. *Talmud (Babylonian)*, Baba Batra 75a.

6. St. Methodius of Olympia, *The Symposium* (ed. and trans. Herbert Mursillo) 9. 5 (pp. 124–125); cf. Jean Danielou, *The Bible and the Liturgy*, p. 337.

7. Acts of the Apostles 4:11.

8. Matthew 17:4; Mark 9:5, 6; Luke 9:33.

9. John 12:13; cf. Zechariah 9:9.

10. Apocalypse 7:9–17.

11. Ibid., 7:15, 12:12, 13:6, 21:3.

12. Erwin R. Goodenough, *Jewish Symbols in the Graeco-Roman Period*, vol. 12, p. 86–87.

13. Baldwin Spencer and F. J. Gillen, *The Native Tribes of Central Australia*, pp. 16–23.

14. Baldwin Spencer, *The Native Tribes of the Northern Territory of Australia*, pp. 28–31.

15. Spencer and Gillen, p. 307; Geza Roheim, *The Riddle of the Sphinx*, pp. 123–126.

16. A. P. Elkin, *The Australian Aborigines*, pp. 16–17.

17. Sir Ernest Alfred Thompson Wallis Budge, *The Book of the Dead*, vol. 2, p. 371 (cap. cxxv b).

18. Ibid., vol. 3, p. 414 (cap. cxxxvii a).

19. Franz Boas (*Indian Sagas*), quoted in Vladimir J. Propp, *Le Radici storiche dei racconti di fate*, p. 98.

20. Lord Raglan, *The Temple and the House*, p. 98.

21. *Jewish Encyclopedia*, s.v. "Huppah."

22. *Talmud de Jerusalem*, Sotah 9. 15; cf. *Jewish Encyclopedia*, s.v. "Huppah."

23. *Talmud de Jerusalem*, Sukkah 2. 5.

24. *Pirkê de Rabbi Eliezer*, pp. 88–89.

25. Menorath-ha-Moar.

26. Susan Isaacs, *Social Development in Young Children*, pp. 362–364.

27. Norman O. Brown, *Love's Body*, p. 59.

BIBLIOGRAPHY

Aelianus, Claudianus. *Varia historia*. Edited by A. Gronov (Gronovius). 2 vols. Leiden, 1731.

——. *On the Characteristics of Animals*. Translated by A. F. Scholfield. 3 vols. London, 1958–59.

Afanasev, K. I.; Afanasev, V.; and Chasanova, B. E., eds. *Iz Istorii Sovetskoy Arkhitekturi*. 2 vols. Moscow, 1963.

Alberti, Leon Battista. *L'Architettura (De re aedificatoria)*. Edited by Paolo Portoghesi; translated by Giovanni Orlandi. 2 vols. Milan, 1966.

Algarotti, Francesco. *Opere scelte*. 3 vols. Milan, 1823.

Alkaios, see Lobel, E., and Page, D.

Apollodorus. *The Library*. Edited and translated by Sir James George Frazer. 2 vols. London and New York, 1921.

Apollonius Rhodius. *The Argonautica*. Edited and translated by R. C. Seaton. London and New York, 1902.

Aristophanes. [*Aristophane*]. Edited by Victor Coulon; translated by Hilaire van Daele. 5 vols. Paris, 1923–30.

——. *The Plays*. Edited and translated by Benjamin Bickley Rogers. 3 vols. London and New York, 1924.

Astour, Michael C. *Hellenosemitica: An Ethnic and Cultural Study in West Semitic Impact on Mycenaean Greece*. Leiden, 1965.

Athenaeus of Naucratis. *The Deipnosophists*. Translated by Charles Burton Gulick. 7 vols. London, 1927–41.

Baron, Hans. *The Crisis of the Early Italian Renaissance*. Princeton, N. J., 1966.

Batteux, Charles. *Les Beaux-Arts réduits à un même principe*. 2 vols. Paris, 1746.

Bayet, Jean. *Histoire politique et psychologique de la religion romaine*. Paris, 1957.

[Belgrado, P. Jacopo]. *Dell'architettura egiziana*. Parma, 1786.

Biblia Sacra Hebraica, Chaldaice, Graece et Latine. Edited by Benedictus Arias Montano. 8 vols. Antwerp, 1572.

Biblia Sacra Polyglota. Edited by Brian Walton. 6 vols. London, 1657.

Blondel, François. *Cours d'architecture enseigne dans l'Académie Royale d'Architecture*. 5 parts. Paris, 1675–83.

Blondel, Jacques-François. *Cours d'architecture, ou traité de la décoration, distribution et construction des bâtiments, contenant les leçons données en 1750 et les années suivantes, par J.-F. B.* 6 vols. (later vols. edited by P. Patte). Paris, 1771–77.

Börsch-Supan, Eva. *Garten- Landschafts- und Paradiesmotive im Innenraum*. Berlin, 1967.

Boswell, James. *Life of Johnson*. Edited by Augustine Birrell. 6 vols. London, 1896.

Boullée, Etienne-Louis. *The Treatise on Architecture*. Edited by Helen Rosenau. London, 1953.

——. *L'Architecture, essai sur l'art*. Edited by Jean-Marie Pérouse de Montclos. Paris, 1968.

Brelich, Angelo. *Tre variazioni romane sul tema delle origini*. Rome, 1955.

Brown, Frank E. "The Regia," *Memoirs of the American Academy in Rome*, vol. 12 (Rome, 1935), pp. 67–88.

———. *Roman Houses*. Typescript, 1968.

Brown, Norman O. *Love's Body*. New York, 1966.

Budge, Sir Ernest Alfred Thompson Wallis. *The Book of the Dead*. 2nd ed. London, 1909.

———. *From Fetish to God in Ancient Egypt*. London, 1934.

Burke, Edmund. *The Works*. 3 vols. Dublin, 1792.

Butterworth, E. A. S. *Some Traces of the Pre-Olympian World in Greek Literature and Myth*. Berlin, 1966.

Callimachus. *Fragments*. Translated, with notes, by C. A. Trypanis. London and Cambridge, Mass., 1958.

Capell, Lodovicus. *Trisagion, sive templi Hierosolymitani triplex delineatio*. In *Biblia Sacra Polyglota*, vol. 1.

Caramuel de Lobkowitz, Juan. *Architectura civil recta y obliqua considerada y dibuxada en el templo de Jerusalem, erigido en el Monte Moria por el Rey Salomon . . . promovida a suma perfeccion en el templo y palacio de S. Lorenco cerca del Escurial, que invento con su divine Ingenio, delineo y dibuxo con su real Mano y con exemplarios Gestos rempleando los mexores artifices de Europa erigio el Rey D. Philipe II*. Vigevano, 1678.

Cenival, Jean Louis de. *Living Architecture: Egyptian*. London, 1964.

Chamberlain, Basil Hall, and Mason, W. B. *A Handbook for Travellers in Japan*. London, 1903.

Chambers, Sir William. *A Treatise on the Decorative Part of Civil Architecture*. London, 1759.

———. *A Treatise on the Decorative Part of Civil Architecture, with Illustrations and Notes*. Edited by Joseph Gwilt. London, 1825.

Charles-Picard, Gilbert. *Les Religions de l'Afrique antique*. Paris, 1954.

Childe, V. Gordon. *The Danube in Prehistory*. Oxford, 1929.

———. *Prehistoric Migrations in Europe*. Oslo, 1950.

Choisy, Auguste. *Histoire de l'architecture*. 2 vols. Paris, 1899.

Cicero, Marcus Tullius. *De natura deorum; Academica*. Translated by H. Rackham. London and New York, 1933.

———. *Tusculan Disputations*. Translated by J. E. King. Cambridge, Mass., 1950.

Claudian. *Works*. Translated by Maurice Platnauer. 2 vols. London and New York, 1922.

Clemen, Karl. *Fontes historiae religionis Germanicae*. Berlin, 1928.

Cluver, Philip of. *Italia antiqua*. 3 vols. Leiden, 1624.

———. *Germania antiqua*. Leiden, 1631.

Coleridge, Samuel Taylor. *The Philosophical Lectures*. Edited by Kathleen Coburn. London, 1949.

Controspazio. (Special number on Futurism), vol. 3, nos. 4–5 (April–May 1971).

Corbusier, Le, *see* Le Corbusier.

Dacus, Fridericus Bernhardus, illustrator. *Talmudicis Babylonici Codex Succa sive de Tabernaculum Festo.* Frankfort, 1726.

Danielou, Jean. *The Bible and Liturgy.* London, 1960.

Defoe, Daniel. *The Life and Surprising Adventures of Robinson Crusoe of York, Mariner.* London, 1962.

Delitzsch, Franz. *Biblical Commentary on the Psalms.* Translated by Rev. David Eaton. 3 vols. London, 1889.

Diels, Hermann. *Die Fragmente der Vorsokratiker.* Edited by Walther Kranz. 9th ed. 3 vols. Berlin, 1959–60.

Dio Cassius. *Roman History.* Edited and translated by Ernest Cary. 9 vols. London and New York, 1914.

Dionysius of Halicarnassus. *The Roman Antiquities.* Edited and translated by Ernest Cary. 7 vols. London and Cambridge, Mass., 1937.

Dumézil, Georges. *Le Problème des centaures.* Annales du Musée Guimet, no. 41. (Paris, 1929).

———. *La Religion romaine archaïque.* Paris, 1966.

Durand, Jean-Nicolas-Louis. *Précis des leçons d'architecture données à l'Ecole Royale Polytechnique.* 2nd ed. 2 vols. Paris, 1821–23.

Edwards, I. E. S. *The Pyramids of Egypt.* Harmondsworth, Middlesex, 1961.

Einhard. *Vita Karoli Magni (Scriptores rerum Germanicarum ad usum scholarum).* Edited by G. H. Fertz and G. Waitz. 6th ed. Hannover, 1911.

Eliade, Mircéa. *Birth and Rebirth: The Religious Meanings of Initiation in Human Culture.* Translated by Willard R. Task. New York, 1958.

———. "Dimensions religiuses du renouvellement cosmique," *Eranos Jahrbuch,* no. 28 (Zurich, 1959), p. 241.

Elkin, A. P. *The Australian Aborigines: How to Understand Them.* London, 1964.

Emery, Walter B. *Archaic Egypt.* Harmondsworth, Middlesex, 1961.

Empson, William. *Seven Types of Ambiguity.* London, 1956.

Erman, Adolf. *The Ancient Egyptians: A Sourcebook of Their Writings.* Translated by Aylward M. Blackman, with an introduction by William Kelly Simpson. New York, 1966.

Euripides. *The Plays.* Translated, with notes, by A. S. Way. 4 vols. London and Cambridge, Mass., 1962.

Eustathius Archiepiscopus Thessalonicensis. *Comentarii ad Homeri Odysseam Iliadem as fidem exempli Romani Editi.* 7 vols. Berlin, 1827.

Fakhry, Ahmed. *The Pyramids.* Chicago, 1961.

Félibien, André des Avaux. *Des Principes de l'architecture, de la sculpture, de la peinture.* 3rd ed. Paris, 1697.

Fergusson, James. *A History of Architecture in All Countries from the Earliest Times to the Present Day.* Edited by R. Phene Spiers. 3 vols. London, 1855 (5 vols., 1893).

Festus Sextus Pompeius. *De Verborum significatu quae supersunt cum Pauli Epitome.* Edited by Wallace M. Lindsay. Leipzig, 1913.

Filarete's Treatise on Architecture, Being the Treatise by Antonio di Piero Averulino, Known as Filarete. Translated, with an introduction and notes, by John R. Spencer. 2 vols. New Haven, Conn., and London, 1965.

Fischer von Erlach, Johann Bernhard. *Entwurf einer historischen Architektur in Abbildung . . . berühmter Gebäude des altertums und fremder Völker.* Vienna, 1721.

Fletcher, Banister, and Fletcher, Banister F. *A History of Architecture, Being a Comparative View of the Historical Styles.* London, 1896 (4th ed., 1901; 14th and latest ed., 1964; later editions ascribed to Banister F. Fletcher alone).

Focillon, Henri. *Giovanni-Battista Piranesi, 1720–1778.* Paris, 1918.

Fontanesi, Giuseppina. *Francesco Milizia, scrittore e studioso d'arte.* Bologna, 1932.

Fontenrose, Joseph. *Python: A Study of Delphic Myth and Its Origins.* Berkeley and Los Angeles, 1959.

Frankfort, Henri. *Cylinder Seals.* London, 1939.

———. *Kingship and the Gods.* Chicago, 1948.

———. *The Art and Architecture of the Ancient Orient.* The Pelican History of Art. Harmondsworth, Middlesex, 1954.

———. *Ancient Egyptian Religion.* New York, 1961.

Frankfort, H., and Groenewegen-Frankfort, H. A., eds. *Before Philosophy: The Intellectual Adventure of Ancient Man.* Harmondsworth, Middlesex, 1949–59.

Frankl, Paul. *The Gothic: Literary Sources and Interpretation.* Princeton, N.J., 1960.

———. *Gothic Architecture.* Harmondsworth, Middlesex, 1962.

Fraser, Douglas; Hibbard, Howard; and Lewine, Milton J., eds. *Essays on the History of Architecture Presented to Rudolf Wittkower.* London, 1967. See also Hermann, W.; Nyberg, D.; Taylor, R.

Frazer, Sir James George. *The Golden Bough.* 12 vols. London, 1911.

Fréart de Chambray, Roland. *Parallèle de l'architecture antique et de la moderne.* Paris, 1650.

———. *A Parallel of the Ancient Architecture with the Modern.* Translated by John Evelyn. London, 1723.

Frobenius, Leo. *Kulturgeschichte Afrikas: Prolegomena zu einer historischen Gestaltlehre.* Zurich, 1933.

Gennep, Arnold van. *The Rites of Passage.* London, 1960.

Giedion, Siegfried. *Mechanization Takes Command.* New York and Oxford, 1958.

———. *The Eternal Present.* Vol. 1: "The Origins of Art"; Vol. 2: "The Origins of Architecture." London and Oxford, 1962.

Gjerstad, Einar. *Early Rome.* Vol. IV: *Synthesis of Archaeological Evidence.* Lund, 1966.

Goethe, Johann Wolfgang von. *Gedenkausgabe der Werke.* Edited by Ernest Beutler. 24 vols. Zurich, 1948–54.

Goff, Beatrice Laura. *Symbols of Prehistoric Mesopotamia.* New Haven, Conn., and London, 1963.

Goldman, Bernard. *The Sacred Portal: A Primary Symbol in Ancient Judaic Art.* Detroit, 1966.

Goldmann, Nicolaus. *Vollständige Ausweisung zu der Civil-Bau-Kunst.* Wolfenbüttel, 1696 (Leipzig, 1708).

Goodenough, Erwin R. *Jewish Symbols in the Graeco-Roman Period.* 12 vols. New York, 1958—.

Griffiths, J. Gwyn. *The Conflict of Horus and Seth.* Liverpool, 1960.

Groenewegen-Frankfort, H. A. *Arrest and Movement.* London, 1951.

Grose, Francis. *The Antiquities of England and Wales.* 4 vols. London, 1773–89.

Hall, Sir James, Bart. *Essays on the Origins, History and Principles of Gothic Architecture.* London, 1813.

Harden, Donald. *The Phoenicians.* London, 1962.

Harrison, Jane Ellen. *Prolegomena to the Study of Greek Religion.* London, 1921.

———. *Themis: A Study of the Social Origins of Greek Religion.* London, 1912 (1963).

Hegel, Georg Wilhelm Friedrich. *Sämtliche Werke, Jubiläumausgabe,* 26 vols. Stuttgart, 1926.

———. *Aesthetik.* 2 vols. Berlin and Weimar, 1965.

Hentze, Carl. *Bronzgerät, Kultbauen, Religion in ältesten China der Shang Zeit.* 2 vols. Antwerp, 1951.

———. *Das Haus als Weltort der Seele.* Stuttgart, 1961.

Herbert, Jean. *Shinto at the Fountain-Head of Japan.* London, 1967.

Herodotus. *The Histories.* Translated, with notes, by A. D. Godley. 4 vols. London and New York, 1926.

Herrmann, Wolfgang. *Laugier and Eighteenth-Century French Theory.* London, 1962.

———. "Unknown Designs for the 'Temple of Jerusalem' by Claude Perrault." In Fraser, Douglas, et al., eds. *Essays on the History of Architecture Presented to Rudolf Wittkower.* London, 1967. Pp. 143–158.

Hesychius. *Hesychii Alexandrinii Lexicon.* Edited by Kurt Latte. 2 vols. Copenhagen, 1953–66.

Hooke, S. H. *Middle Eastern Mythology.* Harmondsworth, Middlesex, 1963.

Holton, D. C. *The Japanese Enthronement Ceremonies.* Tokyo, 1928.

Horace. *Satires, Epistles and Ars Poetica.* Edited and translated by H. Rustin Fairclough. London and New York, 1926.

———. *The Odes and Epodes.* Edited and translated by C. E. Bennett. London and Cambridge, Mass., 1964.

Horn-Oncken, Alste. *Uber das Schickliche.* Abhandlungen der Akademie der Wissenschaften in Göttingen (Philosophisch-Historische Klasse, 3rd series, no. 70). Göttingen, 1967.

How, W. W., and Wells, J. A. *A Commentary on Herodotus.* 4 vols. Oxford, 1928.

Isaacs, Susan. *Social Development in Young Children.* London, 1933.

Jacoby, Felix. *Die Fragmente der griechischen Historiker.* 14 vols. Berlin, 1923 (Leiden, 1955).

James, E. O. *Seasonal Feasts and Festivals.* London, 1961.

Jastrow, Morris. *The Religion of Babylonia and Assyria*. Handbooks on the History of Religions. Boston and New York, 1898.

Jeanmaire, H. *Couroi et couretes*. Travaux et mémoires de l'Université de Lille, no. 21. Lille, 1939.

Jensen, A. E. *Mythos und Kult bei Naturvölkern*. Wiesbaden, 1960.

Jewish Encyclopedia. Edited by Isidore Singer *et al.* 12 vols. New York and London, 1928.

Johnson, Philip C. *Mies van der Rohe*. 2nd ed. New York, 1953.

Johnson, Samuel. *A Dictionary of the English Language*. 2 vols. London, 1755.

Jones, Ernest. *Sigmund Freud: Life and Work*. 3 vols. London, 1953.

Josephus Flavius. *Works*. Introduction by H. St. J. Thackeray. 9 vols. London and New York, 1926 (later vols. by Louis H. Feldman, Ralph Marcus, and A. Wikgren).

Kames, Henry Home, Lord. *Essays on the Principles of Morality and Natural Religion*. Edinburgh, 1751.

———. *Elements of Criticism*. 3 vols. Edinburgh, 1762.

———. *Sketches of the History of Man*. 2 vols. Edinburgh, 1774 (enl. ed., London and Edinburgh, 1788).

Kant, Immanuel. *Works*. 5 vols. Wiesbaden, 1957.

Kaufman, Yehezkel. *The Religion of Israel from Its Beginning to the Babylonian Exile*. Translated and abridged by Moshe Greenberg. London, 1961.

Kidder, J. Edward. *Early Japanese Art: The Great Tombs and Treasures*. London, 1964.

Kircher, Athanasius. *Latium, id est nova et parallela Latii tum veteris tum novi descriptio*. Amsterdam, 1671.

Klein, Melanie. *Narrative of a Child Analysis*. International Psychoanalytical Library, no. 55. London, 1961.

Koch, Herbert. *Von Nachleben des Vitruvius*. Deutsche Beiträge zur Altertumswissenschaft, no. 1. Baden-Baden, 1951.

Koppers, Wilhelm. *Primitive Man and His World*. Translated by Edith Rybould. London and New York, 1952.

Kramer, Samuel Noah. *Sumerian Mythology*. New York and London, 1944 (1961).

———. *History Begins at Sumer*. 2nd ed. London, 1961.

Kraus, Hans-Joachim. *Gottesdienst in Israel*. Munich, 1962.

Lagrange, Marie-Joseph. *Etudes sur les religions semitiques*. Paris, 1905.

Lamy, Bernard. *De Tabernaculo Foederis, de Sancta Civitate Jerusalem, et de Templo eius Libri Septem*. Paris, 1720.

Lang, Susan. "The Principles of the Gothic Revival in England," *Journal of the Society of Architectural Historians*, vol. 25, no. 4 (December 1966), pp. 240–267.

Langdon, Stephen. *Le Poème sumérien du paradis, du déluge et de la chute de l'homme*. Paris, London, and New York, 1919.

———. *The Babylonian Epic of Creation, Restored from Recently Recovered Tablets at Assur*. Oxford, 1923.

Langer, Susanne K. *Feeling and Form: A Theory of Art*. New York, 1953.

Latte, Kurt. *Römische Religionsgeschichte*. Handbuch der Altertumswissenschaft, sec. 5, pt. 4. Munich, 1960.

Laugier, Marc-Antoine. *Essai sur l'architecture*. Paris, 1753.

——. *Observations sur l'architecture*. The Hague, 1765.

Le Bonniec, Henri. *Le Culte de Cérès à Rome*. Etudes et Commentaires, 27. Paris, 1958.

Le Corbusier (Charles-Edouard Jeanneret). *Vers une architecture*. Paris, 1926.

Lefèvre, André. *Les Merveilles de l'architecture*. Paris, 1880.

Leon, Jacob Jehudah Arie. *Retrato de templo de Solomon*. Middleburg, 1642.

Leroi-Gourhan, André. *Le Geste et la parole*. Vol. 1: *Technique et langage*; vol. 2: *La Mémoire et les rythmes*. Paris, 1964.

Lichtenberg, Reinhold Freiherr von. *Haus, Dorf, Stadt*. Leipzig, 1909.

Lightfoot, John. *The Temple, Especially as it Stood in the Dayes of Our Saviour*. London, 1650.

Lobel, E., and Page, D., eds. *Poetaram lesbioram fragmenta*. Oxford, 1955.

Lobkowitz, Juan Caramuel de, see Caramuel.

Loos, Adolf. *Gesammelte Schriften*. Vol. 1 (only one published). Vienna, 1962.

L'Orme, Philibert de. *L'Architecture*. Rouen, 1648.

Lucanus, Marcus Annaeus. *The Civil War*. Translated by J. D. Duff. London, 1928.

——. *Pharsalia*. Translated by Robert Graves. London, 1956.

Lucian of Samosata. *Works*. Edited and translated by A. M. Hamilton. 8 vols. London and New York, 1921.

Lucretius Carus, T. *De rerum natura*. Translated, with notes, by H. A. J. Munro. 3rd ed. 2 vols. Cambridge, 1875.

——. *De rerum natura*. Edited and translated by W. H. D. Rouse. London and New York, 1924.

Lugli, Giuseppe. *Roma antica, il centro monumentale*. Rome, 1946.

——. *Fontes ad topographiam veteris urbis Romae pertinentes*. 6 vols. Rome, 1952–.

Lurçat, André. *Architecture*. Paris, 1929.

Lydus, Johannes Laurentius. *De magistratibus, de mensibus, de ostentis*. Corpus scriptorum historiae Byzantinae, edited by I. Bekker. Bonn, 1837.

Macrobius, Aurelius Ambrosius Theodosius. *Opera quae supersunt*. Edited by F. Eyssenhardt. Leipzig, 1893.

Marini, Gaetano. *Gli atti e monumenti de fratelli Arvali*. 2 vols. Rome, 1795.

Martini, Francesco di Giorgio. *Trattati di architettura ingegnerìa e arte militare*. Transcribed and edited by Corrado and Livia Maltese. 2 vols. Milan, 1967.

McKelvey, R. J. *The New Temple: The Church in the New Testament*. Oxford, 1969.

Mead, Margaret. *Male and Female: A Study of the Sexes in a Changing World*. Harmondsworth, Middlesex, 1950 (1962).

Meillet, A. *Esquisse d'une histoire de la langue latine*. Paris, 1928–52.

Memmo, Andrea. *Elementi d'architettura Lodoliana; ossia l'arte del fabbricare con solidita scientifica e con eleganza non cappriciosa*. 2 vols. Milan, 1833–34.

Mendelsohn, Erich. *Das Gesamtschaffen des Architekten*. Berlin, 1930.

Methodius, St., of Olympia. *The Symposium*. Edited and translated by Herbert Mursillo. London, 1958.

Midrash. *The Midrash on the Psalms*. Translated by William G. Braude. New Haven, Conn., 1959.

Migliorini, Ermanno. *Studi sul pensiero estetico del settecento*. Florence, 1966.

Milizia, Francesco. *Memorie degli architetti antichi e moderni*. 3rd ed. 2 vols. Parma, 1781.

———. *Principii di architettura civile*. 3 vols. Bassano, 1823.

Mishnah. Translated, with introduction and notes, by Herbert Danby. Oxford, 1933 (1958).

Monboddo, James Burnett, Lord. *Of the Origins and Progress of Language*. Edinburgh, 1773.

———. *Ancient Metaphysics, or the Science of Universals*. 6 vols. Edinburgh, 1779–99.

Montanus, Benedictus Arias. "Exemplar, sive de Sacris Fabricis Liber." In *Biblia Sacra Hebraica, Chaldaice, Graece et Latine*. Vol. 8. Antwerp, 1572.

Mowinckel, Sigmund. *The Psalms in Israel's Worship*. Translated by D. R. Ap-Thomas. 2 vols. Oxford, 1962.

Neumann, Erich. *The Great Mother*. Translated by Ralph Mannheim. New York, 1955.

Nilsson, Martin P. *Geschichte der griechischen Religion*. Handbuch der Altertumswissenschaft, sec. 5, pt. 2. 2 vols. Munich, 1941, 1950.

Nyberg, Dorothea. "La Sainte Antiquité: Focus of an Eighteenth-Century Architectural Debate." In Fraser, Douglas, *et al.*, eds. *Essays on the History of Architecture Presented to Rudolf Wittkower*. London, 1967. Pp. 159–169.

Ouvrard, René. *Architecture harmonique, ou application de la doctrine des proportions de la musique à l'architecture*. Paris, 1679.

Ovidius Naso, Publius. *The Fasti of Ovid*. Translated, with commentary, by Sir James George Frazer. 5 vols. London, 1929.

———. *Fasti*. Translated by Sir James George Frazer. London, 1931.

Page, Denys. *Sappho and Alcaeus: An Introduction to the Study of Ancient Lesbian Poetry*. Oxford, 1955.

Paine, Robert Treat, and Soper, Alexander. *The Art and Architecture of Japan*. Harmondsworth, Middlesex, 1955.

Pallis, Svend Aage. *The Babylonian Akitu Festival*. Copenhagen, 1926.

Panofsky, Erwin. "Der Begriff des Kunstwollens," *Zeitschrift für Asthetik*, vol. 14 (1920), pp. 321–339.

———. *Studies in Iconology: Humanistic Themes in the Art of the Renaissance*. New York and Evanston, Ill., 1939 (1962).

Parke, H. W. *Greek Oracles*. London, 1967.

Parke, H. W., and Wormell, D. E. W. *The Delphic Oracle*. 2 vols. London, 1953.

Patai, Raphael. *Man and Temple: In Ancient Jewish Myth and Ritual.* New York, 1947 (2nd ed., 1967).

Pausanias. *Description of Greece.* Translated, with an introduction, by Sir James George Frazer. 6 vols. London, 1897 (2nd ed., 1913).

————. *The Description of Greece.* Edited and translated by W. H. S. Jones. 6 vols. London and New York, 1918.

Percy, Thomas. *Reliques of Ancient English Poetry, Consisting of Old Heroic Ballads, Songs and other Pieces of our Earlier Poets.* 2nd ed. 3 vols. London, 1767.

Perrault, Charles. *Parallèle des anciens et des modernes en ce qui regarde les arts et les sciences, dialogues.* 4 vols. Paris, 1688–1694.

Perrault, Claude. *Ordonnance des cinq espèces de colonnes selon la méthode des anciens.* Paris, 1683.

————. *A Treatise on the Five Orders of Columns in Architecture.* Translated by John James. London, 1708.

Petrocchi, Massimo. *Razionalismo architettonico e razionalismo storio-grafico.* Rome, 1947.

Pevsner, Sir Nikolaus. *Studies in Art, Architecture and Design.* 2 vols. London, 1968.

Photius. *Bibliothèque.* Edited and translated by René Henry. 5 vols. Paris, 1959–67.

Pindar. *The Odes of Pindar, Including the Principal Fragments.* Translated, with an introduction, by Sir John Sandys. London, 1937.

————. *Siegesänge und Fragmente.* Edited and translated by Oskar Wener. Munich, 1967.

Piranesi, Giovanni Battista. *Della magnificenza ed architettura de'romani.* Rome, 1761.

————. *Osservazione di G. B. P. sopra le lettere di M. Mariette.* Rome, 1765.

————. *Una Prefazione ad un nuovo trattato della introduzione e del progresso delle belle arti in Europa ne tempi antichi.* Rome, 1765.

————. *Diverse maniere di adornar i cammini ed ogni altre parte degli edifizi desunte dall'architettura egizia, etrusca e greca.* Rome, 1769.

Pirke de Rabbi Eliezer. Translated by Gerald Friedlander. London, 1916.

Plutarch. *Lives.* Translated by Bernadotte Perrin. 11 vols. London and New York, 1914–26.

————. *Moralia.* Translated by Frank Cole Babbitt et al. 15 vols. London and New York (later vols. Cambridge, Mass.), 1927–61.

Poleni, Giovanni. *Exercitaiones Vitruvianae.* Padua, 1739.

Pope, Alexander. *The Works.* Edited by T. Warburton. 21 vols. London, 1760.

Pradus, Hieronymus, and Villalpandus, Ioannes Baptista. *In Ezechielem explanationes et apparatus Urbis ac Templi Hierosolymitani.* 3 vols. Rome, 1596–1604.

Pritchard, James B., ed. *Ancient Near Eastern Texts Relating to the Old Testament.* 2nd ed. Princeton, N.J., 1955.

Propertius, Sextus. *Poems.* Translated by H. E. Butler. London and Cambridge, Mass., 1912.

Propp, Vladimir J. *Le Radici storiche dei racconti di fate.* Translated by Clara Coïsson. Turin, 1949 (Russian ed., 1946).

————. *Morfologia della fiaba*. Turin, 1966 (Russian ed., 1926).

————. *Morphology of the Folktale*. American Folklore Society Publications, vol. 9. Austin, Tex., 1968.

Pugin, A. Welby. *Contrasts, or A Parallel between the Noble Edifices of the Middle Ages and Corresponding Buildings of the Present Day, Shewing the Present Decay of Taste.* London, 1836.

————. *The True Principles of Pointed or Christian Architecture, Set Forth in Two Lectures.* London, 1841.

Quatremère de Quincy, Antoine Chrysostome. *De l'architecture égyptienne considerée dans son origine, ses principes et son goût et comparée sous les mêmes rapports à l'architecture grecque.* Paris, 1803.

————. *Dictionnaire historique de l'architecture*. 2 vols. Paris, 1832.

Quilici, Vero. *L'Architettura del construttivismo*. Bari, 1969.

Quitzsch, Heinz. *Die asthetischen Anshauungen Gottfried Sempers.* Berlin, 1962.

Raffaello Sanzio. *Tutti gli scritti.* Edited by Ettore Comasecca. Milan, 1956.

Raglan, Lord. *The Temple and the House.* London, 1969.

Reinach, Salomon. *Orpheus: A History of Religions.* Translated by Florence Simmonds. New York, 1930.

Ribart de Chamoust, M. *L'Ordre François trouvé dans la nature, presenté au Roi le 21 septembre 1776.* Paris, 1783.

Riegl, Alois, *Stilfragen.* Berlin, 1893.

————. *Spätrömische Kunstindustrie.* Vienna, 1927.

Roberts, E. S. *An Introduction to Greek Epigraphy.* 2 vols. Cambridge, 1887–1905.

Robertson-Smith, W. *Lectures on the Religion of the Semites.* Edinburgh, 1889.

Roheim, Geza. *Animism, Magic and the Divine King.* London, 1930.

————. *The Riddle of the Sphinx, or Human Origins.* London, 1934.

Rousseau, Jean-Jacques. *Oeuvres complètes.* Edited by B. Gaguebin and M. Raymond. Paris, 1959. 4 vols. to date.

————. *Essai sur l'origine des langues.* Paris, 1969.

Royal Society of Edinburgh. *Transactions of the Royal Society of Edinburgh.* Edinburgh, 1788–.

Ruskin, John. *The Poetry of Architecture.* London, 1893.

Saton, Ernest. "Ancient Japanese Rituals," *Transactions of the Asiatic Society of Japan,* vol. 9 (Yokohama, 1881), pp. 118–211.

Scamozzi, Vincenzo. *L'Idea della architettura universale.* Venice, 1615.

Schlegel, Friedrich von. *Works.* Edited by Ernst Behler, Jean-Jacques Anstett, and Hans Eichner. 12 vols. to date. Munich, 1959–.

Schlosser, Julius von. *Schriftquellen zur Geschichte der karolingischen Kunst, gesammelt und erläutert.* Quellenschriften zur Kunstgeschichte & Kunsttechnik, New Series, vol. 4. Vienna, 1896.

Semper, Gottfried. *Der Stil in den technischen und tektonischen Kunsten oder praktische Aesthetik.* Frankfort and Munich, 1861–63 (2nd ed., 2 vols., Munich, 1878).

————. *Wissenschaft, Industrie und Kunst.* Edited by Hans M. Wingler. Mainz, 1966.

Seneca, Lucius Annaeus. *Letteres a Lucilius.* Edited by Francis Prechac; translated by Henri Noblot. 5 vols. Paris, 1945–64.

Seneca, Marcus Annaeus. *Controverses et Suasoires.* Edited, translated, and annotated by Henri Bornecque. 2 vols. Paris, 1932.

Servius. *Marius Servius (Honoratus): In Virgilium commentarius.* See Virgil.

Sethe, Kurt Heinrich. *Aegyptische Lesestücke zum Gebrauch im akademischen Unterricht.* Leipzig, 1927–28.

Severyns, Albert. *Recherches sur la chrestomathie de Proclos.* Bibliothèque de la Faculté de Philosophie et Lettres de l'Université de Liège, facs. 78, 79. 3 vols. Paris, 1938.

Sidonius Apollinaris, C. Solinus Modestus. *Poems and Letters.* Translated, with notes, by W. B. Anderson. 2 vols. Cambridge, Mass., and London, 1936–65.

Silius Italicus, Ti. Caius. *Punica.* Edited by Ludovicus Bauer. 2 vols. Leipzig, 1890.

Smith, Norris Kelly. *Frank Lloyd Wright: A Study in Architectural Content.* Englewood Cliffs, N. J., 1966.

Snaith, Norman H. *The Jewish New Year Festival.* London, 1947.

Soane, Sir John. *Lectures on Architecture, as Delivered to the Students of The Royal Academy from 1809 to 1836.* Publications of Sir John Soane's Museum, no. 14. Edited by Arthur T. Bolton. London, 1929.

Solinus, C. Julius. *Collectanea rerum memorabilium.* Berlin, 1895.

Soriano, Marc. *Les Contes de Perrault.* Paris, 1968.

Spencer, Baldwin. *The Native Tribes of the Northern Territory of Australia.* London, 1914.

Spencer, Baldwin, and Gillen, F. J. *The Native Tribes of Central Australia.* London, 1899.

Spenser, Edmund. *The Poetical Works.* Edited by J. Payne Collier. 5 vols. London, 1891.

Strabo. *The Geography.* Translated by Horace Leonard Jones. 8 vols. London and New York, 1917–32.

Strzygowski, Josef. *Altai-Iran und Völkerwanderung. Zeitgeschichtliche Untersuchungen über den Eintritt der Wander- und Nordvölker in die Triebhäuse geistigen Lebens.* Leipzig, 1917.

————. *Der Norden in der bildenden Kunst Westeuropas. Heidnisches und Christliches um das Jahr 1000.* Vienna, 1926.

————. *Europas Machtkunst im Rahmen des Erdkreises.* Vienna, 1941.

Sturm, Leonhard Christof. *Sciagrafia Templi Hierosolymitani.* Leipzig, 1694.

————. *Der ausserlessneste und vernenerle Goldmann . . . mitgetheilet von* L. C. S. Augsburg, 1721.

Suidas. *Lexicon* (Lexicographi Graeci, Part I). Edited by Ada Adler. 5 vols. Leipzig, 1928–38.

Summerson, John. *Heavenly Mansions, and Other Essays on Architecture.* London, 1949.

Tacitus, C. Publius Cornelius. *The Histories*, translated by Clifford H. Moore; *The Annals*, translated by John Jackson. 4 vols. Cambridge, Mass., and London, 1928–30.

Talmud (Babylonian). Edited and translated, with notes, by Rabbi I. Epstein. 35 vols. London, 1935–52.

Talmud de Jerusalem. Translated by Moise Schwob; introduction by Maurice Liben. 11 vols. Paris, 1932–33 (photocopy of 1871–90 ed.).

Tange, Kenzo, and Kawazoe, Noboru. *Ise: Prototype of Japanese Culture*. Cambridge, Mass., 1965.

Taylor, Renée. "Architectural Magic: Considerations on the Idea of the Escorial." In Fraser, Douglas, et al., eds. *Essays on the History of Architecture Presented to Rudolf Wittkower*. London, 1967. Pp. 81–109.

Thompson, Stith. *Motif-Index of Folk-Literature*. Rev. and enl. ed. 6 vols. Bloomington, Ind., 1955.

Thureau-Dangin, François. *Rituels accadiens*. Paris, 1921.

Tibullus. *Tibulle et les auteurs du corpus tibullianum*. Edited and translated by Max Ponchont. Paris, 1924.

———. *Poems*. Edited and translated by J. B. Postgate. In *Catullus, Tibullus, and Perviglium Veneris*. London and Cambridge, Mass., 1950.

Torcellan, Gianfranco. *Una figura della Venezia settecentesca: Andrea Memmo*. Rome, 1963.

Ugolinus, Blasius [and Foscari, Francesco]. *Thesaurus Antiquitatum Sacrarum complectens selectissima clarissimum virorum opuscula in quibus veterum Hebraeorum mores . . . illustrantur*. 34 vols. Venice, 1744 ff.
Vol. 8 (1747): Salomonis Van Til, Commentarius de Tabernaculo Mosis. Johannes Buxtorf, Historia Arcae Foderis. Theodorus Hasaeus, Dissertationes de Ligno Sittim, de Rubo Mosis, de Lapide Fundamenti. Jo. Henri Antonius Dorien, Diss. de Cherubinis Sancti Sanctorum. J. Buxtorfi, Diss. de Manne, Maimonide Vita a Jo: Buxtorfo descripta. Roberti Clavigeri de Maimonide, Humfridus Prideaux, Praefatio ad Maimonidem. Ludovicus Compiegne de Veil, Praefatio in Maimonidis opera. Maimonidis Constitutiones. Leonhardus Christophorus Sturm, Sciagraphia Templi Hierosolymitant.
Vol. 9 (1748): R. Abraham Filius Davidus Arie, Commentarius de Templo Ex Ejo qui Schitte Haggiborim inscribitur excerptus . . . Johannes Lightfoot, Descriptio Templi Hierosolymitani Praesertim quale erat tempore Servatoris Nostri.

Valerius Maximus. *Factorum dictorumque memorabilium*. 3 vols. London, 1823.

Vandier, Jacques. *Manuel d'archéologie égyptienne*. 6 vols. Paris, 1952–58.

Varro, M. T. *On the Latin Language*. Edited and translated by Roland G. Kent. Cambridge, Mass., 1958.

Vaux, Roland de. *Ancient Israel: Its Life and Institutions*. Translated by John McHugh. New York and London, 1961.

Vico, Giovanni Battista. *Opere, illustrate da G. Ferrari*. 7 vols. Naples, 1858–65.

Villalpanda, Juan Bautista. See Pradus, Hieronymus.

Viollet-le-Duc, Eugène. *Histoire de l'habitation humaine*. Paris, 1875.

———. *The Habitations of Man in All Ages*. Translated by Benjamin Bucknall. London, 1876.

————. *Lectures on Architecture.* Translated by Benjamin Bucknall. 2 vols. London, 1877.

Virgil. *Virgilii Maronis Opera.* 2 vols. Louvain, 1718. (This ed. contains complete commentaries of Servius.)

Vitruvius. *M. Vitruvius per Jucundum solito Castigator factus.* Venice, 1511.

————. *Di Lucio Vitruvio Pollione de architectura libri dece traducti in vulgare Affigurati: Commentati: et con Mirando Ordine insigniti* [by Cesare Cesariano]. Como, 1521.

————. *Vitruvius Teutsch. Nemlichen des Aller namhafftigsten und Hocherfarnesten romischen Architecti . . . Zehen Bucher von der Architectur und Kunstlich Bauen* [Opera D. Gualthierius H. Rivius (Walter Hermann Riff)]. Nuremberg, 1548.

————. *I Dieci libri dell'architectura di M. Vitruvio tradotti et commentati da monsignor* [Daniele] *Barbaro.* Venice, 1556.

————. *M. Vitruvii Pollionis de architectura libri decem, cum commentariis Danielis Barbari.* Venice, 1567.

————. *M. Vitruvius Pollionis de architectura libri decem cum notis, castigationibus e observationibus . . . Omnia in unum collecta, digesta, et illustrata a Ioanne de Laet.* Antwerp and Amsterdam, 1649.

————. *Les Dix livres d'architecture de Vitruve, corrigés et traduits nouvellement . . . par M. Claude Perrault.* 2nd ed. Paris, 1684.

————. *Vitruvius on Architecture.* Edited and translated by Frank Granger. 2 vols. London and Cambridge, Mass., 1931 (1955).

————. *Vitruvii architettura.* Edited and translated, with notes, by Silvio Ferri. Rome, 1960.

Volz, Paul. *Das Neujahrfest (Laubhütenfest).* Tübingen, 1912.

Wachsmann, Konrad. *Holzhausbau: Technik und Gestaltung.* Berlin, 1930.

Warde, Fowler, W. *The Religious Experience of the Roman People.* London, 1911.

————. *The Roman Festivals of the Period of the Republic.* London, 1933.

Warton, Rev. T.; Bentham, Rev. T.; Grose, Capt.; and Milner, Rev. J. *Essays on Gothic Architecture.* London, 1800.

Watson, William. *China Before the Han Dynasty.* London, 1961.

Wheeler, Post. *The Sacred Scriptures of the Japanese.* London, 1952.

White, Morton, and White, Lucia. *The Intellectual Versus the City: From Thomas Jefferson to Frank Lloyd Wright.* Cambridge, Mass., 1962.

Whitney, Lois. *Primitivism and the Idea of Progress in English Popular Literature.* Baltimore, 1934.

Wildenstein, Georges. "Note sur un projet d'ordre français," *Gazette des Beaux-Arts* (May, 1964), pp. 257–260.

Winckelmann, J. J. *Gedanken über die Nachahmung der griechischen Werke in der Malerei und in der Bildhauerkunst.* Dresden, 1755.

————. *Geschichte der Kunst des Altertums.* Dresden, 1764.

————. *Storia delle arti e del disegno presso gli antichi.* Translated by the Cistercian Monks of Sant' Ambrogio in Milan; edited by the Abate Carlo Fea. 3 vols. Rome, 1783.

Wind, Edgar. *Art and Anarchy: The Reith Lectures, 1960*. London, 1963.

Wingler, Hans M. *Das Bauhaus*. Cologne, 1968.

Wischnitzer-Bernstein, R. "Die messianische Hütte in der jüdischen Kunst," *Monatschrift für Geschichte und Wissenschaft des Judentums*, neue folge, vol. 80 (Berlin, 1936), pp. 377–392.

Wissowa, Georg. *Religion und Kultus der Romer*. Munich, 1902.

Wittkower, Rudolf. *Architectural Principles in the Age of Humanism*. London, 1952.

Wood, John. *The Origin of Building, or the Plagiarism of the Heathen Detected*. Bath, 1741.

———. *Choir Gaure, Vulgarly Called Stonehenge, on Salisbury Plain, Described, Restored and Explained in a Letter to the Rt. Hon. Edward, Late Earl of Oxford and Earl Mortimer*. Oxford, 1747.

Wood, John George. *Homes without Hands, Being a Description of the Habitations of Animals, Classed According to Their Principles of Construction*. London, 1875.

Wright, Frank Lloyd. *The Future of Architecture*. New York, 1963.

———. *The Living City*. New York, 1963.

———. *The Natural House*. New York, 1963.

Zimmern, D. Heinrich. *Das babylonische Neujahrsfest*. Vol. 25: *Der alte Orient*. Leipzig, 1926.

Zonaras, Joannes. *Annales*. Edited by Charles du Fresne, Sieur du Canges. Paris, 1686–87.

———. *Annales*. Edited by M. Pinder. 3 vols. Bonn, 1841–97.

PICTURE CREDITS